The new politics c

Issues in Environmental Politics

Series editors Tim O'Riordan *and* Albert Weale

already published in the series

Environment and development in Latin America: The politics of sustainability *David Goodman and Michael Redclift editors*

The greening of British party politics *Mike Robinson*

The politics of radioactive waste disposal *Ray Kemp*

The new politics of pollution

Albert Weale

Manchester University Press

Manchester and New York

Distributed exclusively in the USA and Canada by St. Martin's Press

Published by Manchester University Press
Oxford Road, Manchester M13 9PL, UK
and Room 400, 175 Fifth Avenue, New York, NY 10010, USA

British Library Cataloguing-in-Publication Data
A catalogue record for this book is available from the British Library

Library of Congress Cataloging-in-Publication Data
Weale, Albert.
    The new politics of pollution / Albert Weale.
        p. cm. — (Issues in environmental politics)
    Includes index.
    ISBN 0-7190-3066-8 (hardback). — ISBN 0-7190-3067-6 (paperback)
    1. Pollution — Government policy — European Economic Community
countries. 2. Pollution — Economic aspects — European Economic Community
countries. 3. Environmental policy — European Economic Community countries. I. Title. II. Series
HC240.9.P55W43 1992
363.73'094—dc20

                                                                92–5507

Reprinted 1993

ISBN 0 7190 3067 6 *paperback*

Printed on recycled paper

Printed in Great Britain
by Bell & Bain Ltd, Glasgow

Contents

List of tables and figure

To JFH
who bore the external costs

Acknowledgements

To take on a subject as vast and complicated as the politics of pollution requires more than a little foolhardiness and a great deal of personal and collegial support. The foolhardiness is my own; for the support I must acknowledge others.

Although I have had a long-standing interest in the politics of the environment, it was Timothy O'Riordan who first encouraged me to take the issues seriously. This book should have been our third collaborative project, but the other demands on his time prevented his being the joint author on this occasion. None the less, he has been an invaluable source of advice and support, and, though this is in no way a book he would have written, I hope he can see some evidence of our collaboration in what is here.

Other colleagues at East Anglia have been generous with their time, particularly John Greenaway, John Street and Steve Smith who all read a draft typescript and made detailed comments. Their characteristic mixture of enthusiasm and criticism, as well as their acute specific comments, helped me see more clearly where I was going wrong and how things could be done better. Louise Kramme, with whom I worked on an earlier project, left an enormous amount of valuable research material when she returned to Germany, and I am especially grateful to her for the characteristic thoroughness with which she unearthed sources, particularly on the subject of social learning. Andrea Williams, with whom I am now working, not only made valuable comments on the draft, using her best editorial skills, but also has provided a source of insights and material on problems related to the North Sea. Martin Hollis revived an old interest in methodological problems, and I hope he sees something of his influence herein.

Elsewhere, a number of people have been of great help. Arild Underdal took time to read and comment upon the draft, comments that had his typical precision and insight. Erik Lykke has drawn my attention to aspects of international environmental diplomacy that I otherwise should have missed. Sonja Boehmer-Christiansen provided valuable detailed comments on the draft as well as useful material more generally. Percy Lehning was kind enough to allow me the use of his flat in Amsterdam during research trips, and proved that it is possible to mix business and pleasure whilst explaining to me the complexities of Dutch politics. Gerd Wagner has kept me up to date with German developments, spent an enormous amount of time helping me understand the logic of German policy discourse and generously provided me with an opportunity to visit the Ruhrgebiet - an essential experience for anyone who wants to understand what a positive environmental policy can do for the quality for life. Comments from Mick Moran revived my spirits when I began to fear that the best might be the enemy not simply of the good, but also of the mediocre.

I have taken up a great deal of the time of busy public officials in various countries. I am particularly grateful to George Meurders for first alerting me to the significance of Dutch developments, and for providing me with opportunities to visit him and his colleagues in Arnhem to see what implementation meant in practice. Officials in The Hague, in particular Paul de Jongh and Bert van der Sluijs, were also of enormous help as were the staff at DG-XI in the Commission of the European Communities. The usual conventions of confidentiality (as well as a journalistic interest in keeping my sources) prevent me from naming the British officials from whom I have received information and advice, but I have learned much from conversations with civil servants over the years and I remain constantly impressed by their ability to weather the vicissitudes of the British political system.

In a book that stresses the importance of ideas in their institutional context, I must thank those who have provided support in the institution in which I worked on this book. Carole Forward and Julie Parsons, as successive secretaries in the Centre for Public Choice Studies, undertook large amounts of work with great speed and efficiency. Sue Rowell provided secretarial services above and beyond the call of duty one busy summer. Anne Martin, as usual, managed to keep us both cheerful whilst manipulating huge chunks of text on the computer. She also fielded the phone calls and other intrusions at crucial times when I needed peace to write.

Other institutional acknowledgements reflect the material dimension that any piece of comparative policy analysis requires. This work draws upon research generously funded by the Anglo-German Foundation for Industrial Society and the European Science Foundation and was helped by grants from the Research Committee of the School of Economic and Social Studies and the Centre for Public Choice Studies at the University of East Anglia.

Richard Purslow at Manchester University Press provided a commitment to the project that was only exceeded by his patience with the author.

My greatest debt is to Jan Harris. Her love, affection and support allowed me to think that it was important to finish the work, not least so that once it was over we could get on and do all the other things we were planning.

Albert Weale
Norwich
December 1991

1

The new politics of pollution

Protecting the environment from pollution has now become one of the central issues in the politics of industrial and post-industrial societies. Acid rain, global climate change with its threat of greenhouse warming, the dispersal of chemicals in the environment, keeping waters clean for drinking and recreational purposes and the national and international management of toxic wastes have ceased to be the concerns of a few specialists or committed ecologists and instead are widely discussed and argued about in the press and the media, among political parties, between citizens and their representatives, or among governments in international negotiations. Ensuring that affluent societies do not transgress the boundaries imposed upon their production and consumption by the renewing and cleansing cycles of the ecosphere, or 'making peace with the planet' as Barry Commoner eloquently expresses it, is increasingly likely to be one of the means by which democratic governments secure their legitimacy and their right to exercise power.[1]

During the 1980s politicians previously schooled in the conventional language of economic growth and material prosperity began responding to the pressing environmental issues coming on to the political agenda. In 1982 the government in the Federal Republic of Germany was shifted from its cautious stance on the environment by the sudden upsurge in public concern over issues of forest death and damage. The early period of the Reagan presidency had been characterised by hostile action against existing environmental policies. For example, the US Council on Environmental Quality had its budget substantially reduced, its personnel cut and its ability to carry out research work curtailed. Reagan also appointed

Anne Gorsuch, a well-known sceptic on environmental regulation, as administrator of the Environmental Protection Agency. Yet, by 1988, George Bush, who as Vice-President had headed Reagan's task force on deregulation, part of the function of which was to identify environmental regulations that were burdensome to industry, was required to run as a pro-environment candidate in his own presidential contest.[2] In September 1988 even the British government, after nine years in which it had been expounding the virtues of material prosperity and economic growth, appeared to undergo a conversion with Mrs Thatcher's speech to the Royal Society, on the threat to the environment, although as its subsequent transport plans showed the resolve of the old materialism was still a powerful force in government thinking.

The transformation of Eastern Europe during 1989, with its rapid and dramatic falls of communist orthodoxy, revealed that the problems of pollution were not simply a feature of the operation and politics of capitalist societies. Under systems of so-called socialist planning factories and plants had been allowed to pollute not only their local neighbourhoods but also the international environment. Levels of pollution related diseases were high in many East European towns and cities as out of date factories produced ever more obsolete goods in ways that disgorged pollution in plenty. If the capitalist West could be characterised, in Galbraith's famous phrase, as producing private affluence and public squalor, the socialist East could be said to have managed the unenviable combination of private poverty and public squalor. Indeed, much of the impetus behind East European reform movements was motivated by a concern with the environment, and so great had been the international repercussions of the pollution in Eastern Europe that West Germany had already subsidised the installation of air pollution control technology into East Berlin and Sweden had contemplated paying for part of Poland's clean-up of the Vistula to prevent further degradation of the Baltic.

This newly emerging concern with issues of pollution control did not take place in a vacuum, however. The intense public and political attention paid to pollution in the 1980s had been preceded by an earlier wave of international concern in the late 1960s and early 1970s. Indeed, as I shall seek to show in this chapter, many of the 1980s developments can be seen as the result of reflection upon the experience of policy-making in that earlier phase, and much that was characteristic of the 1980s would have been impossible had there not been an earlier generation of policies, laws, regulations and institutions. Moreover, for some countries and political movements, the issue of pollution had been continuously high on the political agenda for many years. Thus, the Scandinavian countries had throughout the 1970s been concerned about air pollution from factories and transport, the vast bulk of it originating outside their own boundaries, and falling as acid rain, thereby damaging trees and lakes. In the 1970s Norway took the lead in sponsoring a major research programme on the effects of acid precipitation on forests and fish,[3] and from the early 1970s Norway and Sweden have been diplomatically active in seeking international controls on air pollution. The Nordic concern with environmental issues was also symbolised by Mrs Brundtland's, the Norwegian Prime Minister, chairing of the UN World Commission on Environment and Development between 1982 and 1987, which produced its influential report *Our Common Future*.[4] Thus, the surge of interest in environmental issues in the 1980s needs to be understood against an earlier background of public policies and political ideas. It also needs to be understood in terms of the characteristics of pollution as an issue, and it is those characteristics we shall look at in the next section.

Pollution as a policy issue

The scientific definition of pollution is a hotly contested issue. Fortunately, for the purposes of political science and policy analysis we do not need a definition that will cover all possibilities, merely one that will indicate what the main problems are. I shall define pollution, then, as the introduction into the environment of substances or emissions that either damage, or carry the risk of damaging, human health or well-being, the built environment or the natural environment. There is no implication in this definition that the substances involved stem purely from human sources. Some, like sulphur dioxide for example, will be present from natural sources. The assumption is simply that emissions or substances introduced into the environment in quantities or concentrations greater than those that can be coped with by the cleansing and recycling capacity of nature constitute pollution. Table 1.1 provides an illustrative set of examples of the sort of problems

Table 1.1 *Illustrative problems in pollution control policy*

Pollution problem	Main pollutants	Related human activities	Expected effects
1. Global climate change	Carbon dioxide, methane, CFCs	Fossil fuel burning for power, heating and transport	Various and uncertain. Global temperature rise in next century; sea level rise; desertification
2. Ozone depletion	CFCs	Aerosol use; refrigeration	Loss of protective function of atmosphere against ultra violet radiation
3. Acidification	Sulphur, dioxide, nitrogen oxides, ammonia, hydrocarbon	Fossil fuel burning	Human health, building damage, forest and freshwater damage
4. Eutrophication	Phosphates, nitrates	Fertiliser use	Overenrichment of rivers and estuaries, leading to algae growth
5. Dispersal of chemicals and wastes in the environment			
(i) Seas and oceans	Sewage, pesticides, heavy metals	Concentrated habitation and untreated sewage, industrial waste disposal, marine disposal	Soil, groundwater and seas pollution. Species effects Species loss, economic losses to fisheries, tourism
(ii) Soil and groundwater	Pesticides, toxic waste	Industrial and domestic waste disposal	Species loss, contamination of water supplies
(iii) Freshwater	Nitrates, phosphates, acid rain	Farming, fossil fuel burning	Species loss
6. Urban pollution	Smoke, noise	Traffic, production	Stress, dirt, physical ill health

with which modern pollution policy is confronted.

As with any other policy issue, pollution has its own distinctive characteristics which condition the type of politics that develops around the problem. Theodore Lowi once suggested that policies determine politics.[5] It is not necessary to share this view completely to understand that the characteristics of an issue can be expected to have an important influence upon the political coalitions and the policy discourse that surround pollution. Thus, even without endorsing Lowi's generalisation, we can still expect that the type of policy problem that is at issue will limit and shape the type of political conditions and policy solutions that are possible.

The most obvious feature of these pollution problems is that they concern issues that are public goods as economists use the term. A public good is one in which 'each individual's consumption leads to no subtraction from any other individual's consumption of that good.'[6] A public good in this sense is non-rival and non-excludable in consumption. When action is taken to protect the environment from pollution, the benefit of this action will typically be widespread. Thus, if anyone living in a particular location enjoys clean air then all others living nearby enjoy clean air. In this sense, since one person's consumption does not limit the consumption of others, the good in question can be regarded as non-rival. Similarly, if some nations enjoy the benefit of a stable global climate then all nations will enjoy those benefits. With some nations taking action to prevent greenhouse warming, other nations cannot be excluded from the benefits that result and the benefit is therefore non-excludable. Unlike private goods, for example the consumption of washing machines or houses, where potential rivals for the benefit can be excluded by conventional rules of property or entitlement, the public good of environmental protection typically has the characteristic of non-exclusion.

This does not mean that the effects of pollution are equal in their effects upon all people. Those down wind or down river of a polluting source will suffer more from uncontrolled pollution than those upwind or upstream. Contrast the examples of a clean river and a stable global climate. The first will affect fewer people than the second and hence the level of publicness of public goods may well vary considerably. But relative to a particular set of affected parties, the prevention of pollution always has the characteristic of being a public good. If environmental protection from pollution is achieved for one member of the affected group, the relevant 'public', then protection is achieved for all members.

The public character of environmental protection leads some analysts to identify a problem of collective action in the supply of environmental protection. Since public goods are non-rival and non-excludable in consumption, it follows that individuals can enjoy the benefits of the public good, whether or not they have contributed to its production. Moreover, many public goods display threshold effects in their production. Provided there is a general, but not universal, willingness to contribute to their production, the good will be supplied. For example, nitrate pollution of drinking waters will be prevented provided a sufficient number of farmers reduce their fertiliser use, or harmful sulphur dioxide emissions can be reduced provided a sufficient number of manufacturers can be induced to install scrubbers or burn low sulphur coal. In these circumstances, there is a temptation for individuals to free-ride upon the efforts of others, hoping to secure the benefits without paying the costs. Thus, farmers will be tempted to continue using nitrogenous fertilisers in the hope that sufficient others will give up, or manufacturers will hope that others will install scrubbers. Yet, if everyone seeks to free-ride in this way, the net effect will be mutually frustrating for all involved, rather like everyone trying to stand on tiptoe. Hence, protection from pollution always potentially involves a dilemma of collective action, in which there is a risk that societies will not secure the public good of environmental protection.

As well as its public dimension, the control of pollution also has the characteristic that the harm of pollution often arises as the by-product of otherwise legitimate activities within society.[7] The consequence is that pollution control is typically a regulatory policy, in the sense that the role of the political authorities is seen to be to circumscribe the damage that one set of persons can impose on others or upon the public commons. This does not necessarily mean that pollution control regulation takes place by means of legal instruments, such as laws limiting permissible emissions from certain types of processes or the licensing of certain persons to carry out activities, although this is its usual form. Pollution policy may also be pursued by economic instruments, for example taxes on environmentally harmful products, or by public education, for example encouraging people to use bottle banks. To say that policy is regulatory is not therefore to say that it is accomplished by means of particular policy instruments, but it is to contrast it with policies whose essential aim is to alter the distribution of disposable resources by a mixture of taxes and public spending. Distributive policy in this sense has the aim of altering the allocation of claims over consumption that arises from market processes. The usual form that this takes in the welfare state is to shift resources over the life-cycle, so that individuals are protected from the economic insecurity associated with childrearing, unemployment, disability or old age, and this cannot be done without the government controlling a high proportion of the national income. Pollution control, by contrast, does not use public spending as its primary policy instrument. In this sense it is a post-welfare state sector of public policy.

A further characteristic of pollution control policy is that it normally has a large technical core. Of course people can feel the ill effects of pollution without knowing the atmospheric chemistry of fossil fuel burning or the biological processes that lead to the accumulation of heavy metals in the food chain, and experts who have denied the possibility of human health effects or environmental damage from particular sources have often had to eat their words. None the less, there is a clear technical core to the vast majority of contemporary pollution problems, and this fact imposes its own requirements upon the way that pollution policy can be conducted.

The most obvious effect is that professional expertise has to be called upon at the stage of identifying and framing a problem of pollution policy, let alone at the stage of determining possible answers. Even something as obvious as a lake in which fish stocks have died has to be identified as a case of damage by acid precipitation before a pollution problem can be identified. Similarly, the world would not know that it was facing the possibility of global atmospheric warming were it not for the activities of professional scientific communities interpreting ambiguous and sometimes conflicting evidence. This dependence upon professional expertise affects both the character of the policy community around pollution issues and the manner in which problems are understood. Thus, scientific teams are inevitably drawn into the process of policy-making and the type of expertise that is called upon will be significant in giving lay policy-makers an understanding of the problem. We should not expect environmental scientists to share the same understanding of a problem as engineers or lawyers, nor should we necessarily expect consistency of interpretation across experts from different national policy systems.

Consequently, the level of complexity involved in pollution control policy can be considerable. In some cases it may be difficult to identify environmental problems or the parameters that characterise emission streams. For example, there is a great deal of modelling involved in knowing whether acid precipitation is proportional to distance from source or has some other relationship. Even when parameters can be reliably estimated or modelled, the cause and effect relationships that underlie the generation of those parameters may be uncertain. It may be reasonable to hold that sulphur dioxide deposition is not good for trees, but whether observed forest damage is primarily due to sulphur deposition or some other factors, for example tropospheric ozone or soil degradation, is far from clear. It has been claimed that there are 186 scientific hypotheses for observed tree damage.[8] Since potentially expensive choices about the priorities for control may depend upon rival cause and effect hypotheses, the difficulty of establishing such hypotheses becomes an important element in understanding the policy-making process.

A fourth feature of the emerging politics of pollution is that the problems created will often have effects over the long term, affecting future generations whose interests are poorly represented in policy-making processes. Increased consumption of fossil fuels may well have beneficial consequences for members of present generations in terms of increased economic development, but only at the cost of generations living in the middle of the twenty-first century. In itself this raises difficult and complex issues of social justice, but the problems are compounded when it is probable that those in the present generation who are asked to refrain from consuming present benefits in order to protect future generations can plausibly claim that they are not primarily responsible for the problem. The protection of the ozone layer will require India and China to refrain from using relatively cheap CFC gases in their refrigerators, but their populations can argue that they are being prevented from the benefits of cheap industrialisation because Western countries have already consumed a disproportionate share of the global commons. In this sort of case, issues of intergenerational justice inevitably become confused with issues of international justice, and the potential conflict between the eradication of economic underdevelopment and pollution control have long soured international environmental diplomacy, as far back as the 1972 UN Conference on the Environment in Stockholm.[9]

The final feature of pollution policy is that, in so far as it is concerned with reducing the causes of pollution rather than simply limiting or mitigating its effects, it is a policy area that cuts across the established sectors of public policy. The origins of pollution are to be found in industrial production, consumption, farming practices, energy consumption and traffic patterns. All of these areas of social life are the province of particular ministries within the governmental structure of developed liberal democracies. Moreover, the age and status of these ministries is typically greater than that of relatively recent environment ministries. Hence, in addition to the technical problems of how industrial, farming or transport processes might be adapted to be made compatible with environmental protection, policy actors responsible for the environment confront the political problem of how to gain the leverage on other traditionally more powerful actors. Since political interests tend to congregate around ministries, in the form of policy communities comprised of interest groups, professional associations, journalists, academics and so on, many of whom will usually share an understanding of policy priorities for that policy sector, the problems of confronting the entrenched practices of sectors that impinge upon the environment can be considerable.

In summary, then, we can say that the characteristics of pollution control as a policy issue are that it is a matter of providing public goods with the attendant risk of the dilemma of collective action, that is involves complex technical issues, that the scale of the problems often exceeds the boundaries of those living within a political system at any one time and that difficult questions of political diplomacy are involved in seeking to solve pollution problems at their source rather than merely dealing with their effects.

However, although we can identify these intrinsic features of pollution control as an issue, we should not assume that there is a simple deterministic relationship between the nature of the policy problems and the types of political action to which they give rise.

The definition of the relevant public, the construction of expertise and the willingness to intervene at national and international levels are not constants but depend upon the system of institutions and ideas, as well as individual motivations and social structures, within which policy strategies are debated and chosen. One way in which to see this is to examine the development of pollution control policies over time. The 1980s had been preceded by other periods in which the issue attention cycle was high. At the end of the 1960s and beginning of the 1970s environmental concerns had secured a prominent place on the political agenda of every developed nation. Moreover, the environmental challenge of the 1970s did not go without a policy response. During the 1970s policy and legislative initiatives occurred in all developed societies. If we are to understand the peculiar and distinctive features of the politics of the 1980s, and what this politics promises for the 1990s, we should do well to examine the earlier stage of the story.

The strategies of the 1970s

The late 1960s and early 1970s saw a great upsurge of public interest in environmental policy in Europe and North America, symbolised by the demonstration of twenty million Americans on Earth Day in April 1970. Media coverage, pressure group campaigns and popular interest increased dramatically in a short period. It is not easy to date exactly the point when political and public interest became significant, nor is it easy to trace its antecedents. There were certain events, for example when the Cuyahuga River near Cleveland caught fire because of chemical discharges in June 1969 or the supertanker *Torrey Canyon* spilled over 120,000 tonnes of oil when it was grounded in 1967, that undoubtedly played a role. But there had been significant pollution events before, for example the smoke pollution incidents in Donora, Pennsylvania, in 1948 or London in 1952, that had not led to an upsurge of political activism.[10] There is certainly no precedent for the combined and simultaneous movement of public opinion occurring across so many countries. It seems reasonable to assume, therefore, that behind that tide of activism there lay long-term structural changes in patterns of social organisation and social relations: rising educational standards that enabled an attentive public to absorb the message of Rachel Carson's *Silent Spring*;

growing international coverage by the media that both focused attention on specific pollution events and enabled the transmission of ideas to take place at rapid speed; the maturing of a generation in which post-materialist values were prevalent; and the effects of the post-war long boom that had provided an unprecedented quantity of commodities for citizens in developed economics but only at the cost of ambiguous effects on the quality of life. The policy response to this upsurge involved legislation specifying more stringent controls on pollutants and toxic substances, and regulating the use of the air and water. Typical of this legislation was the 1970 Clean Air Act in the United States, the 1974 Federal Immission Control Act in the Federal Republic of Germany and the 1974 Control of Pollution Act in the United Kingdom. The policy response also involved the creation of new organisations and institutions or the adaptation of existing institutions to new purposes. Thus, the Swedish Environmental Protection Act of 1969 gave the National Environmental Protection Board the powers to develop policy, the US Environmental Protection Agency was created in 1970 and the German government concentrated environment functions in the Interior Ministry in 1969 and in 1974 created its Federal Environment Office to provide the research background to regulation. A particularly noteworthy feature of these new institutions was the creation of bodies to provide high level technical and scientific advice ranging from the Council of Environment Experts in the US to the Royal Commission on Environmental Pollution in the UK to the German *Rat von Sachverständigen für Umweltfragen* (Council of Environmental Experts). These developments are summarised for a range of countries in Table 1.2.

Each of these national developments reflected the circumstances and history of the political system in which they were adopted, and examined in detail the legislation and policies varied greatly. For example, Lundqvist has shown that whereas Swedish air pollution initiatives reflected a concern for economic and technological feasibility, in which private bargaining between public officials and industry was an essential element in the application of flexible, plant-specific standards, US air pollution legislation stressed uniform emission limits set without serious regard to economic and technological feasibility and implemented within a context in which public participation was widespread.[11] Despite

Table 1.2 *Developments of pollution control policy during the 1960s and 1970s*

Measures	Canada	France	Germany	Netherlands	Sweden	UK	USA
Organisational:							
Expert council	Canadian Environment Advisory Council, 1972	High Committee for the Environment, 1970	Council of Environmental Experts, 1972	Temporary Council on Air Pollution Control, 1970	Environmental Advisory Committee, 1968	Royal Commission on Environmental Pollution, 1969	Council on Environmental Quality, 1969
Ministry/agency	Department of the Environment, 1970	Ministry for the Protection of Nature and the Environment, 1971	Interior Ministry acquires responsibility for environmental issues, 1969 Federal Environment Office (research) 1974 Federal Ministry of the Environment, 1986	Ministry of Public Health and Environmental Protection, 1971	National Environmental Protection Board, 1969 Franchise Board for Environmental Protection, 1969	Department of the Environment, 1970	Environmental Protection Agency, 1970
Policy developments:							
Air	Clean Air Act, 1971	Air Pollution Law, 1961 Decree on Air Pollution, 1974	Federal Immission Control Act, 1974	Air Pollution Act, 1970	Environmental Protection Act, 1969	Health and Safety Act, 1974	Clean Air Act, 1970

Table 1.2 (contd)

Measures	Canada	France	Germany	Netherlands	Sweden	UK	USA
Surface waters	Canada Water Act, 1970 Canada Shipping Act, 1970 Fisheries Act, 1970 Northern Inland Water Act, 1970	Water Law, 1964	Federal Water Resources Act, 1957 Federal Water Law, 1976 Effluent Charge Law, 1976	Surface Water Pollution Act, 1969	Environmental Protection Act, 1969	Rivers Act, 1951 Control of Pollution Act, 1974	Federal Water Pollution Control Act, 1972
Chemicals/toxics	Environmental Containments Act, 1975	Law on Chemical Substances, 1977	Chemicals Law, 1980	Chemical Wastes Act, 1976	Act on Chemical Products, 1986	Deposit of Poisonous Wastes Act, 1972 Control of Pollution Act, 1974	Toxic Substances Control Act, 1976
EIA	Environmental Assessment and Review Process, 1973	Requirement for Environmental Impact Assessment, 1976	Requirement for Environmental Impact Assessments, 1975	General Administrative Order, 1987	Proposals in 1990/91	Only under EC Directive, 1985	National Environmental Policy Act, 1969
Integrated pollution control	Environment Protection Act		None	General Environmental Provisions Act, 1979	Environmental Protection Act, 1990	Environmental Protection Act, 1990	None

these important differences of detail, there were none the less significant similarities in the pollution control strategies adopted by different countries. In part these similarities reflected considerable policy borrowing across national boundaries. Innovations and developments in the US were of particular importance in this respect, with key elements of the US approach being taken over by European governments. For example, the US Council of Environmental Quality was taken as a model by the German government for its Council of Environmental Experts, and the idea of environmental impact assessments is one that has been widely followed.[12] However, there is reason to believe that the existence of these similarities goes deeper than simply the practice of policy borrowing, and that what was involved in the similarities of policy developments was a tacit, and often unarticulated, conception of what the policy problem was that confronted governments.

Comparison of policy developments suggests that not only the type of response but also its structure had a number of features in common. If we compare the dates of major legislative and policy developments across countries, then a certain pattern begins to emerge. In the face of growing political and public concern, virtually the first thing that governments did was to establish a council of independent experts (median date 1970) and a branch of the bureaucratic machine (median date 1970) that had responsibility for the development of environmental policy. The purpose of these moves is various. Partly, as with President Nixon's appointment of an Environmental Quality Council in 1969, the purpose is symbolic showing visible presidential activism in the face of a disgruntled Congress. On other occasions, as with Harold Wilson's appointment of the standing Royal Commission on Environmental Pollution, the move can be seen as an expression of the well-established tradition of informal interdependence in Britain between scientific and political elites. Yet, despite these differences of purpose, the underlying logic in this initial response is to identify a distinct area of public policy requiring its own specialist expertise and its own institutions for the conduct of public discussion. Before pollution policy can be developed, it first has to be invented, and this in turn involves constructing the relevant institutions.

These changes in the machinery of policy did not always amount to the creation of a separate environmental ministry, although in each case it did involve a reassembling of the bureaucratic lego bricks that brought previously separate administrative sections together and established some unit or agency whose purpose was to give some central direction to policy. The creation of a separate ministry has much wider ramifications, however, involving as it does political calculations about the balance of portfolios and, in many cases, the composition of coalition cabinets. Thus, the British government quickly established a Department of the Environment in 1970, which is what one might expect in a political system where one party normally forms the government, requiring few complicated calculations of balancing cabinet portfolios among coalition partners. (It is also what one might expect from a government system in which it is easier to change a name than to change the substance of what is done: twenty years later the Department of the Environment was still more preoccupied with the reform of local government finance than with protecting the environment.) In Germany, the most that could be accomplished was the assembling of pollution control functions within the Interior Ministry and it was sixteen years later that the German government established its environment ministry (*Bundesministerium für Umwelt*) and then under considerable political pressure arising from the consequences of Chernobyl. These variations in the speed and structure of policy response suggest that a number of contingent factors influence the form that machinery of government changes take, but there is sufficient similarity in their timing to suggest that some reorganisation in the machinery of government was a necessary condition for further policy developments, as well as being a valuable response for politicians to the public pressure that they faced.

The substantive policy responses themselves also show a certain pattern. Legislative innovation begins with the topics of air and surface water pollution (median date for water 1970 and 1971 for air) where in some cases it was possible to build on existing policies and structures of pollution control. Then control of toxic chemicals emerges on the legislative agenda (median date 1976) followed by control of waste disposal facilities. This pattern is not surprising. Dirty air and waters are the most obviously visible consequences of pollution, and there are well-established public health interests involved in understanding their consequences for the welfare of populations.

However, it is worth underlining how extensive is the selective perception embedded in these policy developments. One way of highlighting this is to note how some important topics have come only very late on to the agenda of pollution politics. One of these is soil pollution. Already in 1962 Rachel Carson had drawn attention to the importance of soil conservation when she wrote:

This soil community, then, consists of a web of interwoven lives, each in some way related to the others – the living creatures depending on the soil, but the soil in turn a vital element of the earth only so long as this community within it flourishes ... Chemical control of insects seems to have proceeded on the assumption that the soil could and would sustain any amount of insult via the introduction of poisons without striking back. The very nature of the world of soil has been largely ignored.[13]

This concern, however, was not reflected in the legislative developments. Protection of the soil only became explicit in interim legislation in the Netherlands in 1982 and in some countries, for example the UK, legislative provision is still very weak. The low priority commonly afforded to some issues of pollution and the high priority correspondingly accorded to others reflects the limitations of selective attention built into the processes of policy development.

One common feature of policy developments in the 1970s was the use of traditional administrative regulatory strategies. Regulation by legal rule was the norm. Of course the exact significance of this approach varied from country to country depending upon constitutional conventions and political culture. Thus in the United States and the Federal Republic of Germany, both political systems in which processes of rule-making are highly formalised, there was provision for explicit legal review of standards set and administrative decisions made, whereas the United Kingdom and Sweden continued to rely upon their traditional preference for wide administrative discretion and close working relationships between the pollution inspectors and the regulated. Yet, despite these differences of policy style, policy substance still relied upon the assumption that control by administrative rule was the appropriate way to deal with the main problems. Other techniques of control, most notably economic ones, were topics of intense discussion in the relevant policy communities, but they did not occupy a central place in the political response of the 1970s.

One important problem with these techniques was the proneness of administrative regulation to 'implementation deficit'. Implementation deficit arises when legislative and policy intent is not translated into practice. The stringent standards legislated for air and water pollution in the US in 1970 and 1972 included timetables for implementation that were not met, so that President Carter, for example, had to relax the air pollution limits in 1977 and in the same year the EPA acknowledged that it had failed to meet the legislative deadlines for the regulation of toxic discharges to water.[14] Similarly, many of the detailed provisions of the UK's Control of Pollution Act remained unimplemented for many years.[15] As early as 1978 Renate Mayntz and her colleagues were able to show that German pollution control systems were prone to implementation deficit as a routine part of their operation.[16] The principal problem was that information about the nature of the process being regulated rested more with the operator than with the regulatory agency. Regulators were therefore forced into bargaining strategies with operators over such matters as timetables, investment in pollution control technologies and the like. One implication of this finding is that if implementation deficit is present in Germany, which is perhaps archetypically an over-administered society, then one would expect such deficits in all forms of administrative control.

Moreover, the informational restrictions on implementation are compounded by another feature of administrative regulation, namely the divergence between the performance requirements on regulators and their own motivational aspirations. In the end administrative regulation comes down to the day to day work of street-level bureaucrats: people in wellington boots whose job it is to go in and take measurements or enforce standards. In a wide range of studies, not only in connection with the environment, but also in public policy fields one might have thought had quite different characteristics like the regulation of nursing homes for the elderly, similar results emerge. Regulators are often faced with a choice between negotiating compliance and enforcing standards. There are strong psychological pressures to negotiate compliance, which itself has a number of different moral and social judgements involved. Regulation by street-level bureaucrats is not simply a matter of enforcing a rule, it also involves judgements about culpability, negligence and the likelihood of compliance in the future. In order to preserve a working relationship and maintain the possibility of compliance, the regulator will typically bargain with the operator to the detriment of the strict implementation of the intended legislation. These features of administrative regulation are inherent in the process and are not restricted to specific administrative systems. They have been observed in societies as diverse as Germany, the UK, Sweden, the US, France, the Netherlands and India.[17]

There is, furthermore, a more prosaic problem with the regulatory strategies of the 1970s, namely the issue of multiple permitting. Controls over emissions to air or water, or limitations on the use of certain chemicals were developed in terms of the problems that were posed by specific forms of pollution. However, a manufacturing or industrial process will typically involve emissions of different types as well as the handling of potentially dangerous substances. To the extent to which the regulatory strategy uses administrative instruments, it will impose a licensing requirement on operators for the various individual forms of pollution in which they might be involved. Hence individual factories could find themselves undergoing inspection and licensing for a variety of discharges with no necessity for consistency between them and considerable cost and disruption. Such features of implementation were an inherent consequence of the regulatory strategies adopted during the 1970s.

One interesting feature of the implementation process was that no devices were put in place to monitor the consequences of legislative and policy initiatives and provide a feedback loop to policy-makers of the difficulties that they were confronting. In part this reflects the political construction of knowledge. Political and administrative systems will characteristically pay more attention to some types of information rather than others not because of the substantive merits of the evidence addressed but because the selection is influenced by the background and the disciplinary specialism of policy elites and perceptions of legitimacy. Thus British governments across a wide range of policy sectors frequently downplay sociological or other behavioural evidence to the advantage of the natural sciences or economics. German administration typically has a large number of lawyers who are sensitive to the niceties of constitutional and legal interpretation, but who are less interested in information on the effectiveness of the pollution control regime in place. On top of these existing biases, there was no evaluation machinery whose task it was to monitor performance and provide information to policy makers-about where future developments should take place. Little work on instrument selection was set in train in the 1970s and there was seldom intellectual preparation for subsequent administrative reforms. For example, there was no intellectual preparation involved in establishing the German Federal Ministry of the Environment, and the UK Royal Commission on Environmental Pollution made recommendations about administrative organisations without ever including an expert in administrative studies amongst its members or in its support staff.[18]

Without a suitable vehicle for evaluation within the process of policy-making it was difficult to provide the impetus for policy development. One symptom of this was the manner in which policy developments were sometimes the product of forces outside policy-making institutions narrowly defined or even in some cases the conventional policy community. Policy developments in Germany emerged from a ferment of activity among the citizens' initiatives and the rise of the Greens. In the UK developments came partly from the transformation of established pressure groups, like the Council for the Preservation of Rural England, into new style campaigning groups and partly from the rise of new groups, like CLEAR which campaigned for lead-free petrol. A similar process happened in the US where old-style amenity groups, like the Sierra Club and the Audubon Society, became politically active. There was also the rise of the public interest organisation, so that it was the Conservation Foundation, for example, which managed to place the issue of integrated pollution control firmly on the policy agenda.[19]

So far we have looked at those features of the 1970 strategy that were in part responsible for implementation failure of one sort or another. However, it can be argued that the 1970s response was flawed not simply in implementation but also in conception. In other words, we need to look not only at the consequences of political decisions, but also at the consequences of political non-decisions. One example of such non-decisions, it has been alleged, was the lack of interest in problems of cross-media transfers. This problem is intrinsic to any system of pollution control and will remain since no government can repeal the law of thermodynamics that states that matter can neither be created nor destroyed. Given this law, the problem for pollution control is simply that a solution to one pollution problem, for example air pollution, may create a landfill or water pollution problem. Work in the US has established that the problem of cross-media transfers is neither marginal nor of secondary significance, but is the norm rather than the exception.[20] The transport and transformation of pollutants through different media are a consequence of the chemicals involved, their concentrations and solubilities, as well as their propensity to interact with other chemicals. Examples include waste-water treatment, where the primary focus of attention is on the protection of surface waters, but where volatile organic compounds can air-strip into the atmosphere and metallic and organic compounds can contaminate soils. Similarly, non-aqueous phase organics can migrate from hazardous waste sites into water or indoor air pollution. The policy problem is that sectoral legislation protecting a particular receiving medium, like the air or surface waters, may achieve its effectiveness in terms of its primary purpose by worsening these secondary effects.

A further common feature was that the environmental policy was treated as a discrete policy area within its own right which was simply to be added to the other concerns of government. The creation of new branches of government or administrative agencies exemplifies this assumption. The EPA or the Department of the Environment were to become the branch of government responsible for the pollution control function. Since government reorganisations or innovations seldom take place without non-substantive considerations of departmental 'turf' entering, it was not always possible to implement policies directly in accordance with this assumption, but it was clearly a powerful force at the time. There was little attention correspondingly given to devising co-ordinating institutions that would allow environmental considerations to affect public policy decisions in transport, agriculture or industry. A good example of the consequences of this fact can be seen in the pollution problems now attributable to agricultural practices. During the 1980s it became clear that agricultural intensification was one of the main contributors to water pollution in the form of nitrate pollution and eutrophication. Such problems had been anticipated by environmental scientists, but the fragmentation of responsibility meant that they could not be addressed.[21] Agricultural intensification itself was a product of public policy developments including the practice of farm price support in the European Community, which provided farmers in member states with an incentive for crop fertilisation and a more intensive rearing of animals. Moreover, the stimulation of food production in the developed world reduced the demand for imports from the Third World, creating for Third World farmers a prospect of declining income from which pressures arose for overstocking and overuse of natural resources.

The neglect of the integration of environmental concerns into the broad range of public policy has implications for the understanding of environmental problem-solving. Knoepfel and Weidner[22] in their study of sulphur dioxide policies have shown how the volume of sulphur dioxide emissions was as much a function of economic and other public policy variables as it is of environmental policy itself. By engineering the economic depression of the early 1980s, Mrs Thatcher's government inadvertently secured an improvement in atmospheric quality since there were fewer factory chimneys emitting to the atmosphere and lower electricity generation. The flip-side of this interrelationship is that environmental commitments can be undermined by an unregulated upswing in economic activity. Just at the time when the UK had succeeded in negotiating an agreement after five years' arduous bargaining with its European partners on the limitation of sulphur dioxide emissions, it emerged that official projections of trends were being undermined by the increase in activity within the economy at large. By the same token, transport policy stands in an intimate relationship to pollution policy through the contribution that vehicles make to a whole range of pollution problems.

Although the general bias of the 1970s' response was towards substantive legislation and control of particular pollutants without any concern for the integration of environmental concerns into wider areas of public policy, there was one noteworthy development which went against this trend. This was the US 1969 National Environmental Policy Act. The main thrust of this legislation was not substantive, but procedural. Federal agencies were required to make an explicit assessment of the environmental consequences of their actions as these concerned major project developments. Considered as a requirement of policy initiatives this may seem to be a modest requirement, and it is not immedi-

ately apparent how it would provide the impetus for a reorienta-
tion of attitudes and priorities among departments of government
that did not have the environment as their main concern. Yet, as
Taylor has shown, NEPA did have a significant effect over a
number of years.[23] In particular, by creating a specialist cadre of
environmental experts within the relevant federal agencies, the
requirement for impact assessment created institutional momentum within the agencies leading to a change of outlook. This is
not to say that procedural devices always had significant, positive
effects. Hazardous waste regulation in the UK imposed a procedural requirement upon waste disposal authorities to draw up
plans without necessarily contributing much to the quality of
environmental policy. This point is that NEPA did provide one
model of how environmental concerns might be integrated into the
broad sweep of public policy, and the widespread development of
the idea only really took off in the 1980s.

One final common feature of the 1970s' legislation is that it
allowed for problem solution by displacement across political and
administrative boundaries. The most potent symbol of this problem
is the tall smokestack, designed to reduce sulphur dioxide concentrations in immediate neighbourhoods, but which is the main cause
of long-range cross-boundary sulphur deposition. European nations
now have a considerable import-export trade in sulphur dioxide
pollution as a result of measures whose intention was to solve local
problems.[24] Not all the policy developments of the 1970s ignored
the international dimension of pollution problems and in some
case it was international agreements that prompted action at the
local level. Thus it was the 1972 Convention on Marine Pollution
that led individual countries to take measures to ban dumping at
sea. However, it proved possible to allow national problems to be
solved at the expense of international ones. By the same token,
international problems to which individual countries contributed,
for example the build-up of carbon dioxide, received no attention
whatsoever.

Summarising these complex developments, we can identify a
number of features that in general marked the pollution control
strategies of the 1970s. They involved institutional adjustments in
the form of new organisations and institutional forms. They relied
primarily upon the techniques of administrative regulation. They
involved selective attention, stressing some problems at the ex-

pense of others. They were prone to implementation deficit. They favoured the regulation of pollution by legislation that was specific to receiving medium. They rested on the assumption that environmental policy could be treated as a discrete policy area in its own right. And they allowed problem displacement across time and space.[25] Moreover, environmental trends were such that even had the pollution control strategies been fully effective in solving the problems to which they were addressed, they would not have been able to deal with the more demanding problems that more and more were emerging.

The new pollution and the new politics

By the late 1980s it had become clear that the shortcomings involved in the environmental policy strategies of the 1970s left many problems of pollution unresolved or growing worse. Trends on key environmental indicators suggested a widespread increase in pollution and an associated deterioration in the quality of the environment. For example, emissions of nitrogen oxides, which contribute to photochemical smog and acid rain, increased by an average of 12 per cent in OECD countries between 1970 and 1987, with some countries, for example Canada, The Netherlands, Norway and Portugal recording very large percentage increases.[26] Municipal waste, as measured by the weight produced per person, increased on average by 26 per cent in OECD countries between 1975 and the end of the 1980s.[27] The use of nitrogenous fertilisers increased by 48 per cent in OECD countries between 1970 and 1988, and by 142 per cent for the world as a whole during the same period.[28] Most worrying of all for some people, because of its possible implications in climate change and global warming, carbon dioxide emissions increased by 15 per cent for OECD countries between 1971 and 1988, and by 43 per cent for the world as a whole in the same period. Five countries managed to buck this trend, but for some others, for example Australia, New Zealand, Spain and Portugal, the increases were large in percentage terms, whilst for the USA they were large in absolute terms.[29]

Behind these trends in emissions there lie significant and long-term social and economic developments that are contributing to the increase in pollution. The growth in global population continues to put increasing pressure on available food supplies, so that farmers face various encouragements to increase their productivity by means of fertilisers. Population growth also puts increased pressure on the use of seas and rivers for the disposal of sewage and other forms of waste. Rising standards of living increase commodity consumption, with its accompaniment of solid waste needing disposal. New patterns of transport lead to the building of autoroutes, so that there was an 83 per cent increase in the length of autoroutes between 1970 and 1988 within OECD countries.[30]

Indicators of environmental quality reveal the stress created by these trends. Nitrate concentrations showed an increase over the twenty-year period since 1970 in rivers as diverse as the St Lawrence, the Fraser, the Mississippi, the Loire, the Rhône, the Po, the Thames and the Mersey.[31] In the thirty-year period from the mid-1950s to the mid-1980s ozone concentrations over Antartica declined steadily, with the decreases in total ozone being progressively larger in the 1980s than in the 1960s or 1970s, reaching 50 per cent or more loss of the total column ozone in September 1987 over an area roughly the size of the Antarctic continent. In 1988 the size of the record-setting hole was repeated.[32] Microbial contamination of the seas from sewage disposal was identified as the most serious problem by scientists on the 1987 UN Regional Seas Programme.[33]

As well as these trends, a series of events have occurred which have highlighted the inadequacy of the present policy response to problems of pollution. Oil tankers continue regularly to be involved in massive spillages, of which the example of the Exxon Valdez in Alaska provides a vivid instance. The accident at the nuclear power station in Chernobyl, in the Ukraine, revealed more than the difficulties of managing nuclear power. The international contamination from the fall-out highlighted the inadequacy of many national systems of environmental monitoring and protection. Thus, in the Federal Republic of Germany for example, inconsistent advice by provincial (*Land*) and federal authorities was given about safety precautions to be followed. Algae blooms and seal deaths in 1988 alerted the populations of the North Sea states to the possibility of environmental damage due to pollution. In the hot summer of 1988 many US cities recorded high levels of tropospheric ozone.[34] In Hong Kong the incidence of 'red tides', plankton blooms in which the dominant species is toxic, appears to be increasing. And the reports of the growing 'hole' in the ozone layer over Antarctica provided early warning of the scale of environmental damage that might be registered by global climate change.

Trends were not all negative, of course, between 1970 and 1990. The issue of sulphur dioxide emissions had been kept on the international policy agenda by the Scandinavian countries throughout the period, and partly as a result of this pressure and partly because of changes in the character of production technologies emissions of sulphur dioxide from OECD countries fell by 25 per cent between 1970 and the end of the 1980s.[35] More importantly, perhaps, the link between sulphur dioxide emissions and GDP has been broken, so that trends in sulphur dioxide emissions in Canada, the US, Japan, France, Germany, Italy and the United Kingdom are now negatively correlated with trends in GDP.[36] There has also been a marked decline in OECD countries in the concentrations of particulates in the atmosphere of urban centres.[37] Moreover, behind many pollution problems there lies the inefficient use of energy, so that it is striking that energy intensity, or the use of energy resources per unit of GNP, has declined in most OECD countries between 1970 and 1990 and has only recorded rises in Spain, Portugal and Turkey as a result of their efforts to industrialise. This does not mean that rich countries are necessarily using less energy per capita, but it does mean that energy use is not rising at the same rate as GDP. There is no reason to assume an automatic and unbreakable link between economic growth and increased energy consumption.

Despite these positive environmental trends, there was a widespread feeling by the end of the 1980s that the problems of pollution were growing more serious and that existing policy strategies failed adequately to deal with them. In 1988 and 1989 the Harris polling organisation surveyed public opinion and leadership attitudes around the world. The survey encompassed fifteen countries in all parts of the globe and it found that in all but one country, Saudi Arabia, most of those surveyed thought that the environment had become worse in the previous decade.[38] The Dutch National Environmental Policy Plan caught the prevailing mood when it claimed that current environmental problems pose risks not only to public health and the survival of many plant and animal species, but also to the functions of the environment that are essential for good social and economic development.[39]

This sense of policy failure rested upon several observations concerning the results of previous policy approaches. Despite the establishment of regimes of environmental protection at both national and international level in the 1970s, new and potentially serious problems had emerged in the 1980s. Nitrate pollution, ozone depletion and global climate change were new, largely unanticipated, issues that existing policy processes seemed unable to deal with. Moreover, the selective attention built into existing approaches meant that certain problems, most obviously soil contamination, had simply been ignored in the earlier policy strategies. As scientific instrumentation improved and environmental knowledge grew, so awareness of the scale and seriousness of problems increased.

This awareness was also accompanied by an increased understanding about the sources and consequences of pollution. The origins of pollution came to be seen not simply as a by-product of economic activity but also as something that reflected the policy priorities of the state, most notably in terms of economic support given to farmers and the encouragement given to road transport. Other policy sectors, outside of the designated area of the environment ministry or its equivalents, were thus seen to be pursuing policies that had environmental implications that could be of more importance than the policies of the environment ministry. If the sources were various, the consequences were widespread. The international scale of pollution problems posed hitherto unheard of challenges to the organisation of the international system, premissed as it was on the assumption of the sovereignty of nation states and the practice of ad hoc co-operation on specific issues.[40] The economic consequences of permitting continued pollution also became apparent. A tolerance for pollution because of the costs of reduction was now being seen not as a way of successfully avoiding costs, but as a device by which costs were shifted across space, as with the UK's contribution to acid rain in Scandinavia, or across time, as with the contamination of groundwater that would prevent future generations from using certain sources. How to protect the interests of future generations became, as with the Brundtland report, one of the central themes of environmental concern.[41]

The net effect of these trends, it can be argued, was to intensify some of the distinctive characteristics of pollution control as an issue of public policy, and to change the structure of political processes that dealt with the problem of pollution. The policy response of the 1970s both by its decisions and by its non-decisions, had to give way to the new politics that emerged in the 1980s. As these processes took place they began to unravel the key assumptions of the 1970s' reform strategies, of which one central element was the belief that environmental policy stood in a simple trade-off relation with economic growth and development. According to the conventional wisdom of the 1970s, the pursuit of environmental policy involved a zero-sum game between the protection of the environment and a reduction in the costs of economic production: more of one necessarily means less of the other. The sharing of this assumption meant that less attention was necessarily given to creating and nurturing policy institutions whose task it was to find positive-sum solutions to policy problems, by which both environmental protection and economic prosperity could be secured.

A second key element of the conventional wisdom was the view that public action should essentially be a matter of, to use Matthew Arnold's distinction, 'mechanical' rather than 'moral' reform. On this account, the task of the public authorities is to secure the right rules of the economic game and not worry too much about the attitudes that players bring to the game. Van Gunsteren has noted how throughout Western democracies in the 1950s the belief became firmly established that ethical issues should not be allowed to intrude into public affairs.[42] Despite the widespread questioning of this belief, it is incorporated implicitly into the approach of the 1970s with its failure to pay attention to problems of implementation and compliance. This assumption was, to some extent, shared between both pro-environmental and economic feasibility coalitions. The difference between them was that the pro-environmental coalition favoured an extension of mechanical reform, whereas the economic feasibility coalition was resistant.

A further and related assumption was that the problems of pollution could be solved by an extension of existing policy instruments on an incremental basis. Wholesale refashioning of the relationship between the state and the economy was inappropriate. This was most clearly seen in the extension of the command and control techniques of administrative regulation to the variety of pollution problems that were identified. Many of the policy developments built upon long traditions of regulation for public nuisance that had emerged when pollution had quite a different character. Apart from the invention of the technique of environmental impact assessments, the regulatory strategies were often traditional in style, if novel in scope.

Throughout it was implicit in the conventional wisdom that the administrative apparatus of the nation state was the appropriate way to deal with the central problems of pollution. The European Economic Community treaty had not included provision for environmental regulation in its original version, and the Commission therefore found in the early 1970s that it had to establish its legal competence in the field by stressing the implications for international trade of environmental standards. Outside the framework of the EC, certain issues were dealt with by international treaty, but these clearly rested upon the assumption that independent nation states should be sovereign so that their freedom of action could only be limited by their own voluntary agreement. The notion that the main processes of pollution control might take a cross-boundary form that would create international patterns of mutual interdependence had to await the emergence of acid rain, ozone depletion and global climate change.

The persistence and intensification of old pollution problems and the growth of new issues provided the occasion for a new politics of pollution to emerge in the 1980s. The new politics reflected the new scale of problems, including their international dimensions, new patterns of interaction within the relevant policy communities and, ultimately, new intellectual and ideological conceptions of the policy issues. And yet the new politics of pollution grew out of the old. The strategies of the 1970s and the political movements that developed began the process of creating of a new system of policy actors who participated in the making of policy. Whereas pollution regulation had once been a specialist affair, involving primarily the pollution control authorities, regulated industries and a few members of the legislature, the policy community began to expand and diversify, reflecting more general social trends and the heightened place of pollution control on the political agenda.

A paradigmatic example of this process at work is provided by Christopher Bosso's study of pesticides and politics in the United States.[43] In the 1940s and 1950s, when DDT first emerged as a commercial possibility, public policy towards pesticides in the US depended upon the participation of a small number of groups within a closed policy community. In effect, policy was made by the representatives of producers, members of the bureaucracy and a limited range of politicians. By the 1980s a much wider range of actors came to be represented in the process, including consumer groups and public interest organisations. Foundations, like the Ford Foundation, had played an important role in the early 1970s in funding new public interest organisations, who were thereby able to take advantage of the legal system to challenge prevailing practices in the regulation of pesticides. In other countries analogous processes were at work. For example, in the UK Friends of the Earth transformed itself from an 'outsider' group to an 'insider' group within the space of some ten years, with the turning-point in its credibility coming in 1977 at the public enquiry at Windscale over nuclear reprocessing plans, when the press consistently referred to them as the 'leading objectors' or 'most effective opponents'. In consequence of their success, access to civil servants and ministers became much easier.[44]

One of the reasons why the policy community was able to expand to incorporate new groups and pro-environmental activists was that the new organisations were able to demonstrate technical competence, both in the way that they were able to challenge the premises of policy and in the way that they were able to exploit the political opportunity structures that were open to them. Undoubtedly the anti-nuclear movement of the 1970s and 1980s played an important role in this process. Environmental groups were able to demonstrate as much, if not greater, competence than the 'experts' within nuclear power bureaucracies over such matters as safety features of nuclear reactor designs, the health effects of radiation, the problems of disposing of nuclear waste materials and the economics of electricity generation. Moreover, all liberal democracies have land use planning procedures that allow members of the public to challenge decisions to develop large new generating plant. Variations in the extent and character of these political opportunity structures have been shown to be important in understanding the varying success of the anti-nuclear movement.[45]

The political ability of environmental groups to change the character and functioning of the policy community has depended

upon a number of more general social and economic changes.
Environmental groups have benefited from rising educational
standards, both in terms of support, since the better educated
frequently value environmental amenity highly, and in terms of
providing activists and a constituency that are scientifically and
socially literate. The ability to challenge the policy decisions of
existing elites has in part depended upon showing technical competence, and rising educational standards have supplied new generations of supporters able to handle complex bodies of information.
A related trend has been the development of specialist journalists
in science and environmental affairs who have been able to explain
technical issues in an accessible way. In the UK this development
occurred from the mid-1980s. Geoffrey Lean became environment
correspondent for the *Observer* in the late 1970s, but the prolife-
ration of journalists working in the field began in 1986.[46] There
is of course a self-reinforcing process at work in these developments. Once newspapers appoint environmental correspondents
they are more likely to carry environmental stories which in turn
will raise the salience of the issues on the political agenda. This in
turn provides a context within which environmental activism can
become politically effective.

Yet the political and policy coalitions that formed around environmental interests in the 1970s were in many ways fragile affairs.
As with any policy developments the emergence of environmental
concerns in the 1970s was dependent upon often transitory political conditions. The oil price shocks of 1973–74 and 1979 meant
that balance of payments and economic growth considerations
often loomed large in the thinking of policy elites. Thus the federal
German government under Helmut Schmidt was preoccupied with
economic policy in the late 1970s and it was only a few months
before he left office in 1982 that the Chancellor was said to have
acquired an interest in the environment. The Reagan administration was notoriously antipathetic to the supposed costs of the new
social regulation. Not only did Reagan make appointments to the
EPA of persons who were known to be hostile to environmental
regulation, but he effectively stripped the Council on Environmental Quality of its staff in 1981. Both the Labour government of
1974–79 and the Conservative governments from 1979 in the UK
saw themselves as giving a high priority to economic growth.

Partly under the pressure of these political set-backs, pro-environmental groups would find themselves seeking to develop and extend the initiatives of the 1970s without necessarily being able to go beyond the terms of debate and the intellectual premisses on which those initiatives rested. Yet within the pro-environmentalists there was a new belief system emerging that might be termed 'ecological modernisation' which challenged the fundamental assumption of the conventional wisdom, namely that there was a zero-sum trade-off between economic prosperity and environmental concern. Instead of there being a conflict between concern for the economy and concern for the environment, the argument emerged, most notably in the Brundtland report, that environmental protection to a high level was a precondition of long-term economic development. Without the maintenance of a healthy environment, the economy would be threatened, partly because clean-up costs would inevitably expand and partly because environmental degradation threatened the social and physical resources upon which economic prosperity depended.[47]

Once the conventional wisdom about the relationship between the environment and the economy was challenged, other elements of the implicit belief system might also begin to unravel. Regulation by legal and administrative instruments, for example, may no longer seem to be merely a mechanical matter in which the state plays the role of providing appropriate incentives for compliance. The internalisation of externalities becomes a matter of attitude as well as finance, and a cleavage begins to open up not between business and environmentalists, but between progressive, environmentally aware business on the one hand and short-term profit takers on the other. Moreover, the behaviour of consumers becomes important, so that the role of government policy is not simply to respond to the existing wants and preferences of their citizens, but also to provide support and encouragement of environmentally aware behaviour and discouragement for forms of behaviour that threaten or damage the environment. Once this view has taken root, the line from mechanical to moral reform has been crossed.

The challenge of ecological modernisation extends therefore beyond the economic point that a sound environment is a necessary condition for long-term prosperity and it comes to embrace changes in the relationship between the state, its citizens and private corporations, as well as changes in the relationship be-

tween states. This shift of focus is reflected in the changing pattern
of interest aggregation and interest articulation. Where once it was
possible to contrast an economic feasibility coalition and a clean
environment coalition, ecological modernisation suggests a plural
and variegated set of interests, with competing and different inter-
pretations of what values are at stake in matters of environmental
policy. These changes ramify through the way that environmental
policy is perceived and they include changes in strategies of regulation, emerging styles of public policy, alterations in patterns of
international relations, a changing relationship between science
and policy and ideological competition and debate. It is these
issues that we intend to dissect in subsequent chapters.

Political analysis and the new politics of pollution

The new politics of pollution provides a challenge not merely to
the established workings of the political system within liberal
democracies, but also to our understanding of those political
systems and to the traditions of analysis that are conventionally
employed in political science and policy studies. For example, a
key concept in conventional political science is that of interests, so
that both pluralists and their radical critics conventionally conceptualise politics as a process of interest conflict and aggregation,
even when they provide different accounts of how and with what
results competing interests are settled. The new politics of pollution offers a series of questions to this common-sense way of
proceeding. If the argument is that environmental protection is
now a precondition of sustainable economic growth, how should
we conceptualise the interests of consumers and producers? If
policy communities have expanded to take account of the growth
of political participation by environmental movements, do we have
to postulate a concept of 'knowledge interests' by members of
those movements and, if we do, what is the nature of the processes
by which those interests can be expressed and pursued?[48]

A further range of analytic problems emerges when we consider
the traditional distinction between domestic and foreign policy.
Apart from ad hoc commitments under international agreements,
most importantly the Law of the Sea, pollution control policy has
fallen with the sphere of domestic politics. Yet, in a period when
governments are being invited not only to think, but also to act,

global, it is difficult to maintain that distinction. New forms of international resource control regimes are beginning to emerge in which governments are pooling their sovereignty, for example the environmental policies of the European Community. International restrictions on marine dumping or the export of hazardous waste are being imposed. And the transboundary flow of pollution from stationary sources means that the territorial boundaries of the nation state no longer provide an exclusive sphere within which nations can pursue their own policies in the expectation that other nations will be willing not to interfere. Can the distinction still be maintained between international and domestic politics, and if not what are the implications for our account of political action?

It is clear, moreover, that the legitimacy of the modern state increasingly involves its ability to cope with environmental problems, but in seeking to maintain its legitimacy it cannot rely simply upon established habits and practices that have failed to address the problems at hand. New patterns of political behaviour will at least raise a question about how we understand politics. In the next chapter we shall examine some forms of understanding as a preliminary to applying these forms of understanding to a detailed discussion of some key elements in the new politics of pollution.

Notes

1   B. Commoner, *Making Peace with the Planet* (London: Victor Gollancz, 1990). For the importance of legitimacy in the exercise of power, see D. Beetham, *The Legitimation of Power* (Houndmills: Macmillan, 1991), pp. 56–63.

2   For the German and British cases, see chapter 3. For Reagan's anti-environmental revolution, see A. P. Hays and B. D. Hays, *Beauty, Health, and Permanence. Environmental Politics in the United States, 1955–1985* (Cambridge: Cambridge University Press, 1987), pp. 491–504 and P. C. Yeager, *The Limits of Law. The Public Regulation of Private Pollution* (Cambridge: Cambridge University Press, 1991), pp. 226–34.

3   C. C. Park, *Acid Rain. Rhetoric and Reality* (London and New York: Routledge, 1987), p. 159.

4   World Commission on Environment and Development, *Our Common Future* (Oxford: Clarendon Press, 1987).

5   T. J. Lowi, 'American Business, Public Policy, Case Studies and

Political Theory', *World Politics*, 6 (1964), pp. 677–715.

6   P. A. Samuelson, 'The Pure Theory of Public Expenditure', *Review of Economics and Statistics*, 36, (1954), pp. 387–89, reprinted in J. E. Stiglitz (ed) *The Collected Scientific Papers of Paul A. Samuelson* (Massachusetts: MIT Press, 1966), pp. 1223–25. See also, D. C. Mueller, *Public Choice* (Cambridge: Cambridge University Press, 1979), pp. 12–14 and M. Taylor, *Anarchy and Cooperation* (London and New York: John Wiley and Sons, 1976), chapter 2.

7   A. Underdal, 'Integrated Marine Policy. What? Why? How?', *Marine Policy*, 4:3 (1980), pp. 159–69.

8   F. Pearce, *Acid Rain* (Harmondsworth: Penguin, 1987), p. 96.

9   See L. K. Caldwell, *International Environmental Policy* (Durham and London: Duke University Press, 1990), p. 57.

10   The connection between the London smog of 1952 and the 1956 Clean Air Act is much more complicated than simply viewing the latter as a response to the former. For an excellent account, see R. Parker, 'The Struggle for Clean Air', in P. Hall, H. Land, R. Parker and A. Webb, *Change, Choice and Conflict in Social Policy* (London: Heinemann, 1975), pp. 371–409.

11   L. Lundqvist, *The Hare and the Tortoise. Clean Air Policies in the United States and Sweden* (Ann Arbor: University of Michigan Press, 1980).

12   S. Taylor, *Making Bureaucracies Think* (Stanford: Stanford University Press, 1984).

13   R. Carson, *Silent Spring* (Harmondsworth: Penguin, 1983, originally published 1962), pp. 63–4.

14   See Lundqvist, *The Hare and the Tortoise*, pp. 131–58 (for air) and Yeager, *The Limits of Law*, p. 220 (for water).

15   R. Levitt, *Implementing Public Policy* (London: Croom Helm, 1980).

16   R. Mayntz u.a., *Vollzugsprobleme der Umweltpolitik* (Wiesbaden: Rat von Sachverständigen für Umweltfragen, 1978).

17   See, *inter alia*, P. B. Dowing and K. Hanf (eds), *International Comparisons in Implementing Pollution Laws* (The Hague: Kluwer-Nijhoff, 1983); K. Hawkins, *Environment and Enforcement* (Oxford: Clarendon, 1984); B. Hutter, *The Reasonable Arm of the Law?* (Oxford: Clarendon, 1988).

18   A. Weale, T. O'Riordan and L. Kramme, *Controlling Pollution in the Round* (London: Anglo-German Foundation, 1990), pp. 127 and 149.

19   G. Hartkopf *et al*, *Umweltschutz und Verwaltung* (Bonn: Go-

desberger Taschenbuch-Verlag, 1986), p. 102 (on Germany); P. Lowe and J. Goyder, *Environmental Groups in Politics* (London: Allen and Unwin, 1983), especially pp. 36–7 (on UK); and R. A. Liroff, *A National Policy for the Environment. NEPA and its Aftermath* (Bloomington, Indiana: Indiana University Press, 1976), p. 144 (on foundation funding of US groups).

20   Committee on Multimedia Approaches to Pollution Control, *Multimedia Approaches to Pollution Control. A Symposium Proceedings* (Washington, DC: National Academy Press, 1987), pp. 7–53.

21   J. Conrad, 'Ökologisierung der Agrarpolitik als Politikspiel: Das Beispiel der Trinkwasser – Nitratbelastung', in J. Conrad (Hg.), *Wassergefährdung durch die Landwirtschaft* (Berlin: Edition Sigma, 1988), pp. 23–45.

22   P. Knoepful and H. Weidner, 'Implementing Air Quality Programs in Europe', *Policy Studies Journal*, 11, (1990), pp. 103–15.

23   S. Taylor, *Making Bureaucracies Think* (Stanford: Stanford University Press, 1984).

24   See, for example, Park, *Acid Rain*, p. 165.

25   For a detailed discussion of some of these failings as well as others in the German air pollution case, see H. Weidner, *Air Pollution Control Strategies in the Federal Republic of Germany* (Berlin: Edition Sigma, 1986), especially pp. 109–14.

26   OECD, *Environmental Indicators: A Preliminary Set* (Paris: OECD, 1991), p. 23.

27   OECD, *Environmental Indicators*, p. 47.

28   OECD, *Environmental Indicators*, p. 35.

29   OECD, *Environmental Indicators*, p. 17.

30   OECD, *Environmental Indicators*, p. 61.

31   OECD, *Environmental Indicators*, p. 27.

32   OECD, *The State of the Environment* (Paris: OECD), pp. 18–19.

33   The World Resources Institute, *World Resources, 1990–91* (New York and Oxford: Oxford University Press, 1990), p. 183.

34   World Resources Institute, *World Resources, 1990-91*, p. 209.

35   OECD, *Environmental Indicators*, p. 21.

36   OECD, *The State of the Environment*, p. 37.

37   OECD, *The State of the Environment* , p. 49.

38   World Resources Institute, *World Resources, 1990-91*, p. 10, reporting on a survey in Kenya, Nigeria, Senegal, Zimbabwe, China, India, Japan, Saudi Arabia, Argentina, Jamaica, Mexico, Hungary, Norway and the Federal Republic of Germany.

39   Second Chamber of the States General, *National Environmen-*

tal Policy Plan: To Choose or Lose ('s-Gravenhage: SDU uitgeverij, 1989), p. 42. See chapter 5 for a discussion of this document.

40   D. Held, 'Democracy, the Nation-State and the Global System' in D. Held, *Political Theory Today* (Cambridge: Polity Press, 1991), p. 201.

41   World Commission on Environment and Development, *Our Common Future.*

42   H. van Gunsteren, in F-X. Kaufmann, *et al, Guidance Control and Performance Evaluation in the Public Sector* (Berlin: de Gruyter, 1986), pp. 268–71.

43   C. Bosso, *Pesticides and Politics: The Life Cycle of a Public Issue* (Pittsburgh: University of Pittsburgh Press, 1987).

44   P. Lowe and J. Goyder, *Environmental Groups in Politics*, p. 134.

45   H. Kitschelt, Political Opportunity Structures and Political Protest: Anti-Nuclear Movements in Four Democracies, *British Journal of Political Science*, 14:1, (1986), pp. 57–85.

46   G. Lean, The Role of the Media, in L. Roberts and A. Weale, *Innovation and Environmental Risk* (London: Belhaven Press, 1990) p. 25.

47   World Commission on Environment and Development, *Our Common Future.*

48   For the concept of 'knowledge-interests', see A. Jamison, R. Eyerman and J. Cramer, *The Making of the New Environmental Consciousness* (Edinburgh: Edinburgh University Press, 1990).

2

Idioms of analysis

How should we understand the new politics of pollution? This question raises methodological as well as empirical and substantive problems. The processes I have outlined in the previous chapter are extensive and wide-ranging. They include new issues, new configurations of institutions, new forms of policy discourse and new patterns of international relations. We cannot hope to understand these changes in their full detail, so we shall inevitably have to simplify the story and abstract from the complexity. Such a process of simplification and abstraction is always done within a particular intellectual context, variously called a 'paradigm', a 'model' or, as I shall term it, an 'idiom'. This chapter will explore the possible intellectual modes within which we can understand the changing politics of pollution.

A paradigm, according to Kuhn[1], is 'a set of recurrent and quasi-standard illustrations of various theories in their conceptual, observational, and instrumental applications'. These illustrations are transmitted to a community of scientists by textbooks, lectures and laboratory exercises. It is by studying these paradigms that members of the community learn their trade. Models, according to Allison,[2] are like spectacles that 'magnify one set of factors rather than another and thus not only lead analysts to produce different explanations of problems that appear, in their summary questions, to be the same, but also influence the character of the analyst's puzzle, the evidence he assumes to be relevant, the concepts he uses in examining the evidence, and what he takes to be an explanation'.

Despite the elegance and influence of Kuhn's notion of a paradigm or the usefulness of Allison's notion of a model, the concep-

tual presuppositions they involve seem too rich for the understanding of policy processes. As the quotation from Kuhn reveals,
the concept of a paradigm relies upon an extensive institutional
arrangement of teaching and research formally carried out. It is
doubtful if policy analysis could claim such institutional security.
The notion of a model suggests something coherent, clear and well
developed. In some ways of analysing policy this is certainly true
– but not all. For these reasons I prefer the term 'idiom'. An idiom
is a way of speaking, comprising a set of terms structured into
various patterns of relationships and often bearing a close family
resemblance to other idioms concerned with the same subject
matter. Idioms provide a way of talking about, and therefore
understanding, political processes, but there is no assumption in
referring to an idiom that the connections between its component
parts are particularly tight or elaborate. Nor is there any assumption that one idiom excludes another. Just as children can learn to
speak in one way at home in front of their parents and another
way at school with their classmates, so analysts of public policy
may wish to vary their idiom depending on circumstances.

The four idiomatic modes that I shall be concerned with in this
chapter are rational choice theories; social systems analysis; institutional analysis; and policy discourse approaches. In each case I shall
seek to lay out the central propositions of the different idioms, and
draw out some of their characteristic implications for the understanding of pollution control policy. I have felt free to draw my
account of these different idioms from various sources, partly
because there sometimes is no canonical source to which one can
go, but largely because each approach is capable of being used in
various ways, and it is important to recognise this internal diversity within an idiom as well as the differences between them.

Rational choice theory

Within the idiom of rational choice theory, the basic unit of
analysis is individual actors who are assumed to have preferences
over alternative outcomes. The pattern that we observe in the
politics of pollution will therefore be the result of individual agents
pursuing their own goals in a context in which other agents are
rationally pursuing their goals. In this sense, rational choice accounts of politics are always reductionist, seeking to account for

collective patterns of behaviour in terms of their constituent parts. Nozick, for example, speaks of 'invisible-hand' explanations in this context.[3] He means to draw attention to the fact that reductionist, rational choice explanations account for complicated patterns of collective behaviour as the unintended outcome of individual action and he suggests that such invisible-hand explanations yield greater understanding than do explanations of phenomena in terms of intentional design by agents.

The rationality of the actors is revealed in the way that they choose a course of action, when confronted with a set of options. Rational agents are presumed to be consistent in their preferences over outcomes. A rational choice is the one that enables actors to find the most efficient way of reaching their desired end. Rationality in this context is always instrumental, concerned with the selection of means to ends antecedently given, rather than concerned with the nature of the ends.

The standard example of rational individuals in this sense is supplied by persons trading in a market, who have given tastes and preferences and seek to spend their resources in such a way as to attain their most preferred basket of goods at least cost. But the 'individuals' can also be organisational entities, for example firms competing with one another in a market who have to decide whether to bring out a new product range. Thus, Milton Friedman explicitly compares the decision processes of a firm to those of an individual playing a game, arguing that it is but a short step from the rationality of individual behaviour to the rationality of a firm's decision. Similarly, it has been suggested that a rational actor model can be applied to countries bargaining with one another when each has to decide whether to make a concession to the other side or not[4]. In neither case does rational actor theory enquire into the source or origin of the preferences, but instead considers how individuals would behave if they rationally sought to achieve their goals.

In analysis of environmental protection policy within the idiom of rational choice theory, two questions have traditionally been posed. The first is why is there a politics of pollution at all? The second is that, given that there is a politics of pollution, why does it take the form that it does? Let us look at each of these questions in turn.

According to standard rational choice accounts, the origin of the politics of pollution is to be found in the problem of *market failure*. To understand the concept of market failure, it is useful to look at the concept of market success. Within the tradition of analysis that has drawn most heavily upon the idiom of rational choice theory, namely neo-classical economics, a market is successful if it produces an allocation of resources such that no one can be made better off without making anyone else worse off. This state of affairs is known as a 'Pareto optimum' or an 'efficient' allocation of resources. It can be shown that, provided a certain number of conditions are satisfied, a competitive market will tend towards a Pareto optimum, and where there is this efficient allocation of resources there will also be a market equilibrium, that is a situation from which no agent in the system has an incentive to depart.[5]

Clearly this account of market competition only applies to a fictional world, since no one supposes that the conditions that would need to be satisfied in order for the market to tend to a Pareto optimum are ever found in the world as we know it. However, proponents of this account argue that it is a useful fiction. By identifying the conditions that must obtain if Pareto-optimality is to be achieved, we are in a clearer position to identify the causes of market failure when they occur. (The customary analogy here is with the frictionless world of physical theories, which can nevertheless serve as a useful reference point for what happens on the surface of the earth.[6]) A frequent cause of market failure is to be found in the existence of *externalities* or spillover effects. An externality exists when the consequences of a market trade are not restricted to the willing participants in that trade. Sometimes such externalities can be beneficial, as when beekeepers selling honey also contribute to the productivity of nearby flower beds owned by market gardeners; but often they will be harmful, as when a factory making a product for sale to its customers releases pollution into the atmosphere or rivers of a community.[7] In this case, unless rectificatory action is taken, the members of the community will suffer uncompensated losses. For example, they will have to wash their clothes more frequently or paint their houses more often.

In these sort of circumstances it is tempting to say that the members of the affected community will take action to secure compensation for the damage they suffer or to prevent the damage from occurring in the future. But it is at this point that the characteristic logic of rational choice theory comes into play. From the viewpoint of rational choice theory, the most important characteristic of environmental protection is that it takes the form of a public good, and thereby gives rise to the problem of free-riding.

Suppose that the reduction of pollution is costly and suppose that those who suffer the pollution would be willing to pay towards the cost, because this would be worthwhile from their point of view. Imagine, now, someone seeking to collect subscriptions from individuals to fund the reduction of pollution. As a rational agent, each person can reason as follows. It is unlikely that my subscription will make the decisive difference between the project succeeding and the project failing. Either enough is going to be collected by way of subscriptions from others, without my contribution, or it is not. If it is, then it is pointless in my contributing, since I shall get the benefit of the public good, even though I have not paid for it. If it is not, then it is also pointless in my contributing, for I shall have lost the use of the money between the time the subscriptions are collected and the time that they are returned unspent. Hence, whether or not other people contribute, it seems rational to any solitary individual not to contribute. And when the organiser of the scheme comes round to collect the subscription, our rational individual finds it rational to dissemble about his or her true preferences. But since everyone can think like this, it would seem that the project to reduce pollution will never get off the ground, even though everyone would be better off were they to contribute along with everyone else. Via this rational choice logic the pursuit of individual ends would seem to lead to a self-defeating conclusion.[8]

The point about the logic is that it is impeccable, even though it does lead to individuals being worse off than they need to be. We have here a version of an N-person prisoners' dilemma. A prisoner's dilemma is a situation in which the rational choice for each individual in a set prevents the set of individuals from realising joint gains from co-operation. The purpose of public policy on one version of rational choice analysis is to solve this prisoners' dilemma. Politics exists to solve problems of collective action, of which the control of pollution is a prime example. The explanation as to why there is a politics of pollution is therefore to be found in market failure. Markets on their own cannot be expected to produce an efficient allocation of resources so long as uncompensated externalities exist. The task of politics is to supply the public good of environmental protection. A similar logic can be applied to relations between states. On this account, international regimes of pollution control exist to solve the prisoners' dilemma that nations face when they confront one another over the use of common resources like the global atmosphere or the open seas. In the absence of international co-operation externalities imposed by some nations upon others would prevent the maintenance of global or regional public goods.[9]

The logic of this explanation provides a rational choice account of why there should be a politics of pollution, in so far as it explains why rational agents would find it advantageous to establish some authoritative body to make and impose rules upon themselves to prevent pollution. But it does not provide an account of the form that the politics of pollution will take. This issue is crucial. Presumably the rationality of agreeing to establish a common authority to solve collective action problems depends upon our expectation of how well that political authority is likely to be able to perform its task. Since we are considering rational agents, the most natural way to pose the question is to ask how we should expect rational agents to behave when they participate in policy-making processes in liberal democracies. This takes us into the domain of public choice theory – the portion of rational choice theory that is devoted to the analysis of rational agents in the contexts of collective action. Four main propositions drive the public choice account of environmental politics.

The first of these concerns the motives of politicians. Politicians are assumed to be office-seekers, that is their primary motive for being in politics is to win office. As Downs classically expressed the proposition: 'parties formulate policies in order to win elections, rather than win elections in order to formulate policies'.[10] The effect of this assumption is to suggest that politicians are not interested in issues for their own sake, but only in so far as commitment to certain causes will enable them to win votes and be elected to office. They can therefore be expected to be respon-sive to movements of public opinion in favour of one cause rather than another, but they will be cautious about making principled commitments to particular policy positions in case a majority of the electorate changes its mind. Moreover, winning elections normally involves being sensitive to a wide range of issues, since members of the electorate vary in their concerns. It follows that politicians have little incentive to be interested in the details of policy complexity in any one policy sector. The ability plausibly to put together a package of policy measures is more likely to lead to political success than a reputation for commitment to a popular cause in one department of public issues. As the British Green Party found to its cost, it is electorally inhibiting to be identified with a position in just a limited range of public policy, even if one does hold a popular position in that limited sphere.

Citizens too, according to rational choice theory, have little interest in attending to the details of policy. As Schumpeter put it with his characteristic bluntness: '... the typical citizen drops down to a lower level of mental performance as soon as he enters the political field.'[11] The reason for this is simple. Acquiring an expertise in politics is time-consuming and requires effort. In this sense it is costly. It will only be rational for citizens to incur these costs if it will enable them to achieve their goals more successfully. But for the average citizen the connection between being well informed on a particular policy question and achieving one's most preferred policy is typically remote. The likelihood of being able to influence the policy process at the national level in one's preferred direction is so small that it may as well be discounted entirely, although at the local level it would make more sense. Hence, a prediction of rational choice theory is that typical citizens will think, as well as act, local. They will be preoccupied with what goes on in their backyard, because that is where they are likely to have most effect.

Those who have most incentive to become familiar with the details of policy are producer groups who are likely to face regulations limiting their freedom of action and imposing costs upon their activities unless they take preventive action. Unlike the electorate, the costs of political action are concentrated for producer groups, and hence we can expect that they will organise political pressure groups to act in their favour. Moreover, since producers are relatively few in number they face less of a collective action problem in pursuing their interests than other members of society.[12]

The characteristic attitude of producer groups in respect of political regulation was exquisitely expressed by Adam Smith in the idiom of rational choice theory:

The interest of the dealers, however, in any particular branch of trade or manufactures, is always in some respects different from, and even opposite to, that of the public. To widen the market and to narrow the competition, is always in the interest of the dealers. To widen the market may frequently be agreeable enough to the interest of the public; but to narrow the competition must always be against it, and can serve only to enable the dealers, by raising their profits above what they naturally would be, to levy for their own benefit, an absurd tax upon the rest of their fellow-citizens. The proposal of any new law or regulation of commerce which comes from this order ought always to be listened to with great precaution, and ought never to be adopted till after having been long and carefully examined, not only with the most scrupulous, but with the most suspicious attention.'[13]

Other interest groups, for example those concerned with nature protection or generalised consumer interests, will also have characteristic motivations according to the rational choice idiom. In general one would expect public interest groups to be relatively weak. They suffer from the free-rider problem and so their activities depend upon strongly motivated individuals or upon political entrepreneurs, whose task will be to seek out issues that garner support and income. Other non-producer interest groups fall midway between the public interest group and the producer groups. For example, a residents' group that is affected by pollution will have a greater economic incentive to take collective action than the standard public interest group, but typically this incentive will not be as great as the producer group. Moreover, unlike the producer groups, residents' groups lack the full-time staff and office support that makes collective action easier.

Bureaucrats or public officials are the final group to be considered. Different approaches to bureaucracy can be found in the public choice literature, but the dominant account is related to the size of bureaucratic organisations.[14] Size is thought to stand proxy for the motivations that drive bureaucrats in particular a concern for salary and status. Moreover, since bureaucrats control much of the relevant information in terms of which their performance is to be judged, they are assumed to be able to raise their size above a level that is optimal from the social point of view. Given this motivation, it will not be rational to search for policies of cost-effective regulation. Public officials do not have to examine the private sector cost implications of their regulatory strategies, but instead seek to expand the scope of what they do.

These presumed motivations of key actors within the policy-making process may be combined into a general account of the politics of pollution that addresses questions of agenda formation, policy development and policy implementation.

Thus, the issues that come on to the political agenda will in part depend upon the preferences of voters and in part depend upon the ability of politicians to manipulate issues according to their rhetorical competence. No politician, no matter how competent, can manipulate the agenda without paying a great deal of attention to citizens' preferences. Equally, strong policy preferences among the electorate are insufficient unless there are politicians willing to be responsive to advance their own political careers. The effects on agenda formation will therefore depend on the strength of public preferences and the opportunities available to politicians. In principle, within the rational choice idiom, one would expect environmental issues to have relatively low salience for the mass of electors, that is one would not expect a high proportion of the electorate to make their candidate choice depend upon the candidate's stand on environmental questions. Since environmental benefits are public goods, candidate selection faces a free-rider problem: I may be prepared to make my candidate choice depend upon environmental concerns, if you are prepared to do the same; but if you vote for your economic interest, then I will do the same. The consequence is a political equivalent of Gresham's law: bad issues drive out the good. McLean cites evidence to the effect that in the US environmental concerns have moderate salience: some 2 per cent of a national sample said that they might depart from their normal partisan preference if the candidate were unsympathetic on the environment issue.[15] Whether or not this is in line with the prediction one would obtain from the rational choice idiom is a matter of judgement. The prediction itself is quite clear: environmental concerns will not figure as prominently in the calculus of voting as those issues, like economic well-being, that impinge directly on perceptions of personal welfare. Moreover, the direction of mass preference is as important as salience. Since voters have little incentive to obtain information on complex matters their judgements will underestimate the opportunity costs associated with measures. One would therefore expect to find the direction of preferences to favour environmental improvements, perhaps with an unwillingness to shoulder the costs when they become apparent.

At the stage of detailed policy formulation a different range of actors come into play. Interest groups are unlikely to direct their attention to the choice of electoral candidates, but they are likely to be interested in the range of policy alternatives over which a government must choose. Participation in the policy-making process will not be equal at this stage. In particular, producer groups will have a strong incentive to try to influence the process of decision in a way that is favourable to them. A similar story can be told of the more strongly committed cause groups, particularly those who are able to finance their political lobbying by creaming off income from the provision of selective benefits to their members. Political decision-makers are unlikely to have a strong interest in the substance of issues, so that the prediction from the rational choice approach is that policy will often be characterised by a stress upon symbolic rather than important issues, with little account being taken of social opportunity costs and with an inability to avoid perverse or counterproductive effects.

At the state of policy implementation firms have an incentive to resist profit reduction, and provided that the choice of policy instruments allows, they will exploit opportunities to weaken the impact of a regulatory regime. In particular they will exploit technical complexity in order to soften the blow of regulation. Collusion may well grow up between regulator and regulated, since regulators will wish to preserve harmonious working relationships with the firms with whom they are working and with whom they might find a future career. Moreover, job satisfaction is more likely to arise from acting as a consultant to industry than in adopting the role of enforcer. Cause groups have little capacity to monitor compliance with standards. No one has an incentive to estimate the costs and benefits of regulation.

Systems idiom

The rational choice idiom is based upon the notion of possessive individualists seeking to achieve their own purposes in competition with one another. At the other end of the theoretical spectrum, there is the systems approach. This takes the social system as a whole as the basic unit of analysis, and seeks to derive an account of the politics of pollution from the way in which the component parts of the system respond to system constraints. There are in fact a variety of models that can be specified in this form. However, for our purpose it is most useful to concentrate on the neo-Marxist approach in some of its more widely discussed versions. The essence of this approach is to view the relation between the state and the economy as a system whose components are functionally related to one another so that state and economy have to be seen as a system of relationships. By contrast with the rational choice idiom the focus is not upon the pursuit of individual goals within institutionally given constraints. Instead it is on the way in which components of the system adapt, or fail to adapt, to one another.

In its neo-Marxist variant this approach identifies the main components of the system in terms of the prevailing mode of production. A mode of production is the combination of the forces of production and the relations of production. A capitalist mode of production, in which the relations of production are defined by private ownership, will create its own structural imperatives, that is conditions that will need to be satisfied if the mode of production is going to be able to continue. In particular, it will create the imperative of capital accumulation, that is the continual need to expand the forces of production under the pressure of economic competition. However, the state also exists within the same social system. The state has its own structural imperatives, in particular its need to secure legitimacy. To achieve legitimacy it must meet the democratic aspirations of its citizens. The problem for the system is that the imperative of capitalist accumulation is in conflict with the imperative of political legitimacy.[16]

The social system must therefore establish devices that mediate this conflict. The characteristic logic of the systems approach is therefore to identify the functional prerequisites of system maintenance, for unless these functional prerequisites are maintained, the social system will collapse from the stress of its internal contradictions.

This approach does not imply that understanding system outcomes requires an appeal to the logic of functional explanation. There may be such an appeal in versions of the contemporary neo-Marxist systems approach, but, as Dorothy Emmet pointed out in respect of an earlier generation of structural-functionalists, it is the notion of structure that is explanatory, whereas the notion of function is more like a heuristic device identifying what are important features in the workings and maintenance of the social

system.[17]   Moreover, the neo-Marxist version of systems theory
that I am considering does not presuppose an instrumentalist
theory of the state, in which it is merely a tool of capitalist
interests, but instead sees the state as embedded within a contradictory set of social relationships.[18]

The implications of this approach for public policy have been
clearly discussed by Offe who identifies three subsystems within
modern society: the economic subsystem; the political-administrative subsystem; and the normative subsystem.[19] In this model there
is both a positive and a negative relationship between the subsystems, most clearly exemplified in the relationship between the
economic system on the one hand and the political-administrative
system on the other.

According to Offe the processes of exchange within the economic system create the need for state regulation. The growing
division and differentiation of labour, for example, lead to problems that can no longer be dealt with adequately by the dynamics
of market processes. Market exchanges between owners of commodities create social conditions that threaten to destroy the process of exchange, and these conditions cannot be compensated
through exchange processes themselves. It is also important to
realise that the interdependence of the subsystems creates the need
for specific functional prerequisites within the political-administrative centre. 'The more that steering problems result from a failure
of the exchange mechanism to integrate the process of socializa-
tion, the greater is the degree of independence or relative autonomy required by the political-administrative centre if it is to repair,
compensate for, these problems.'[20]

On the other side of the system, there is the relationship between
the political-administrative subsystem on the one hand and the
normative subsystem on the other. The political-administrative subsystem cannot perform its function within the overall system unless
it relates adequately to the normative claims of members of society.
In particular, this means that it must achieve legitimacy by securing
mass loyalty and support for its actions. This in turn means that it
must show how its actions are consistent with the norms of a
democratic society, including respect for civil and political rights
and the basic equality that is contained in the idea of citizenship.

On this analysis the crucial problem is how to ensure the
identity and maintenance of the whole system, and this in turn

means ensuring an appropriate balance between its component parts. The clearest area in which there is likely to be a problem in achieving this balance is that of public expenditure. Securing mass loyalty will involve acknowledging and to some extent meeting citizens' demands for economic security, and this in turn means providing an adequate system of welfare state benefits. However, the finance of these welfare state benefits will place a strain upon the economic subsystem, to which the state will have to be sensitive. The state is therefore placed in the contradictory position both of needing to ensure a high and satisfactory level of public expenditure and control of the fiscal burden of social services.

However, although the fiscal crisis of the state provides the clearest example of the contradictory situation in which the state is located, there are other areas within which similar contradictory tendencies would be revealed. One of these areas is that of state regulation. Offe sees this as the principal service provided by the political-administrative subsystem to the economic subsystem. In an interesting twist, he argues that the contradictory role of the state is particularly acute in the area of environmental regulation, since the principal demands of the environmental movement, which affect the relationship between the political-administrative subsystem and the normative subsystem involve a concern for autonomy:

The concerns of these 'new social movements' are not geared towards what is to be created or accomplished through the use of state politics or power but towards what should be saved from and defended against the state and the considerations governing the conduct of public policy. The three most obvious of such movements, the peace movement, the environmental movement and various movements centred on human rights (of women, of prisoners, or minorities, of tenants etc.) all illustrate a 'negative' conception of politics trying to protect a sphere of life against the intervention of the state or state-sanctioned policy.[21]

Such a value orientation is of itself likely to be a source of contradiction for public policy since the form in which the state will seek to solve the problems of environmental pollution created by the economy is by closer 'steering' or regulation. Moreover, this conflict will be superimposed upon the one that is intrinsic to the relationship between state and economy, namely that the independence of the political-administrative subsystem, functionally necessary for it to perform its role, contains the danger that it will over-regulate.

It may be worth noting some specific points about the systems idiom. In the first place, there is nothing in the logic of the systems approach that denies the rational choice account of environmental problems as having their origin in production externalities. But in the systems approach the existence of externalities is merely a symptom of the conflict between the social nature of production and the private ownership of the means of production. In effect, capitalist enterprises are merely appropriating an item of common property, for example the air, for their own use. It is clearly implicit in this approach that there can be no final solution to the problem of externalities without changing the nature of the social system itself.

A second major feature of the systems approach is that it identifies a tendency within the capitalist social system towards turning problems of political values into problems of technical rationality.[22] The typical mode of operation in the administration of the modern state is that of instrumental rationality and the reliance upon established expertise. Consequently, another form of displacement that we should expect is that issues are removed from the forum of public debate, to a forum where a technical consensus can be established within systems of communication that can be officially controlled.

It is possible to identify some features of the policy processes that are entailed by the systems model. Since the origin of environmental problems is to be found in the contradiction between the private ownership of the means of production and the social nature of production, this implies that the process of agenda formation, but particularly policy development and policy implementation, will be dominated by the demands of capital rather than labour, or the new social movements. In its attempts to mediate in its conflicting role of servicing the needs of capital and sustaining political legitimacy, the political-administrative subsystem will structure the manner in which the problem is presented, turning it from an issue of political values into one of technical rationality. Moreover, the dominance of capital means that some alternatives, for example nationalisation, will not be considered. There will be closer links between the state bureaucracy and the industries that are to be regulated, and these links will be shielded from the focus of democratic scrutiny. The choice of policy instruments will be affected by this link, and there will be a tendency to avoid the 'polluter pays' principle, for example by choosing state subsidies as policy instruments. If the process of policy decision does by chance result in strong legislation, then implementation of policies will be weak. In all aspects of the policy cycle apparent 'solutions' to problems will in fact be displacements on to other parts of the system.

An important study of the politics of pollution control that has been conducted within this idiom is Yeager's *The Limits of Law*, which examines the characteristics of water pollution policy in the US during the 1970s.[23] This study focuses upon the 1972 amendments to the US Federal Water Pollution Control Act. Yeager draws attention to several features of the political processes involved: the marginal role played by representatives of environmental interests at the stage at which standards were set, in a process dominated by the interests of the public administration and the regulated industries; the tendency towards technical rationality rather than a publicly accountable political rationality in the discourse on pollution policy; the use of techniques, like cost-benefit analysis, that systematically understate potential environmental benefits and so favour the economic feasibility arguments of the regulated; and, most importantly, weak structures of implementation stemming from the regulatory overload placed on the Environmental Protection Agency that was given an impossible standard-setting task and from the absence of a high-level political commitment to prosecution as a strategy of enforcement. In conclusion, Yeager argues that the limits of regulatory law are inscribed in all of its aspects and the outer bounds of social regulation are set 'by the systemic needs of the political economic system of capitalist democracies.'[24] Here, then, we have a clear account of how pollution control policy will look when accounted for in the idiom of neo-Marxist systems analysis.

The idiom of institutions

The two idioms examined so far have been at opposite ends of the theoretical spectrum. Rational choice analysis begins with individuals and examines the outcome of their interaction; the systems model begins with the whole social system and examines its com-

ponents as an interrelated set of parts. However, there is an
intermediate level of analysis, namely one which takes institutions
as the basic unit of explanation. Institutions are not absent from
either the rational choice or the systems approach; they merely
appear obliquely. For the rational choice theorist institutions are
'congealed tastes' and their effect is to constrain the manipulation
of preferences by office-seekers, bureaucrats and so on.[25] For the
systems idioms institutions are the components of a set of interrelationships and their functioning is to be explained by reference
to the role they play in that wider system. In neither approach
do institutional characteristics assert an independent role on the
nature and form of public policy. An idiom of institutions seeks
to rectify this omission.

An institution for these purposes may be defined in terms of
'identifiable practices consisting of recognised roles linked by clusters of rules or conventions governing relations among the occu-
pants of these roles'.[26] Institutions, in this sense, comprise such
things as a system of rules governing electoral processes, the
practices of investment and market exchange, or regimes of international co-operation governing the use of resources, for example
fishing rights or the disposal of wastes at sea. As Young emphasises, institutions should be distinguished from organisations,
which 'are material entities possessing physical locations (or seats),
offices, personnel, equipment, and budgets.'[27] Examples of organisations in this sense are firms, political parties, trade unions,
pressure groups, government agencies, churches and charities.
The argument of those who favour the institutions approach is
that public policies need to be understood in the light of the
specific configuration of institutions and organisations that exist
within the political system. Some configurations will create the
conditions within which certain public policies may be pursued,
whereas other configurations will prevent certain strategies of
policy.

A clear example of this approach is provided by Katzenstein's
discussion of the way in which the organisation of industry and
trade unions in Austria create the possibility of corporatist forms
of economic management by comparison with Switzerland.[28] For
example, trade unions and industrial associations are required to
be members respectively of the Chamber of Labour and the Chamber of Commerce, which bodies are then involved in negotiation

over the direction of economic policy. In countries that have a fragmented trade union structure, it is not possible for governments to pursue corporatist forms of economic management in the same way. The institutional and organisational preconditions are simply lacking. Generalising from this example, we can say that an institutions idiom seeks to identify the specific organisational and other institutional conditions within which distinctive types of policy strategy will emerge. Among those who favour an institutions approach, essential reference must always be made at the basic level of explanation and analysis to the specific institutional settings within which public policies are made.[29]

An example of an institutions approach in the field of pollution control is provided by Crenson's study of the un-politics of air pollution.[30] In Crenson's comparative study of air pollution ordinances in East Chicago and Gary, great weight is placed on the organisational characteristics of the Democratic Party in each of the two towns. In Gary the party was tightly organised, acting as a broker between competing interests. In East Chicago it was a loose coalition of various ethnic groups. This difference in structure meant that the possibilities of individuals pursuing improvements in air quality varied. In the more open East Chicago system, it was not necessary for the leading individual to obtain the mayor's consent before taking action. In the tighter arrangements of Gary such consent was necessary. Moreover, the nature of broker politics imposes limits on what can be attained. Broker politicians find it more advantageous to deal in specific benefits, for example housing construction or public jobs, than they do in collective benefits, such as pollution control. When we have a broker-style political system, therefore, we should expect the relative neglect of collective goods issues. Comparative studies in this mode include Boehmer-Christiansen and Skea on acid rain policy, the collection by Downing and Hanf on implementation, Enloe's comparative study of pollution policy in the 1970s and Lundqvist's comparison of policy in the US and Sweden.[31] Kelman's study of occupational health and safety also for the US and Sweden provides a related example.[32]

In many ways the idiom of institutions replicates the patterns of everyday, commonsensical discussion about policy processes, especially for those involved as actors who as part of their job have to take into account legal and organisational constraints and possibilities in framing their own plans of action. In this sense, the institutions approach resembles systematised common sense, in which there is an attempt to identify what features of the institutional environment are likely to play a particularly important role. However, within the institutions idiom we can find a tendency to go beyond the case study method (which may be biased itself, since institutional differences are the most prominent difference for the policy analyst between countries) and seek for middle-range empirical generalisations about policy behaviour.

An influential stream of analysis within an institutions idiom has begun from the observation of the constraints of organisational process. Governments must use bureaucratic modes of action in order to pursue their policies; as such bureaucracies will be liable to the problems of organisational process. One particular problem is that of informational overload. Organisations possess in Simon's terms, only 'bounded rationality', since they cannot have at their disposal all the relevant information for taking decisions and acting.[33] One important dimension of this is the limitations on the type of information that can be stored in retrievable form; another limitation is the time available to actors within the organisation to understand the issues involved. With limited time issues compete with one another for attention and ways of coping with this information overload will have to be found if the organisation is to manage.

One of the typical ways in which organisations cope is to adapt existing procedures and routines of working to new problems. Moreover, standard operating procedures are the usual ways in which bureaucracies process issues and handle the demands of work. Hence existing practices tend to become important determinants of the way in which new problems are treated. For example, if international obligations, for example an EC directive, require an extension of pollution control, then the most natural way to handle this demand is to find existing legislative or policy provisions that can be adapted to satisfy the new demands. By extending and adapting existing standard operating procedures, a bureau will save itself the time and effort involved in thinking through a wholesale readjustment of its activities.

An auxiliary feature of the information problem for bureaucracies is that they become dependent upon particular sources of information and understanding and upon particular types of expertise. This is the phenomenon behind the idea of policy communities, specific clusters of actors who are drawn into the policy process by their need to share information. The existence of these shared networks of actors serves to reinforce the tendency towards bureaucratic politics, a situation in which different parts of the bureaucracy favour policy strategies that accord with their own perspectives, even though they may be at odds with the policy position of some other part of the policy process. It is a frequently observed feature of public policy that an environment ministry can find itself at odds with other ministries in government particularly those representing industry, transport or agriculture. Since specific policy communities surround different ministries, it is hardly surprising on the bureaucratic politics account to find unresolved policy differences. In consequence the making of a policy is likely to be characterised on any specific issue as a resultant of the competition for influence among players with different interests and varying capacities.[34]

Institutional configurations vary between different countries, and so within the institutions idiom much understanding can be gained by charting the varying institutional arrangements between countries and bringing these into line with variations in policy. Within this context variations in institutional rules are likely to be important. Thus, since some types of interests, for example farmers or industry, are geographically concentrated it will make a difference whether voting rules specify that legislators are elected on the basis of a constituency or a national list, since the two arrangements will affect the composition and orientation of significant policy communities. Similarly, it will make a difference whether a country has a federal or a unitary system of government. With a federal system of government, players in the policy game usually have less room for manoeuvre than actors within a unitary system.

Wider factors than specific institutional arrangements may be accommodated within the institutions approach, not least political culture. For example, when discussing why it was that the USA and the UK diverged in their system of environment regulation, having shared similar institutional forms during the Progressive era, Vogel argues that the old style of regulation remained resilient in the UK because it rested on three elements: a highly respected civil service, a business community that was prepared to defer to public authority and a public that was not unduly suspicious of industry.[35] Vogel's argument illustrates a general feature of the institutions approach: the specific institutional features of a political economy, conditioned by historical circumstance is invoked to explain the nature of the policies adopted, and it may become difficult to generalise across a range of political systems.

Of course it need be no part of the institutions approach to deny that similar institutional forms may evolve in different political systems. The most obvious example of such an institution is the capitalist corporation. If such a corporation is a structured set of roles exhibiting internal diversity, then we may expect it to behave in a different fashion when confronted by regulation than the firm as conceived in neo-classical theory. The neo-classical firm always has an incentive to oppose profit-reducing regulation. The modern corporation in the institutions approach does not always have that incentive, or rather the strength of that incentive may be counter-balanced by other considerations. In particular, certain members of the corporation will favour regulation because it favours their cause within the enterprise. Thus, the safety manager will welcome health and safety regulation because it makes negotiation easier with the finance department. More importantly, perhaps, the modern corporation is often said to favour certainty of future operations over the maximisation of profits, and therefore it will favour regulations and regulatory arrangements that promise to stabilise the market.

Although it is possible to venture some generalisations about organisational behaviour across different political systems, for example that large corporations will often favour regulation to reduce uncertainty or that bureaucratic in-fighting will make it difficult to impose a coherent strategy across the whole range of public policy, the logic of the institutions approach is to place such generalisations in the context of the specific historical and institutional conjuncture of a political system. The motivational generalisations to which rational choice theorists appeal need not be denied within the institutions idiom, but the stress within that idiom will always be upon the initial conditions within which these generalisations are supposed to apply, rather than with the implications of the generalisation *per se*. Thus, it matters less whether or not politicians behave as office-seekers than whether or not they are competing for office in an electoral system of proportional representation or first-past-the-post. Institutional factors dominate the motivational factors.

Since institutional factors vary from country to country, it follows that pollution control policy within any national system cannot be understood in the absence of a specification of the institutional arrangements for the political system in question. Within this approach specific historical features are likely to be of particular importance, for example the legacy of the 'consensual' style of air pollution control established by Angus Smith in nineteenth-century Britain or the Prussian system of licensing and uniform pollution control that still characterises German pollution control. Moreover, the composition of policy communities is likely to be a matter of great importance that will be determined by institutional arrangements and traditions. Thus, the prominent role played by the courts in the policy processes of both the USA and Germany contrasts with the subordinate role of the courts in the UK, and the difference is to be explained in terms of differences in constitutional arrangements and historical development. Yet these institutional differences, it is argued, have serious implications for our understanding of pollution control politics.

Policy discourse idiom

The idiom of institutions is often mechanical, focusing upon the hauling and pushing of bureaucratic and other policy actors within a political game. By contrast the idiom of policy discourse approaches to policy focuses not upon interests but upon understandings. The processes of research, discussion, argumentation, conjecture and refutation take centre stage, not the push and pull of mechanical forces. Policy-making is seen as a problem-solving activity in the sense that there is a cognitive and intellectual component to the formulation and development of policies and these components are non-reducible to considerations of bureaucratic interests. On this view of policy there will be coalitions of actors opposed to one another in a policy system, but their points of agreement and disagreement will depend upon their belief systems, not upon an antecedently identified concept of interest.

From this perspective significant features of public policy cannot be understood without making essential reference to belief systems. Thus, we cannot understand economic policy in the inter-war period without referring to the neo-classical orthodoxy that dominated most finance ministries at the time, nor can we understand post-war economic policy without understanding the rapid, if variable, spread of Keynesianism.[36] Similarly, we cannot understand the 'rediscovery' of poverty in the 1960s in a number of developed economies without understanding the background of work in the theory of relative deprivation that underlay the empirical findings. Nor, to take a quite different example, can we understand the changing character of nuclear strategy between 1960 and the 1980s without understanding the emergence of the doctrine of 'flexible response' and the implications it was thought to have for the conduct of war.

To note these examples is not, however, to provide a reason for making the study of belief systems central to the understanding of public policy for at least two reasons. The first is that, although certain belief systems may be essential for the legitimation of public policy strategies and principles, there is no reason to think that the holding of any belief system by members of the policy elite is the main cause of subsequent policy outcomes. Thus, it would clearly be too simple to ascribe the long boom of the post-war period to the adoption of Keynesian principles among economic policy elites, rather than to more general structural features of the world economy. The specification of belief systems may be essential to the identification of what policy elites take themselves to be doing, but it may not be a leading part of the explanation of subsequent policy outcomes, or perhaps even policy outputs. Secondly, belief systems themselves may be conceived as effects rather than causes, for example as rationalisations of some economic or political interest, so that reference needs ultimately to be made to the interests that underlie belief systems rather than to the belief systems themselves.

Despite these doubts about the centrality of belief systems as the basis for understanding public policy, there has grown up in public policy studies in recent years the view that belief systems are not merely epiphenomenal or incidental but do provide a crucial element in our understanding of policy formation and development. Thus, for Majone policy discussions involve a process of evidence, argument and persuasion in which a central part of policy choice is determined by the core elements of belief systems that function like scientific research programmes, determining what counts as evidence and how potential contradictory information is to be interpreted and reconciled.[37]

On one influential account of the philosophy of science, scientific theories can be distinguished in terms of their core and their periphery. The core of a theory is comprised of the central propositions that guide enquiry and research, for example, the proposition in evolutionary biology that acquired characteristics cannot be inherited, or that selection takes place at the level of the individual. Typically, these core propositions are surrounded by a 'protective belt' in the sense that they are not subject to scrutiny or testing. Tests are applied instead to peripheral propositions, for example what particular characteristics are adaptive for a species in a given environment, and the refutation of any particular peripheral proposition is not thought to have implications for the theory at large. By analogy, Majone argues, public policies exhibit a core and a periphery. The central assumptions of public policies tend to remain stable over long periods of time, and when change occurs it tends to take a form that does not challenge these central assumptions. The important point of this analogy is that it is the logical, not the institutional, features of scientific activity that provide the point of reference for the understanding of public policies.

To this approach Sabatier has added one crucial methodological argument.[38] This is the claim that beliefs are easier to identify and ascribe than are interests. Whereas it is a relatively straightforward matter to know what policy actors are advocating as a policy option along with the arguments and theories that they use to support their preferred position, it is almost impossible to identify their interests with any reasonable intersubjective plausibility. It is possible to take this argument one stage further and suggest that beliefs are, in some sense, logically prior to interests. In order to identify an interest we need to reconstruct the background of beliefs and assumptions from which self-ascribed interests emerge. Thus, even on the simplest model of economic self-interest, we need to assume that agents take their actions to be efficient means to their ends, otherwise we have no way of linking their actions with the preferences they claim to have. That such an identification of belief is often, perhaps typically, uncontroversial does not show that it is redundant.

One reason why the policy discourse approach may be applied

to pollution control policy is that professional expertise is necessarily involved in the making of such policy. Indeed, some items of policy will not come on to the policy agenda unless it is placed there by experts: we would not even know there was a problem of global climate change without the professional work of climatologists and other scientists. Similarly it was the work of the Swedish scientist Svente Oden which in 1968 represented a breakthrough to the politically controversial claim that airborne sulphur from East and West Germany and the UK was responsible for acidification in Scandinavia.[39] This being so, it is clear that the construction and interpretation of a problem will be influenced by the belief systems and conceptual frameworks that professional communities use in the conduct of their work.

A special twist in the idiom of discussive analysis is to draw upon the metaphor of 'social learning'. This perspective on politics and policy was well expressed by Heclo:

Politics finds its sources not only in power but also in uncertainty – men collectively wondering what to do. Finding feasible courses of action includes, but is more than, locating which way the vectors of political pressure are pushing ...

Political and administrative systems from this perspective are to be viewed as mechanisms of social learning. In this view societies are presented with certain problems, and the tasks accomplished by political and administrative evolution are to devise ways of solving these problems. Partly under pressure of these solutions and partly in terms of their own logic, new problems establish the conditions for further evolutionary change.[40]

General remarks

Although I have presented these four idioms of analysis as integrated and discrete entities, this is in many ways an oversimplification. None is as integrated and self-contained as the rather formal outline I have given suggests. For example, I doubt whether any of those who work in one or other of these idioms would say that a particular conceptual apparatus can be applied without amendment or adaptation. There is no perfect fit between the account given by the idiom and our observations of how policy is in practice made. Perhaps this is not surprising, when we consider

the motivational importance of anomalies and discrepancies between theories and observation in science. On Kuhn's account of
a paradigm, the propositions that form the centre of the paradigm
function to guide and structure observations and empirical work,
but it is the persistent anomalies that are thrown up by work
within the paradigm that provide the main focus for scientific
activity. A perfect fit between idiom and observation would mark
the end of the creative function of the idiom.

If the idioms are not self-contained, neither are they necessarily
discrete. Elements of the idioms may be linked together in various
ways. For example, a systems theorist could accept the rational
choice idiom as a valid characterisation of the behaviour of individuals within a system, but argue that it failed to account for why
individuals have the maximising motivations that they do. Here
the rational choice idioms would be nested in or subsumed by the
systems idiom, and our ability to interpret actors' behaviour in
terms of an attempt to achieve maximum preference satisfaction is
simply a consequence of the fact that the structurally specified
roles actors occupy require them, in a particular case, to be value
maximisers. If possessive individualism is an ideology functional
to the survival of competitive capitalism, then it will hardly be
surprising if a logical abstraction from that ideology, in the form
of rational choice theory, turns out to be a way of characterising
the behaviour of agents within the politics of market capitalist
societies.

However, idioms may be linked in other ways than by the
subsumption of one within the other. For example, rational choice
theorists admit that their accounts apply only under *ceteris paribus*
conditions, and that institutional arrangements are part of these
conditions. Any adequate account of the behaviour of actors
within a policy system, therefore, even if one accepts the rational
choice idiom, depends upon complementing one account with
another. But when two accounts are put side by side in a complementary way, which one should be the focus of theoretical
attention? After all, it may be that when all the initial conditions
are specified there is little freedom of decision for actors given the
institutional constraints to which they are subject. Once we accept
that certain types of maximising motivation are characteristic of
key actors within a political system, it may be more important to
know the circumstances of their choice than to reproduce a hypo-

thetical calculus of choice. Understanding the institutional context may simply render the choice unpuzzling. In other words, idioms that are formally complementary may in practice stand in more complex arrangements of pre-eminence and subordination.

Where idioms rival one another there is usually no simple test that will enable us to say whether one is superior to the other. Predictive ability is not a simple matter. Observation may not enable us to distinguish which of two rival idioms is applicable, since they may coincide in their predictions. For example, consistency in policy strategy over time may be taken as confirming an institutional approach that depends upon the idea of national styles of policy making, or it may be taken as confirming a distinction based in the idiom of policy discourse between policy core and policy periphery.

The new politics of pollution is a complex set of processes and it is possible to find elements that correspond to each of the idioms that I have identified. In the account of the politics of pollution that follows I shall seek to draw out elements that touch upon the themes raised by these different idioms. In the next five chapters I shall examine specific features of the new politics of pollution. These may be regarded as an interrelated set of case studies, the purpose of which is not simply to understand the new politics of pollution but also to explore which idioms are best suited to understanding these developments and changes. Only when we have surveyed the processes of pollution control policy can we consider which idiom or idioms are best suited to the task of analysis.

Notes

1   T. S. Kuhn, *The Structure of Scientific Revolutions* (Chicago: University of Chicago Press, 1970), p. 43.

2   G. T. Allison, *Essence of Decision* (Boston: Little, Brown and Company, 1971), p. 251.

3   R. Nozick, *Anarchy, State and Utopia* (Oxford: Basil Blackwell, 1974), p. 19.

4   For the use of rational choice ascriptions to organisational entities, see M. Friedman, *Capitalism and Freedom* (Chicago: University of Chicago Press, 1962) and for the use applied to nation states, see

G. Allison, *Essence of Decision.*

5   See, for example, E. R. Weintraub, *General Equilibrium Theory* (London: Macmillan, 1974), especially pp. 38–40.

6   Friedman, *Capitalism and Freedom.*

7   A. C. Pigou, *The Economics of Welfare* (London: Macmillan, 1920), p. 184.

8   For this logic and the idea of a prisoners' dilemma see, *inter alia*: R. Hardin, *Collective Action* (Baltimore: Johns Hopkins University Press, 1986); S. Hargreaves Heap *et al.*, *The Theory of Choice. A Critical Guide* (Oxford: Basil Blackwell, 1992); R. D. Luce and H. Raiffa, *Games and Decisions* (New York: John Wiley and Sons, 1957), pp. 94–7; D. Mueller, *Public Choice* (Cambridge: Cambridge University Press, 1979), pp. 11–18; and M. Taylor, *Anarchy and Cooperation* (New York: John Wiley and Sons, 1976).

9   O. R. Young, *International Cooperation. Building Regimes for Natural Resources and the Environment* (Ithaca, NY: Cornell University Press, 1989).

10   A. Downs, *An Economic Theory of Democracy* (New York: Harper and Row, 1957), p. 28.

11   J. Schumpeter, *Capitalism, Socialism and Democracy* (London: Allen and Unwin, 1954), p. 262.

12   Downs, *An Economic Theory of Democracy*, p. 254.

13   A. Smith, *The Wealth of Nations*, ed. A. Skinner (Harmondsworth: Penguin 1776, 1974 edition), pp. 358–9.

14   W. A. Niskanen Jnr, *Bureaucracy and Representative Government* (Chicago: Aldine-Atherton, 1971).

15   I. McLean, *Public Choice* (Oxford: Basil Blackwell, 1987), p. 54.

16   R. R. Alford and R. Friedland, *Powers of Theory* (Cambridge: Cambridge University Press, 1985); J. O'Connor, *The Fiscal Crisis of the State* (New York: St Martin's Press, 1973) and *Accumulation Crisis* (Oxford: Basil Blackwell, 1984).

17   D. M. Emmet, *Function, Purpose and Powers* (London: Macmillan, 1958), especially chapters 3 and 4. The best modern defence of functional explanation, strictly so-called, is G. A. Cohen, *Karl Marx's Theory of History : A Defence* (Oxford: Clarendon Press, 1978), chapters 9 and 10.

18   For a clear discussion of this distinction between instrumentalist and structural theories of the state, see S. Lukes, *Power* (London: Macmillan, 1974), pp. 52–6, discussing R. Miliband, *The State in Capitalist Society* (London: Weidenfeld and Nicolson, 1969) and N. Poulantzas, *Political Power and Social Classes*, translation ed. T.

O'Hagan (London: NLB and Shead and Ward, 1973).

19   C. Offe, *Contradictions of the Welfare State* (London: Hutchinson, 1984), p. 52.

20   Offe, *Contradictions*, pp. 48–9.

21   Offe, *Contradictions*, pp. 189–90.

22   J. Habermas, *Communication and the Evolution of Society*, translation T. McCarthy (London: Heinemann, 1979), pp. 178–205.

23   P. C. Yeager, *The Limits of Law* (Cambridge: Cambridge University Press, 1991).

24   Yeager, *The Limits of Law*, p. 306.

25   See W. H. Riker, 'Implications from the Disequilibrium of Majority Rule', *American Political Science Review*, 74:2 (1980), p. 445.

26   Young, *International Cooperation*, p. 5.

27   Young, *International Cooperation*, p. 32.

28   P. J. Katzenstein, *Corporatism and Change* (Ithaca and London: Cornell University Press, 1984).

29   Compare P. A. Hall, *Governing the Economy: The Politics of State Intervention in Britain and France* (Cambridge: Polity Press, 1986).

30   M. A. Crenson, *The Un-Politics of Air Pollution* (Baltimore and London: Johns Hopkins University Press, 1971).

31   S. Boehmer-Christiansen and J. Skea, *Acid Politics* (London and New York: Belhaven Press, 1991); P. B. Downing and K. Hanf (eds), *International Comparisons in Implementing Pollution Laws* (The Hague: Kluwer-Nijhoff, 1983); C. H. Enloe, *The Politics of Pollution in Comparative Perspective* (New York and London: Longman, 1975); and L. Lundqvist, *The Hare and the Tortoise: Clean Air Policies in the United States and Sweden* (Ann Arbor: University of Michigan Press, 1980).

32   S. Kelman, *Regulating America, Regulating Sweden: A Comparative Study of Occupational Safety and Health Policy* (Cambridge, Mass.: MIT Press, 1981).

33   H. A. Simon, *Models of Man* (New York: John Wiley and Sons, 1957).

34   Allison, *Essence of Decision*, pp. 162–84.

35   D. Vogel, *National Styles of Regulation* (Ithaca and London: Cornell University Press, 1986), p. 26.

36   See, *inter alia*, P. A. Hall (ed.), *The Political Power of Economic Ideas* (Princeton: Princeton University Press, 1980) and D. Winch, *Economics and Policy* (London: Fontana, 1972), especially chapter 6.

37   G. Majone, *Evidence, Argument, and Persuasion in the Policy Process* (New Haven and London: Yale University Press, 1989).

38   P. A. Sabatier, 'Knowledge, Policy-Oriented Learning and

Policy Change. An Advocacy Coalition Framework', *Knowledge: Creation, Diffusion, Utilization*, 8:4 (1987), pp. 64–92.

39 C. C. Park, *Acid Rain: Rhetoric and Reality* (London and New York: Routledge, 1987) p. 158.

40 H. Heclo, *Modern Social Politics in Britain and Sweden: From Relief to Income Maintenance* (New Haven and London: Yale University Press, 1974), p. 235.

3
The politics of ecological modernisation

The new politics of pollution have not developed at the same pace everywhere. Some countries have been able to adapt their systems of pollution control and environmental policy more rapidly than others. In all countries some aspects of pollution control have been adapted more extensively than others, and in no country is the transformation anywhere near complete. Yet, we can learn much by comparing systems that have responded differently to the new environmental challenges. In this chapter we shall compare the experience of Britain and Germany in the 1980s.[1] The reason for taking this pair is, in the words of Sonja Boehmer-Christiansen and Jim Skea, 'the widely divergent policy stances which were taken by the two countries on the acid rain issue'.[2]

Acid rain became an important issue of international and comparative policy in the 1980s. 'The term "acid rain" refers to the dilute sulphuric and nitric acids which, many believe, are created when fossil fuels are burned in power stations, smelters, and motor vehicles, and which fall over long distances downwind of possible sources of the pollutants.'[3] Its basic ingredients are sulphur dioxide, nitrogen oxides and ozone, which can be deposited in dry form, and in a wet form in solution with rain or snow or by suspension in fog.[4]

Policy towards acid rain is a good test of the differences in policy development for a number of reasons. Unlike air pollution by particulates, its effects were often widespread and remote. Moreover, although the phenomenon of acid rain has long been identified as a problem of transboundary air pollution, there are considerable scientific controversies about its effects alone or in combination with other pollutants. As we shall see, the widely divergent stances on the issue of acid rain in Britain and Germany involved and reflected a whole series of other institutional and ideological differences, and the difference in policy position over acid rain was replicated across a wide variety of issues. As case studies in contrasting policy approaches to environmental policy, therefore, Britain and Germany provide excellent examples.

Yet the contrast is in many ways a surprising one. At the time of the second oil price explosion in 1979, an observer of comparative environmental policy would have been most likely to conclude that Britain and Germany had a roughly similar position on environmental policy questions. Both countries were more preoccupied with the problems of maintaining economic growth than they were with the protection of the environment, so that the upsurge in environmental interest that had characterised the late 1960s and early 1970s appeared to have receded. Although both countries had legislation and administration in place for controlling pollution, the systems were patchy and prone to failures of implementation. In Britain significant portions of the 1974 Control of Pollution Act had not been put into effect, including those dealing with public access to registers of emission levels, and there was a continuing uncertainty about the future administrative arrangements for pollution control.[5] In Germany the principal legislation for air pollution control at national level, the 1974 Federal Immission Control Act was in place, but regulators were finding it difficult to advance more stringent emission standards under the legislation, and there were many other aspects of pollution that were weakly or inadequately regulated.[6] In both countries the day to day work of enforcing pollution control regulation was prone to bargaining and negotiation over the setting of standards and the timetable for their application. In Germany this phenomenon became identified by the term 'implementation deficit'.[7] At the international level it was a similar story. There was little use of the European Community (EC) as an instrument for internationalising environmental regulation and the governments of both countries were sceptical of the need for further reductions in sulphur dioxide emissions under international agreements and protocols, for example the 1979 Convention on Long-Range Transboundary Air Pollution of the UN's Economic Commission for Europe. In short, Britain and Germany together presented the spectacle of two, medium-sized and industrialised countries that had put in place

the legislation and policy instruments to cope with the most
obvious and visible problems of environmental degradation, but
who were unwilling to become pace-setters in a comparative context.

Slowly building up from 1979, however, German environmental
policy entered what Edda Müller has termed its 'recovery phase'
and revived its 'offensive' potential, and German policy positions
on a whole range of environmental questions have come to diverge
considerably from those in the UK.[8] The most important and most
vivid symbol of this divergence was the adoption in 1983 by the
German government of the Large Combustion Plant Ordinance in
the wake of the public concern over forest die-back (*Waldster-
ben*).[9] The 1983 Ordinance, implemented under the Federal Immission Control Act, imposed stringent limits on emissions of
sulphur dioxide on large furnaces, affecting most significantly
those plants generating electricity from the burning of coal. The
Ordinance required that existing plants meet the new standards
within five years, so that expensive flue-gas desulphurisation
equipment had to be retrofitted. By contrast, the British government's decision to retrofit flue-gas desulphurisation equipment to
a small number of power stations run by the Central Electricity
Generating Board in September 1986 was tardy, and taken after
much domestic and international campaigning. The lack of public
commitment to the programme was shown when it was revealed
in the aftermath of electricity privatisation that the government
would allow the newly privatised electricity generators to meet
emission targets by burning low sulphur coal rather by the installation of flue-gas desulphurisation equipment.

Although the most dramatic symbol of change in policy stance,
the legislation on air pollution was not the only example of
Germany's move to a more stringent pollution control policy.
Restrictions on vehicle emissions, including lead, have been pursued, and Germany favoured the development of an EC directive
requiring the fitting of catalytic converters on cars. Waste recycling
programmes have been implemented at local level, and in 1991 an
Ordinance on packaging was introduced making producers and
retailers responsible for the disposal of their packaging waste.
There have been point source reductions in water pollution by the
application of more stringent standards, and water quality maps
show signs of improvement. In 1986 a new federal ministry of the

environment was created and, although it took some months to establish its style and political resource base, it became a powerful force for environmental improvement by the late 1980s.[10] In international negotiations, Germany became anxious to use existing institutional regimes, like that of the European Community, to advance the international regulation of pollution, and it took the initiative in convening the first International Conference on the Protection of the North Sea in Bremen in 1984, thereby inaugurating a new regime of international environmental protection. In regard to problems of global climate change and the control of greenhouse gases, Germany had by the beginning of the 1990s committed itself to the ambitious target of a unilateral reduction in carbon dioxide emissions of between 25 and 30 per cent by the year 2005.

This is not to say that German environmental policy is solving the substantial problems of environmental protection that still exist. Whereas total sulphur oxide emissions fell by some 46 per cent between 1985 and the late 1980s, total nitrogen oxide emissions were more or less stable over the same period.[11] This discrepancy is consistent with a continuing decline in German forest health and reflects the growth of private vehicle use in the period. In the agricultural sector there is a neglect of non-point sources of pollution. The problem of hazardous waste has often been solved by the simple expedient of exporting it to countries with less stringent environmental regulation. Despite these weaknesses, it remains true to say that within Europe Germany has earned for itself the title of an environmental leader during the 1980s. In many ways the unification of Germany in 1990 consolidated the impetus towards stringent environmental standards. The discovery of the magnitude of the clean-up costs resulting from the environmental neglect of the former East German regime was shocking in itself and galvanised action, resulting in the federal government allocating DM800 million over two years for pollution control measures related primarily to drinking water and waste.

Britain's reputation as an environmental policy laggard or 'dirty man of Europe' has been won through a dogged determination not to take action in fields with international repercussions, most notably action to reduce emissions of sulphur dioxide. Although the UK's total emissions of sulphur dioxide fell by some 23 per cent in the first half of the 1980s,[12] the principal explanation for this was the downturn in the economy following Sir Geoffrey Howe's deflationary budget of 1981. By the late 1980s, rapid rates of economic growth led to speculation that official sulphur dioxide projections were too optimistic and would be exceeded. During the 1980s the UK government put up fierce resistance to the adoption of an EC large combustion plant directive that had been originally modelled on the German Large Combustion Plant Ordinance of 1983. The UK's resistance was prolonged over five years, and the issue was only resolved in 1988 after much manipulation of timetables and reduction targets by those responsible for drafting the directive.[13] Since the UK was given a relatively generous target figure because of the comparatively high costs it faced in installing flue-gas desulphurisation equipment, any attempt to meet the target by alternative measures like the burning of low sulphur coal will increase scepticism in Europe about the UK's environmental commitment.

In other areas of EC and international policy, the UK has also been a laggard. The UK has been an unwilling participant in the EC's efforts to clean up Europe's rivers and coastal waters, for example by initially identifying only twenty-seven beaches under the Bathing Waters Directive, fewer than land-locked Luxembourg.[14] For some time the British government held up the process that eventually led to the Montreal Protocol, to the Vienna Convention and an international agreement to phase out the use of chlorofluorocarbons.[15] The British government has also been reluctant to commit itself to the reduction of carbon dioxide emissions unilaterally, tying its willingness to take action to simultaneous action by others. It is true that, at the International Conference on the Protection of the North Sea in The Hague in 1990, Britain did accept the case for ending the dumping of sewage sludge in the North Sea, but this was a relatively late change of heart, and it can be interpreted less as a sign of long-term commitment and more as a desire to avoid politically embarrassing public exposure.

These international dimensions of the UK's policy record have been mirrored in domestic aspects of its pollution control policy. Administrative arrangements have been reformed in ad hoc and incremental ways, following on the privatisation of the water supply companies and the creation of Her Majesty's Inspectorate of Pollution in 1987. The latter never settled into its stride, and there have been continuing difficulties in its relationship with the National Rivers Authority which acquired the responsibility for water pollution control with the breakup of the former Regional Water Authorities as a result of privatisation. The new water companies were allowed to breach water pollution standards to sustain their profitability. Continuing doubts have been raised about the management of hazardous waste. And the much vaunted white paper on the environment, published in September 1990, was generally regarded as a damp squib.[16]

Since 1980, therefore, Britain and Germany's environmental policies have followed divergent paths of development. Germany has moved from a position of reluctant environmentalism to one in which it is now legislating some of the most stringent pollution control standards in Europe and pressing internationally for more vigorous action on a wide range of issues. The UK, by contrast, has been laggardly in its adoption of environmental measures, and has acquired the reputation in international negotiations of resisting the development of more forceful pollution control.

It is useful at this point to consider the underlying political structure of those groups that have traditionally dominated air pollution control policy, and here a comparison with the USA is useful. In the case of US air pollution policy, Sabatier has shown that there were two competing interests over clean air policy.[17] On the one hand there was the 'clean air coalition', which was dominated by environmental and public health groups, their allies in congress, a few labour unions, many state and local pollution control officials (especially those in large cities with serious problems) and some researchers. This clean air coalition was united around a set of propositions concerning the role of industry and the state in respect of environmental protection. These propositions included a belief about the inability of markets to deal with pollution externalities and an assumption that the serious health problems created by these externalities would be ignored by state and local governments in their attempts to attract and retain industry. Against this clean air coalition was an 'economic feasibility' coalition that was dominated by industrial emissions sources, energy companies, their allies in Congress, several labour unions, some state and local pollution control officials and a few economists. This coalition was united around a belief system that gave high place to the role of markets in promoting economic welfare in general and also involved a mistrust of federal government involvement in regulation and an insistence that the benefits of human health gains be traded-off against the costs of making the necessary capital and technical investments. This pattern of coalitions around the elements of those competing belief systems could be replicated in the clean air case for both Britain and Germany in the 1970s. For example, during the 1970s and 1980s in the UK, the clean air coalition comprised a wide range of environmental and public health groups, some elements of the Labour Party, and some members of the policy elite including influential members of the scientific advisory system. On the other side was a coalition of groups who stressed the uncertainties attached to the benefits supposedly flowing from costly investments in acid rain abatement policies, including the Central Electricity Generating Board, the industrial emitters, the Confederation of British Industry, most of the Conservative Party and some members of the policy advisory elite.[18] The debate between these two coalitions was essentially framed in terms of costs and benefits, with much attention being paid to the question of how far the putative benefits had to be discounted in light of the scientific uncertainties that attached to them. A similar constellation of interests formed around competing belief systems in the Federal Republic of Germany. In the clean air coalition could be found the environmental movement, pollution control officials, some parts of the Social Democrats and members of the policy elite. In the economic feasibility coalition could be found the power generating companies, the industrial emitters, the Christian Democrats, some Social Democrats particularly from North Rhine-Westphalia, the German Industrial Federation (BDI) and some members of the policy elite.[19] But in Germany, unlike Britain, the balance of advantage shifted to the clean air coalition.

It is no doubt possible to give an account of these contrasting developments in the idioms of rational choice theory and institutional analysis. Within these idioms, the most obvious factor to point to as explaining these divergent policy developments is the difference in the party systems between the two countries and the effects of Germany's system of proportional representation upon the incentives facing office-seeking politicians by comparison with the UK's system of simple plurality voting. A system of proportional representation like that used in Germany will typically deprive any one political party of a majority in the legislature, and indeed in the 1987 elections German voters showed great sophistication in casting their second list votes in such a way as to deprive the CDU/CSU of an overall majority. The UK's system of simple plurality has the opposite effect, magnifying an electoral plurality into a legislative majority. Thus, throughout the 1980s Germany was governed by parties in coalition, and for a large part of the decade the Greens were a potential threat to the Christian-Liberal coalition at federal level and pivotal in the formation of a number of governments at *Land* level. For rational choice analysts it is a well-known result within the theory of political coalitions that small, pivotal groups can extract large concessions from potential coalition partners, and from this perspective it is not surprising that environmental issues become prominent on the political agenda.[20] Britain's electoral system, by contrast, allowed a political party with little more than 40 per cent of the vote to remain in office throughout the 1980s, free to pursue its overriding ideological objective of seeking to transform the ailing state of the British economy by reducing the scope of public intervention in its management. From this viewpoint the divergent policy developments corresponded to quite distinct political incentives and institutional constraints.

Notice, incidentally, that in such an account we do not need to posit any underlying difference of political culture or citizen preference about environmental policy in order to account for differences in policy trends, but we merely need to locate rational action within distinct institutional settings. To be sure, Germany has consistently scored a higher level of post-materialism than Britain among members of its population since the phenomenon was first identified in the mid-1970s, and some observers have pointed to potentially more deep-seated cultural differences between the two societies.[21] But against this must be set other evidence, most notably the share of the vote received by the British Green Party in the European Parliament elections of 1989, which at 15 per cent was the largest in any country. Moreover, a committed wielder of Occam's razor would not need to invoke these factors within the rational choice idiom. From the basis of social choice theory it is clear that identical preference profiles will yield quite distinct collective choices, provided only that the processes for amalgamating popular preferences vary sufficiently.[22] The institutional differences of electoral and party systems, by themselves, would be quite capable of explaining the divergence of public policies, without resorting to hypothetical conjectures about underlying cultural differences, or observed differences in the prevalence of post-materialist values.

Although the simplest model of office-seeking politicians within different institutional contexts goes some way to explaining divergent policy developments between Britain and Germany, it may be said to miss an important dimension of the story, namely how German policy initiatives were legitimised and justified within the relevant policy communities and in society at large. For a complex variety of historical reasons there are elaborate mechanisms of political accountability built into the German system of government. The influential ideological traditions associated with the idea of the *Rechtsstaat*, by which public action should take place through lawful procedures and with explicit justification in terms of principles, form one element of this historical complex. Another is formed by reaction to the totalitarian excesses of the Third Reich, leading post-war constitution builders to design a system in which public accountability for public action was high. As a result of these historical pressures there is in Germany a striking (to the outsider at least) amount of institutional attention devoted to the detailing and elaboration of policy principles and programmes, and there are firm institutional safeguards to ensure that administrative and political action is underpinned by an account of its rationale. Together with the frequently observed juridification of politics in Germany, by which for example the courts play a significant part in reviewing and defining the permissible scope of administrative measures, there are powerful processes of policy legitimisation built into the German policy system. These discursive features of policy development are ignored within the conventional idiom of rational choice analysis.

In their famous opening to *The German Ideology* Marx and Engels describe how, according to German ideologists, Germany underwent an unparalleled intellectual revolution within a short period 'principles ousted one another, intellectual heroes overthrew each other with unheard-of rapidity and in a three year period more was cleared away in Germany than at any other time in three centuries'.[23] Yet the problem with the German ideology, according to Marx and Engels, was that all this was supposed to have taken place in the realm of pure thought, and it did not occur to any of the philosophers to enquire into the connection of the new critical ideology with the philosophers' material surroundings.

In seeking to understand the divergent policy developments of Britain and Germany, we need to understand how a transformation took place in the legitimating discourse of German environmental policy but not British environmental policy if we are to capture the processes of policy justification and rationalisation in the German case. Unlike the German ideological revolution that Marx and Engels described, the contemporary revolution in intellectual orientation is still incomplete and it has been taking place more slowly. It is also unlike the earlier revolution in one respect: it can only be understood once we place it in the context of its material surroundings, for it is by reference to the interaction of ideas and institutional context that we can best appreciate how and in what ways this ideology has developed. Along with other commentators I shall refer to this ideology as one of 'ecological modernisation'. In the next section I turn to the principal features of this body of ideas.

Ecological modernisation as an ideology

There is no one canonical statement of the ideology of ecological modernisation as *The General Theory* is a source for Keynesianism. It is a view about the relationships between the environment, the economy, society and public policy that has to be pieced together from various sources. One way to understand it is by way of reflection upon and reaction to the assumptions underlying the policy strategies of the 1970s. In chapter 1, I argued that there were a number of assumptions presupposed in the pollution control strategies of the 1970s: that environmental problems could be dealt with adequately by a specialist branch of the machinery of government; that the character of environmental problems was well understood; that environmental problems could be handled discretely; that end-of-pipe technologies were typically adequate; and that in the setting of pollution control standards a balance had to be struck between environmental protection and economic growth and development.

The structure of ecological modernisation as an ideology is given by the denial of the general validity of these assumptions. According to the proponent of ecological modernisation, serious environmental problems are frequently not obvious and the link from cause to effect is often long and indirect. Fundamental problems of environmental protection cannot be dealt with by end-of-pipe technologies, but need to be tackled at source. One reason for this is that from the perspective of the mass balance approach to pollution the solution of one disposal problem will merely displace the problem into another medium. Indeed, if anything forms the leitmotif of the modernist's critique of 1970s environmental policy it is that the policy strategies adopted characteristically resulted in problem displacement, across time and place, rather than problem solution.

However, it is in reconceptualising the relationship between economy and environment that the ideology of ecological modernisation probably marks the most decisive break with the assumptions that informed the first wave of environmental policy. There are a number of themes that are pursued in the reconceptualisation. One of these takes the form of a simple critique. If the 'costs' of environmental protection are avoided the effect is frequently to save money for present generations at the price of an increased burden for future generations. In other words, the costs do not disappear, they are merely pushed forward and possibly magnified in the process. Thus, a failure to regulate industrial waste disposal or agricultural pesticide use in one generation will simply have the effect of creating soil clean-up costs for future generations.

The claims of ecological modernisation go deeper than this, however. Instead of seeing environmental protection as a burden upon the economy the ecological modernist sees it as a potential source for future growth. Since environmental amenity is a superior good, the demand for pollution control is likely to increase and there is therefore a considerable advantage to an economy to have the technical and production capacity to produce low polluting goods or pollution control technology.For example, the EC's *Fourth Environmental Action Programme* makes the point that its proposals:

are rooted in the generally acknowledged fact that, as a key factor in economic decision-making, environmental protection policy and strict environmental protection standards are no longer an optional extra but a *sine qua non* for the quality of life which the Community's citizens expect.[24]

The point is sometimes linked to the fact that skilled workers in new technology industries (electronics, biotechnology, software and so on) have shown a tendency to wish to live in attractive and pleasant surroundings that do not display the environmental degradation of traditional industrial areas. Thus, Baden-Württemberg and Bavaria have seen a growth of the new middle classes precisely because of their environmental appeal.

Moreover, with the advent of global markets, the standards of product acceptability will be determined by the country with the most stringent pollution control standards. Hence the future development of a post-industrial economy will depend upon its ability to produce high value, high quality products with stringent environmental standards enforced. This aspect of the ideology of ecological modernisation was well brought out by Mr Laurens Brinkhorst, the Director-General of the environment directorate of the European Commission, speaking before a House of Lords select committee about the draft *Fourth Environmental Action Programme*:

Secondly – and here it is the old Japan hand who is speaking – I have become very much concerned – and I think this is a view largely shared by other departments – that environment and technology, environment and competition, have become brothers and sisters. It is not because of the low prices of Japanese products that the Japanese are making inroads in all kinds of areas (whether we speak about cars or computers), but it is largely because of the quality of their products and in the field of cars, for instance, the very high emissions standards.[25]

The same point is made in the *Fourth Environmental Action Programme* itself:

The Commission is convinced that hte (*sic*) future competitiveness of Community industry on world markets will depend heavily upon its ability to offer goods and services causing no pollution and achieving standards at least as high as its competitors. Small firms in particular can play their part. Technological innovation allied with a commitment to high supply standards can open up new opportunities, by developing new markets and putting to work the technologies of the future.[26]

Both of these passages are explicit in linking the prospects for future economic development in an era of global markets with higher standards of pollution control and environmentally safe products and processes.

This account of the relationship between economic competitiveness and environmental regulation is also linked to a view about the proper role of the public authorities in ensuring the condition for economic development. Public intervention, along with other decision processes, is an essential part of ensuring a progressive relationship between industry and the environment. Mr Brinkhorst put it as follows to the House of Lords Select Committee:

proper care and environmental standards actually make our society more competitive ... Europe as a technological power is falling behind because we do not put enough pressure from the government and industry, together with the consumer, in seeing that an effective environmental policy is a necessity for our industrial survival in many areas.[27]

Implicit in this account is a positive role for public authority in raising the standards of environmental regulation, as a means of providing a spur to industrial innovation.

In stating the ideology of ecological modernisation I do not want to present it as a coherent, well-formulated doctrine on which there is substantial agreement by many of those active in environmental politics. Each of the central propositions is capable of great elaboration and illustration, and the relative stress and importance given to each one of them will yield different styles of critique with quite distinct policy implications. For example, if more stress is laid upon the need to move from effects to causes then a radical version of policy is likely to emerge, whereas if the stress is the potential growth stimulated by an environmentally sound economy, then a more pro-industry version of policy is likely. However, despite the undoubted differences of emphasis that these distinct propositions will receive, ecological modernisation forms a category of discourse that is a flexible and powerful instrument for criticising the assumptions built into the first wave of environmental protection.

This body of ideas became appealing to many members of the policy elite in European countries and international organisation during the 1980s. Not only the EC, but also the World Commission on Environment and Development and the OECD took up the themes. Part of its appeal, I conjecture, is that it has the potential to break the political stalemate between the clean air advocacy and economic feasibility advocacy coalitions. Once it is recognised that pollution control can itself be a source of economic growth, both in terms of a rising demand for clean products and in terms of an emerging high-tech pollution control industry, then the balance of argument in terms of economic feasibility is tipped towards clean air rather than away from it. In particular, it weakens the economic feasibility arguments against anticipatory environmental policy, since it will highlight the costs of failing to act as much as the costs of acting. This does not imply that all actors in the policy system will recognise the case for improved pollution control. On the contrary, those who incur the costs of stringent pollution control will have an incentive to argue against its introduction if they cannot capture the economic benefits, and undoubtedly the operators of many coal-fired power stations fall into this category. All they see are economic benefits to pollution control companies or nuclear power operators arising from higher prices for coal-fired electricity generation. Nevertheless, it becomes more difficult to argue the economic feasibility case when there are economic, as well as political, arguments in favour of clean air.

My main thesis can now be stated. It is that there were elements in the ideological and institutional traditions of German public policy that made certain elements of ecological modernisation both a legitimising device of public policy developments and a potential source of policy principles. In making this claim I am not saying that the ideology of ecological modernisation was absorbed whole-sale by German policy elites in the 1980s. Indeed it will be part of my purpose to claim that the ideological and institutional features of German public policy that found ecological moderni-sation congenial also predisposed the discourse towards certain specific elements of the new programme. Nevertheless, by com-parison with the equivalent ideological and institutional traditions in the UK, ecological modernisation had a much better oppor-tunity in Germany.

Ecological modernisation in Britain and Germany

The basic principle in terms of which German policy developments were justified in the 1980s was the *Vorsorgeprinzip*, or principle of precaution. There is no simple or single meaning to be given to the principle of precaution. Indeed one analyst has distinguished no less than eleven different meanings assigned to the principle of

precaution within German policy discourse.[28] However, the typical context within which the principle of precaution is used in
which policy-makers are forced to go 'beyond science' in the sense
of being required to make decisions where the consequences of
alternative policy options are not determinable within a reasonable
margin of error and where potentially high costs are involved in
taking action. The installation of flue-gas desulphurisation equipment conforms to this pattern. At the time at which the decision
on the Large Combustion Plant Ordinance was taken, there was
considerable scientific controversy over the extent to which sulphur deposition was the cause of forest die-back, so that it was
unclear how much environmental benefit would be derived from
the implementation of a costly measure. Another example, where
similar levels of uncertainty pertains, is the dumping of wastes in
the seas, in connection with which the German Council of Experts
on Environmental Questions argued for a principle of precaution
in relation to the North Sea, even though the complexity of the
natural system was such that it would be difficult to bring the
costs of measures into any clear relationship with putative benefits.
A final example is provided by the uncertainties surrounding
global climate change, where the costs and benefits of either action
or inaction are difficult to conceptualise, let alone quantify. In all
these cases, proponents of the principle of precaution would argue
that precaution would indicate possibly costly measures to prevent
the possibility of serious environmental degradation.

During the 1980s in Germany the principle of precaution became a widely used justificatory principle among members of the
environmental policy community, but the idea was also taken up
by other policy elites in Europe, including those who drafted the
EC's *Fourth Environmental Action Programme*, who sought to
develop an approach to environmental policy that was preventive
rather than reactive. Commenting upon a draft of this programme
Mr William Waldegrave, as Minister of State at the UK's Department of Environment, said:

I have been struck by how often we appear to be dealing with subjects
not really on the basis of an objective assessment of environmental
priorities but as a result of the changing fashions in pressures from
outside. It is necessary in an area which should be science-based to put
up pretty formidable hurdles and tests of a scientific nature if we are to
make rational priorities ...[29]

In stating this view, Mr Waldegrave was only expressing an established feature of the British approach to environmental policy, namely that a scientific understanding of cause-and-effect relationships in natural systems is a necessary condition for adequate and rational policy-making. This emphasis was restated in the British government's 1990 white paper on the environment, where it was asserted that precipitate action on the basis of inadequate evidence is the wrong response.[30]

There are here, therefore, two competing principles of action: the principle of precaution and the principle of the scientific burden of proof. It is clear that these principles will pull in opposite directions over issues like acid rain or the protection of the seas. Why do we find that one principle is favoured in one country and a contrary principle in another?

The beginnings of an answer to this question can be found by contrasting German and British policy styles.[31] By tradition British policy making is conducted in a mode appropriate to a 'flexible' rather than a 'rigid' constitution (to use Bryce's vocabulary[32]). Policy is conceived as a series of problems, constituting cases that have to be judged on their merits. General norms are to be avoided if the decision can be left to the exercise of continuous administrative discretion. There is a desire to avoid programmatic statements or expositions of general principles governing particular areas of policy. The preference is for the particular over the general, the concrete over the abstract and the commonsensical over the principled. These features of policy-making lead to the absence of principled policy choice in many sectors of policy, including economic and health policy as well as environmental policy. Thus Hayward has characterised the British style in terms of an absence of explicit and medium- or long-term objectives on the one hand and unplanned, and incremental decision-making in which policies are arrived at by a continuous process of mutual adjustment between a plurality of actors on the other.[33] As Richardson and Watts point out, the specialised knowledge co-opted via the advisory group system is an essential element in this plurality of actors.[34]

The German policy style, by contrast, is consistent with the operation of a rigid constitution. A programmatic statement of general principles is seen as an essential prologue to legislation and policy development, a tendency that is probably reinforced by the

practice of coalition government in which political parties of
different ideological persuasions have to come to some agreement
on the running of government. Moreover, the emphasis upon
constitutionalism in the conduct of government also has the effect
of making the policy process more formal. Thus, as part of the
process involved in securing constitutional changes enabling it to
legislate on air pollution, the federal German government set out
the principled basis of its programme in a general statement in
1971.[35] The programme established the principles of the polluter
pays, the common burden principle in case where it would not be
possible to identify polluting source, the principle of social co-
operation in environmental policy and the principle of international co-operation. Within the logic of German policy discourse,
particular policy measures are seen as the 'concretisation' of
general principles, by contrast with the logic of British policy
discourse in which principles are seen as a generalisation of particular policies.

However, it may be argued that these differences of policy style
show that issues of policy principle will be handled by different
methods and under different assumptions within the two systems,
but they do not explain why particular principles, like the principle
of precaution, could play a creative role in German policy developments but not in British ones. After all, the principle of precaution
addresses an aspect of many contemporary pollution problems
where the science is generally only poorly understood. Since this is
an intrinsic feature of problems, how was the British government
able to side-step the challenges that it produces?

One answer here is to look at the composition and background
of typical members of the policy communities that gather around
pollution control. The high esteem accorded to respecting the
finding of science in the British system in part reflects a procedural
reality. Given the non-technical background of virtually all civil
servants involved in environmental policy-making, many elements
of choices are simply remitted to expert advisory committees or
the office of the chief scientist in the department. The intellectual
disposition of those with such a background is to look for evidence
to confirm a hypothesis, and if no evidence is to hand to suspend
judgement until it can be accumulated. By contrast the system of
uniform emissions set according to the principle of *Stand der
Technik,* as it operates in Germany, relies heavily upon the exper-

tise of lawyers and engineers, reinforced by the role that the Federation of German Engineers has traditionally played in the setting of pollution control standards. From these backgrounds the intellectual predisposition is not to ask for confirmation of an hypothesis, but to ask whether there is an enforceable technical proposal for dealing with a pollution problem and then ask whether policy can be built around that solution.

In one important respect, however, the policy community for pollution control is usually wider in Germany than the UK. The constitutional formalism of German policy-making means that the courts play an important role in the setting of standards, since proposed regulations or decisions may be referred to the courts by interested parties under procedures for judicial review of constitutional or administrative issues. Two important court decisions affected the interpretation of the precautionary principle.[36] In its decision on the licensing of the nuclear reactor at Whyl, the Federal Administrative Court refused to accept a distinction between the principle of precaution on the one hand and the generally accepted principle of protection from hazards on the other. The logic of the court's judgement was to argue that potential risks and known hazards are on a continuum, and that both protection from hazards and the principle of precaution required an approach in which the dangers and risks associated with nuclear power should be reduced as far as possible taking into account the state of science and technology. The logic of this position is to refuse to draw a sharp distinction between dangers that have been demonstrated and risks that are suggested but about which there is little current evidence. In the Federal Administrative Court's *Voerde* judgement, where the court held that a district heating scheme should be subject to more stringent air pollution controls, it was held that stringent controls were justified because the costs of pollution abatement had to be considered from the point of view of the economy as a whole, and air quality standards had to be taken into account beyond the immediate vicinity of the plant. In this latter judgement, in particular, there is therefore an acknowledgement of one of the key propositions within the ideology of ecological modernisation, namely that a failure to address a pollution problem does not save costs but merely displaces them elsewhere around the economy, for example in the form of forest damage or damage to buildings.

The net effect of the development of the principle of precaution was the tightening of emission standards within the framework of traditional legal regulations. The stress upon anticipation essentially entailed a movement away from a narrow cost-benefit calculation when considering the implementation of stricter standards and a willingness to see costs as part of a wider process of improving the social environment.

In addition to the development of these specific regulatory policies, another traditional instrument of German public policy has been used to promote environmental protection, namely public investment and subsidy. For example, between 1979 and 1985 the German government subsidy for environmental research and development rose from the equivalent of $144.3m to $236.4m, or from 2.1 per cent of R and D expenditures to 3.1 per cent. (The equivalent figures for Britain were $51.6m, that is 0.8 per cent of R and D, to $76.4m, or 1.1 per cent of R and D). By 1985 German public subsidy had in fact taken over from the US as being the largest absolute level of expenditure.[37] German public investment has also been used to provide financial support in the field of energy conservation, including investment help for firms installing energy-saving devices.[38] The use of public investment subsidies and tax concessions is a familiar element of German public policy. As Andrew Shonfield pointed out in his discussion of the phenomenon in *Modern Capitalism*, such a use of public funds derives from two sources: an ideological tradition of national economics, in which the aim of public policy is seen as that of building up the basic capacity of the national economy; and close organisational and institutional links between government and peak associations in which bargains can be struck about the terms of subsidies and performance targets.[39]

Looked at from this viewpoint, we would expect that certain elements only within the ideology of ecological modernisation were to be taken up and used in the course of policy arguments, and that other elements would be discarded or ignored. For example, the stress upon setting emissions standards implies a focus on effects, rather than causes, and hence a focus upon end-of-pipe solutions. We should not expect a great emphasis, then, in policy discourse on the need for structural changes in production and consumption to reduce pollution. It is striking in this context how much emphasis has been placed in German policy strategies on the installation of pollution control technologies, and how little on behavioural change, for example the imposition of strict speed limits on *Autobahnen*. By contrast we might expect a more positive responsiveness to the theme that there was a potential complementarity between economic growth and environmental protection, and hence a willingness to see the pollution control industry as a part of the expanding sector of the economy. The rise in expenditure on environmental research and development is consistent with this approach.

Of course this does not mean that arguments about the costs of environmental protection are redundant. Even if there is a net gain to the economy from investment in environmental protection, we should still expect some sectors to lose, especially if they are required to undertake new investment to upgrade existing plant. But the existence of costs, and hence of political arguments about costs, is consistent with a positive internalisation of environmental responsibility by leading economic actors, and one symptom has been the willingness of German firms to undertake environmental protection. The conception of the state playing a developmental role has, thus, provided an ideological framework within which elements of ecological modernisation could be incorporated into the thinking of policy elites.

When we turn to the contrasting case of Britain, there are a number of reasons why there was a lack of policy momentum. Scientific scepticism about the effectiveness measures like flue-gas desulphurisation rested on the claim that the proposed reduction in sulphur dioxide and nitrogen oxides would not yield significant benefits to forest health, and this in turn rested on the claim that the observed damage to forests could not be clearly related to sulphur deposition. It is tempting to take this as a bad faith argument on the part of the CEGB, but there are grounds for doubting this interpretation. One reason for doubt is that the scientific scepticism was not confined to CEGB scientists. Scientists at the Forestry Commission, whose institutional affiliation ought perhaps to sensitise them to forest health, were equally sceptical of the sulphur dioxide hypothesis.[40] Moreover, when CEGB-funded research revealed that continual sulphur deposition was contributing to the build-up of sulphur banks with potentially long-term consequences, this finding proved to be a turning point in CEGB policy.[41]

Even without the scientific scepticism, however, there were other trends at work that made it difficult to develop vigorous environmental policy. One was a preoccupation with machinery of government questions among policy elites. As part of the creation of the Health and Safety Executive, the Industrial Air Pollution Inspectorate, that is the old Alkali Inspectorate, was integrated with the inspectorates that had been responsible for occupational health and safety. The Royal Commission inveighed against this decision in its 1976 report on air pollution, but it took eleven years for the decision to be reversed and a new location to be found for the air inspectorate along with other inspectorates in Her Majesty's Inspectorate of Pollution.[42] This preoccupation with machinery of government issue was not confined to this one case. A continuation of the theme can be seen in the 1990 strategic white paper, *This Common Inheritance*, the bulk of whose positive proposals were procedural rather than substantive, and directed to improving the co-ordination of policy within government. Current Labour Party thinking duplicates the preoccupation.

This was reinforced by the Royal Commission's pursuit of one of its principal themes during this period, namely its concern with the cross-media effects of pollution control. The development of this theme by the Royal Commission is of interest since it clearly has a strong relationship to one of the central themes of ecological modernisation that stresses the interconnectedness of natural systems. In its 1976 report on *Air Pollution* the Royal Commission highlighted the problem of cross-media transfers by pointing out that the solution to an air pollution problem can sometimes involve a technology that worsens pollution in some other medium.[43] Its solution to this problem was to create a unified pollution inspectorate which would operate under the principle of best practicable environmental option. In effect the Royal Commission was recommending an incremental adaptation to the traditional British approach to pollution control, by which an inspectorate in central government could use its wide discretion and powers of negotiation to secure optimal reductions of pollution from operators of scheduled works at low cost. No doubt had the recommendations of the Royal Commission been accepted shortly after they were made, Britain would have entered the 1980s with a more efficient and effective system of environmental administration than it did, although it is questionable whether with the widespread attachment to the old informal procedures it still would have been adequate to meet the environmental challenges that the international context was beginning to impose.

One way of highlighting this point is to note how wide in formal, legal terms was the discretion of the air pollution inspectorate to regulate in matters of atmospheric emissions. Under the legislation operators of licensed premises, known as 'scheduled works', were required to use the 'best practical means' to reduce their pollution within specified limits. The head of the air pollution inspectorate, the chief inspector, had the discretion to say what constituted 'best practicable means' for any given type of process. Formally, therefore, the chief inspector could simply have decided that flue-gas desulphurisation was the best practicable means for reducing sulphur dioxide emissions from large combustion plants. The absence of action at this level reflects the constraints of governing party preference under which all civil servants work.

There were, in addition, two features of the Thatcher government programme that were always going to make the vigorous development of pollution control unlikely. The first was its desire to maintain strict controls on public expenditure. The second was its adherence to neo-liberal, laisser-faire economics. The control of public expenditure was relevant because the electricity generating industry was in public ownership throughout most of the 1980s, and technically any investment undertaken by a nationalised industry adds to the level of public expenditure. Similar considerations applied to water pollution control, which was the responsibility of the Regional Water Authorities. In order to meet improved environmental standards for either water or air, new investment would have been needed, and the public expenditure implications of this encountered resistance from the Thatcher government's desire tightly to constrain public spending.

But the policy of the Thatcher government was informed not simply by a desire to balance expenditure against income but also by a vision of the role of the state in relation to the economy and civil society. According to this conception the role of the state is to provide the framework within which economic agents can pursue their own goals; it is not to impose some collective view about where and how economic development is to take place. According to the most sophisticated account of the theory behind this view, in the work of Hayek, public officials are simply unable to know enough about the detailed workings of the economy to substitute their view of what will be profitable to pursue for the view of private entrepreneurs. It follows from this assumption that it ought not to be the role of the state to plan for the future or to promote new technologies. In so doing, it would merely be trying to second guess the outcomes of future market transactions, and this it will inevitably do badly. In this respect the libertarian conservatism of the Thatcher administration was unable to grasp one of the central elements of the ideology of ecological modern-isation, namely that the public authorities needed to promote high environmental quality standards, in order to accomplish the goal of promoting greater global competitiveness. In this respect too, ecological modernisation is mercantilism with a green twist; liber-tarian conservatism is its antithesis.

For a variety of ideological and institutional reasons, therefore, the German policy process provided a more hospitable environ-ment for the ideas of ecological modernisation than did the British policy process. British debates never escaped the belief that there was an inevitable tension between environmental protection and economic development. German debates did, but they selected those elements of the ideology of ecological modernisation they found most congenial. We have in these contrasting examples, then, identified some of the main sources of policy development and sought to understand the political dynamics of the Anglo-Ger-man comparison. What does the case study say about more general analytic issues?

Implications for analysis

I have argued in this chapter that the widely divergent stances of the British and German governments cannot be understood solely in the idiom of rational choice politics, even when that idiom is supplemented by an emphasis upon institutional variations that would make it rational for politicians and policy-makers to de-velop policies in one way in one country and in a contrary way in another country. Such an approach threatens to obscure the dis-cursive and justificatory aspects of policy development, and there-fore threatens to understate how changing ideological perceptions can tilt the balance of argument in favour of one advocacy coali-tion rather than another. This is not say that changes at the level of ideology provide the sole basis for understanding policy developments. Rational choice analysis may provide key actors within the policy system with the incentive to take up some arguments rather than others, and institutional contexts may provide circumstances within which some arguments carry greater weight than others. Indeed, it will be true that the possibility of mounting some arguments, for example those connected with constitutional principles, are only possible given a certain institutional context, because their use depends upon an ability of the courts to intervene in the processes of environmental standard-setting. Policy argument does not take place in an 'ideal speech situation', but in the rough and tumble of political competition and in the historically determined circumstances of those institutions given and transmitted from the past. Nevertheless, although the self-interested motivations of key policy actors and the institutional realities of bureaucratic politics may limit the rationality of policy discourse they do not entirely supplant it, and ideas and principles may play an independent role in the determination of policy outputs.

Such a conclusion also has implications for the idiom of systems analysis. There is no doubt that the functions of legitimating state action and securing mass loyalty do have to be discharged by the political-administrative subsystem, and it may be that these functions are in tension with the imperative of capital accumulation. But the emergence of the ideology of ecological modernisation may show that this conflict is not as fundamental as may be thought. In societies in which one of the central legitimating devices rests upon the ability to deliver to populations increasing standards of living, the capacity to redefine the terms under which that will be accomplished is a potentially important political weapon. The challenge of environmental protection suggests that how the function of legitimation is carried out is as important as whether it is carried out. Moreover, it may be significant that the home of the theory of the legitimation crisis has been Germany, a society in which a high emphasis has traditionally been placed both on capital accumulation and on the processes of public accountability through the principles of the *Rechtsstaat*. Hence, the specification of system functions may well itself depend upon an intellectual understanding of political cultures that are themselves affected by the dominant ideologies within any particular political system.

The contrast between Britain and Germany suggests therefore

that our idioms of analysis may need to be combined in complex ways when we examine the effects of new conceptions of pollution control policy. But, as critics of the strategy of the 1970s will point out, there are other dimensions to the critique of pollution control policy apart from technology enhancement and economic competitiveness. To one of those other elements we now turn.

Notes

1 Since unification in 1990, the nomenclature for the Federal Republic has become confused and tortuous. To avoid having always to refer to the 'former Federal Republic' or 'the former West Germany', I shall most often simply speak of 'Germany' meaning the Federal Republic established in 1949 and contained in the same boundaries until 1990.

2 S. Boehmer-Christiansen and J. Skea, *Acid Politics* (London and New York: Belhaven Press, 1991), p. 4.

3 C. C. Park, *Acid Rain* (London and New York: Routledge, 1987) pp. 1–2.

4 Strictly the term to describe the phenomenon should be 'acid deposition', since this covers the variety of pathways that acidification takes. However, the term 'acid rain' is so widely used that it is rather pedantic to stick to the strictly scientific designation.

5 R. Levitt, *Implementing Public Policy* (London: Croom Helm, 1980) and A. Weale, T. O'Riordan and L. Kramme, *Controlling Pollution in the Round* (London: Anglo-German Foundation, 1991), chapter 5. See also A. Blowers, 'Transition or Transformation? Environmental Policy under Thatcher', *Public Administration*, 65:3 (1987), pp. 277–94; H. Weidner, *Clean Air Policy in Great Britain. Problem-Shifting as Best Practicable Means* (Berlin: Edition Sigma, 1987).

6 For a good discussion reflecting the experience of the late 1970s as well as the 1980s in Germany, see H. Weidner, *Air Pollution Control Strategies and Policies in the Federal Republic of Germany* (Berlin: Edition Sigma, 1986).

7 R. Mayntz u.a., *Vollzvgsprobleme der Umweltpolitik* (Wiesbaden: Rat Van Sachverständigen Umweltfragen, 1978).

8 E. Müller, *Innenwelt der Umweltpolitik* (Opladen: Westdeutscher Verlag, 1986), especially pp. 114–43.

9 Boehmer-Christiansen and Skea, *Acid Politics*, chapter 10.

10 Weale, O'Riordan and Kramme, *Controlling Pollution in the Round*, chapter 4.

11 OECD, *Environmental Indicators: A Preliminary Set* (Paris:

OECD, 1991), pp. 21–3.

12   OECD, *Environmental Indicators*, p. 21.

13   Boehmer-Christiansen and Skea, *Acid Politics*, chapter 12.

14   N. Haigh, *EEC Environmental Policy and Britain* (London: Longman, 1987 edition, revised 1989), pp. 61–9.

15   G. Lean, 'The Role of the Media', in L. Roberts and A. Weale (eds.) *Innovation and Environmental Risk* (London and New York: Belhaven Press, 1991), p. 23.

16   Compare chapter 5.

17   P. A. Sabatier, 'Knowledge, Policy-Oriented Learning and Policy Change', *Knowledge: Creation, Diffusion, Utilization*, 8:4 (1987), pp. 661–2.

18   Compare Park, *Acid Rain*, chapter 10.

19   Boehmer-Christiansen and Skea, *Acid Politics*, chapter 10.

20   W. H. Riker, *The Theory of Political Coalitions* (New Haven and London: Yale University Press, 1962).

21   R. Inglehart, *The Silent Revolution* (Princeton: Princeton University Press, 1977) and 'Value Change in Industrial Societies', *American Political Science Review*, 81:4 (1987), pp. 1289–303; for the alleged cultural difference between Britain and Germany, see Boehmer-Christiansen and Skea, *Acid Politics*, pp. 58–63.

22   W. H. Riker, *Liberalism versus Populism* (San Francisco: W. H. Freeman and Co., 1982).

23   K. Marx and F. Engels, *The German Ideology*, in K. Marx and F. Engels, *Collected Works*, vol. 5 (London: Lawrence and Wishart, 1976), pp. 27–8. Marx and Engels note in this passage that '... when the German market was glutted ... the business was spoiled in the usual German manner by cheap and spurious production, deterioration in quality, adulteration of the raw materials, falsification of labels, fictitious purchases, bill-jobbing and a credit system devoid of any real basis.' It will be no part of my argument to uphold this as an accurate account of the contemporary German economy, whatever may have been true in the 1840s.

24   Commission of the European Communities, *Fourth Environmental Action Programme, 1987–92*, COM (86) 485 final (Luxembourg: Office for Official Publications of the European Communities, 1986), p. 3.

25   House of Lords, Select Committee on the European Communities, *Fourth Environmental Action Programme* (London: HMSO, 1987), 1986–87 Sessions, HL 135, pp. 53–4.

26   Commission of the European Communities, *Fourth Environ-*

mental Action Programme, 1987–92, COM (86) 485 final.

27   House of Lords Select Committee on the European Communities, *Fourth Environmental Action Programme*, p. 54.

28   E. Rehbinder, 'Vorsorgeprinzip in Umweltrecht und präventive Umweltpolitik', in U. E. Simonis (Hg.) *Präventive Umweltpolitik* (Frankfurt: Campus Verlag, 1988).

29   House of Lords Select Committee on the European Communities, *Fourth Environmental Action Programme*, p. 85.

30   Her Majesty's Government, *This Common Inheritance* (London: HMSO, 1990), Cm. 1200, p. 11.

31   For the discussion on policy styles, see also J. J. Richardson (ed.), *Policy Styles in Western Europe* (London: George Allen and Unwin, 1982).

32   J. Bryce, *Studies in History and Jurisprudence* (New York: Oxford University Press, 1901), chapter 3.

33   J. E. S. Hayward, 'National Aptitudes for Planning in Britain, France and Italy' *Government and Opposition*, 9:4 (1974), p. 398, quoted in J. J. Richardson and N. S. J. Watts, 'National Policy Styles and the Environment', International Institute for Environment and Society, Wissenschaftszentrum Berlin, Discussion Paper 85–16.

34   Richardson and Watts, 'National Policy Styles and the Environment', p. 12.

35   *Umweltprogramm der Bundesregierung*, BT-Druck 6/2710, reprinted as *Umweltschtuz* (Stuttgart: Kohlhammer, 1972).

36   See, in particular, the *Voerde* judgement, B VerG, Urt. v. 17.2.1984 – 7C 8/82, Mannheim, especially at pp. 373–4.

37   A. J. Heidenheimer *et al.*, *Comparative Public Policy* (London and Basingstoke: Macmillan, 1990, third edition), p. 343.

38   S. Boehmer-Christiansen, *Forests versus Fossil Fuels?* (Brighton: Science Policy Research Unit, University of Sussex, 1989), p. 71.

39   A. Shonfield, *Modern Capitalism* (London: Oxford University Press, 1969).

40   Interview evidence by author from member of Forestry Commission.

41   Weale, O'Riordan and Kramme, *Controlling Pollution in the Round*, p. 181.

42   Weale, O'Riordan and Kramme, *Controlling Pollution in the Round*, chapter 5.

43   Royal Commission on Environmental Pollution, *Air Pollution Control: An Integrated Approach*, Fifth Report (London: HMSO, 1976) Cmnd. 6371. See discussion in next chapter.

4

Controlling pollution in the round

The typical pattern for the development of pollution control policy legislation and administration in the late 1960s and 1970s was in terms of the specific receiving media of air, water or land. But the environment is a whole, and it is not divided according to the neat categories of public policy. Sulphur dioxide emissions are a problem of atmospheric pollution, but the acid precipitation that results contaminates the soil and freshwaters. Toxic chemicals dumped at waste sites can find their way into groundwater supplies. Pollutants released in one place can end up in distant locations as the presence of pesticides' residues in penguins testifies. Behind these processes there lie the basic principles of thermodynamics: matter is neither created nor destroyed; instead, substances undergo cycles of change within the total mass balance of nature.

Against this holism of nature there is the fragmentation of pollution control arrangements. Administrative arrangements are typically divided not only in terms of their scope – air, water or land – but also in terms of their location within the hierarchy of government, for example, at national, regional or local levels. National government ministries may have responsibility for the protection of one part of the environment but not another. Legislatures and legislative committees focus upon one set of environmental problems, and ignore others. Legislative authority and policy principles may vary from one substance or receiving medium to another, without there being any systematic rationale for the difference of approach. And no one has responsibility or competence to examine the totality of pollution effects that processes of production and consumption have upon the natural or social worlds.

The disjunction between the holism of the natural world, within which pollution occurs, and the fragmentation of the administrative and organisational relationships for the development and implementation of pollution control policy has often been criticised, and as experience grew of medium-specific pollution control strategies, the argument that administrative arrangements were inappropriate was developed. Yet, there is no system of pollution control administration in the world that overcomes the tendency towards fragmentation. The purpose of this chapter is to investigate the barriers to greater administrative integration, and to consider the implications for strategies of pollution control of the currently divided state of environmental administration.

Environmental interdependence and administrative fragmentation can lead to ineffectiveness and inefficiency in pollution control policy. Since polluting substances move between different media, the solution to, say, a water pollution problem may involve the intensification of an air or soil pollution problem. It is tempting to think that this is a technical nicety of relevance to control engineers and environmental scientists, but with no significant implications for the design of public policies. However, evidence is now beginning to accumulate suggesting that the cross-media transfer of pollutants is not a marginal or incidental feature of pollution control, but a central and typical feature, involving a wider range of processes than have hitherto been identified. Harris, for example, shows that contaminants from hazardous waste sites can travel not simply by a process of dissolution by groundwater, but also in solid form according to the slope of a clay layer or the incline of bedrock.[1] Similarly, Loehr and Ward point to the problems associated with waste-water treatment facilities. Volatile organic compounds and metals may be air-stripped during aeration or contained in sludge to be incinerated or disposed to land.[2] Teclaff and Teclaff point out how municipalities on Long Island, forced by state pollution control officials to stop refuse incineration, started to bury wastes in soils which, because of their porosity, leaked toxic chemicals into underlying groundwater.[3] In all these cases the potential arises from the cross-media transfer of pollutants that may lead to worsening environmental quality in one respect while improving it in another.

All end-of-pipe technologies have the potential for solving one pollution problem at the expense of worsening another, effectively displacing the problem across time or space. Catalytic converters will reduce emissions of nitrogen oxides into the atmosphere, but risk creating a solid waste disposal problem because of their heavy metal content. Similarly, flue-gas desulphurisation will reduce emissions of sulphur oxides, but involves techniques that may create a gypsum sludge that has to be disposed of. Even when an economic use can be found for the gypsum in the manufacture of plasterboard, transportation may well involve increased noise and vehicle emission.[4]

Apart from the lack of technical effectiveness that may be involved in single-medium pollution control, there is also the problem of economic inefficiency. Where different agencies and legislative agencies are involved in the administration of pollution control, problems arise that are associated with the phenomenon of 'multiple permitting'. A single industrial process may be responsible for discharges in the air, the water or to land. If different pollution control agencies are responsible for regulation into each of these receiving media, the operators of the process will find themselves subject to different, and possibility inconsistent, procedures and requirements. Thus, air pollution officials may impose a requirement for an operating permit that involves a plant in fitting flue-gas filtration equipment to remove metals, but the disposal of the filtered waste may infringe the permits granted for water or solid waste disposal. Dealing with such inconsistent demands is time-consuming and administratively complex in itself, and is likely to add to the transactions costs of the firm. Just as there is no reason why the sum total of these decisions made by different permitting authorities should amount to a balance of emissions that are optimal from the environmental point of view, so there is no reason to suppose that multiple permitting is the least costly way of obtaining effective environmental regulation.

Since legislative provision for different pollution problems is made under a variety of political circumstances, there is also a tendency for regulation by single-medium discharge to incorporate policy principles and decision criteria of quite different types and demands. Thus, the US Clean Air Act is based upon the principle of 'best available technology' with regard to the environmental need for a particular level of pollution control, whereas the Toxic Substances Control Act is based upon the principle of balancing costs and benefits.[5] Similarly, German environmental regulation varies in setting the control limits for air and for water, with the former requiring limits set in accordance with the state of technology (*Stand der Technik*) and the latter limits set in accordance with generally accepted engineering practice. In the German case it has been argued that the difference of principle may be less significant than at first sight it would seem, since the only distinction resides in whether a majority of engineers in a particular field accept a certain practice.[6] Although no doubt true in strict logic, the point remains that different criteria of control for different media allow the possibility for conflicting standards to be applied in the case of different media.

The shortcomings of single-medium pollution control have been acknowledged for some time. Indeed, at the very opening of the modern phase of environmental policy in 1969, Richard Nixon emphasised the importance of cross-media control in the presidential message announcing the establishment of the Environmental Protection Agency:

Despite its complexity, for pollution control purposes the environment must be perceived as a single interrelated system. Present assignments of departmental responsibilities do not reflect this interrelatedness. Many agency missions, for example, are designed primarily along media lines – air, water, and land. Yet the sources of air, water, and land pollution are interrelated and often interchangeable ... A far more effective approach to pollution control would: identify pollutants; trace them through the entire ecological chain; ... determine the total expense of man and his environment; examine interactions among forms of pollution; and identify where in the ecological chain interdiction would be most appropriate'.[7]

Moreover, it is clear that this was not merely an isolated and idiosyncratic statement from the pen of a presidential adviser, but represented a high level of consensus among informed environmental opinion at the time. The case for controlling pollution paying special attention to cross-media effects was one the central arguments of the 1976 report of the UK's Royal Commission on Environmental Pollution.[8] Subsequently, greater integration of pollution control has been called for by the OECD, the World Commission on Environment and Development and the EC in its *Fourth Environmental Action Plan*. It is also recognised by a number of governments in general statements of principle governing pollution control policy.[9]

Despite a high degree of consensus among informed observers, there has been little practical movement towards integrated pollution control in systems of public administration and policy. Legislation governing the use of toxic chemicals probably comes close to an integrated approach in a number of countries, since it is based upon a recognition that toxic substances migrate from one medium to another and may be dangerous to human health at even very low levels of concentration. Regulation in this instance therefore tends to be of the substance rather than the receiving medium, and control of substances has to be reckoned as one element of an integrated strategy.[10] However, this form of regulation has not proved to be a model for pollution control regulation in general. Moreover, even where governments have made legislative provision for integrated pollution, as with the Dutch 1980 General Environmental Policy Act, implementation has been slow and hesitant. Despite Richard Nixon's ringing statement and the high degree of consensus among opinion formers in the relevant policy community, the US EPA is still neither organised nor legislatively mandated to regulate pollution in an integrated way. Most other systems of pollution control are characterised by high levels of administrative, legislative and procedural fragmentation.

The exception to the trend is provided by Sweden, which, in comparative terms, has a highly integrated system dating back to 1969.[11] In that year comprehensive pollution control was established by the Environmental Protection Act and the associated Environmental Protection Ordinance, the latter revised in 1981. The main feature of the Swedish approach is its focus upon the regulation of all the polluting emissions from a plant according to the principle that disturbances to the environment should be prevented 'to the greatest possible extent'. Installations that require permits are therefore licensed in terms of whether they have reduced their pollution to a level judged optimal by the control authorities. There is, moreover, a commitment to improve pollution control standards in line with developments in technology. There are no uniform emission standards in any particular medium, but national guidelines are laid down. The process of licensing includes provision for public participation and legal challenge to the decisions that are taken, and there is also explicit provision for self-policing by firms with a procedure for checking and approving their internal systems of environmental monitoring.

However, even within this highly integrated process of permitting, the administration of pollution control has diverse elements made up of the National Environmental Protection Board, the Franchise Board for Environmental Protection and the local authorities. The Environmental Protection Board has a supervisory and co-ordinating role, laying down the lines of policy and national guidelines, whilst the Franchise Board is the body that grants licenses to particular installations, and the local authorities carry out inspections. At local authority level there is an uneven and variable distribution of labour between county authorities and municipal authorities depending on where they are located in the country. This administrative separation between national policy and licensing on the one hand and local monitoring and enforcement on the other was the result of a political compromise struck during the formulation of the 1969 legislation, and reflected both the established power of local authorities and an ideological commitment to democratic accountability.

Although there is some fragmentation within the Swedish administrative system, it is none the less true that the degree of integration is high, and the coherence of the licensing process is considerable. To a significant extent, the Swedish system does seek to take into account the totality of polluting activities arising from a particular plant and aims to find a best practicable environmental option minimising total impact. However, the Swedish arrangements cannot be used simply as a model or benchmark with which to compare other systems. The Swedish approach depends upon social and political circumstances and conditions that it is not always possible to replicate elsewhere. Thus, Swedish political culture has been usually characterised as consensual and non-adversarial, with a high premium placed upon finding rational solutions to problems. One would expect the processes of standard-setting and rule-making to be easier in these circumstances than in political cultures characterised by mistrust between leading social actors and a readiness to resort to litigation to solve differences of opinion. Moreover, by comparison with North America, there is an acceptance of an interventionist, regulatory role for the state, stemming from the ideological traditions of the '*overhet* state' and the historic role of the state in the industrialisation of the economy.[12] These same traditions have also contributed to an emphasis in Swedish economic management on technological innovation as a way of enabling an economy otherwise at a comparative disadvantage in a number of respects, to compete successfully in world markets. Finally, whatever political resistance the local authorities were able to put up in 1969 to the nationalisation of pollution control functions, they inevitably had fewer institutional resources at their disposal within the unitary Swedish state than subnational governments have within federal systems. Thus, if centralisation can be resisted in Sweden, we should expect that it can be resisted more forcibly elsewhere.

There is one further reason why the Swedish example cannot be taken as a definitive model for integrated pollution. So far the problem of integrated pollution control has been discussed in the context of proposals to reform the pollution control systems of nation states. But it is clear that in some ways the need for integrated pollution control arises most urgently in relation to the tasks of protecting international natural resources, for example the Great Lakes or the North Sea. The Swedish system focuses upon the plant as the locus of integrated pollution control. Yet this is only one possible focus, and it is equally necessary in certain areas to take note of the receiving region.[13] In the case of the North Sea, for instance, contaminants come both from sources like waste dumping or sewage treatment works, and from highly diffuse sources such as atmospheric deposition of metals. No amount of attention simply to identified activities causing pollution, for example stopping the dumping of sewage sludge, will address the problem of atmospheric deposition. A satisfactory pollution control strategy for the North Sea requires those responsible for control to take an ecosystem perspective based on the characteristics of the receiving region.

For a variety of reasons, therefore, the politics of integrated pollution are not identical with the politics involved in creating a national system of environmental administration, although undoubtedly the two often do amount to the same process. To understand why there has not been a greater development of integrated pollution control, we need to understand the general structural features of an integrated pollution control regime. Arild Underdal has provided a useful definition of integrated policy in this regard. For Underdal:

... a policy is integrated to the extent that it recognises its consequences as decision premises, aggregates them into an overall evaluation, and penetrates all policy levels and all government agencies involved in its execution.[14]

As Underdal recognised, the creation of an integrated policy system in this sense would be equivalent to the creation of a system of 'synoptic' decision-making. The usual contrast with synoptic decision-making is a system of 'disjointed incrementalism', that is a system of policy in which policy is assessed in terms of continuous steps from the status quo, and where a variety of actors, holding diverse and sometimes inconsistent perspectives, impinge upon the same decision-making process.[15] To ask why integrated pollution control is not more developed is to ask therefore why it has proved difficult to develop systems of pollution control distinguished by synoptic rationality rather than disjointed incrementalism.

A key element in identifying the answers to this question is to recognise that the organisational changes involved in creating a system of synoptic decision-making may be divided into two categories. Following Szanton, we can identify these as changes in *structure* on the one hand and changes in *process* on the other.[16] Structure is defined by the way in which the constituent part of the machinery of government are put together. This is the 'hardware' of government, the collection of agencies, bureaux, sections and departments that constitute the structure of government as an organisation. *Process* refers to the activities that take place within the structure, and comprises the 'software' of government, the principles and procedures that define what takes place within the organisation. Barriers to integrated pollution control may affect either the possibilities of structural reorganisation, or the possibilities of process innovation. To understand the barriers to integrated pollution control, we need to understand both the structure and their process aspects, and the relationship between them.

Integration and structural constraints

Since the US EPA was created and given a rationale in terms of integration, the failure to achieve a non-medium specific organisational structure can be instructively analysed in that case. During the formation of EPA, an initial attempt was made to create a structure that would mirror a multimedia approach.[17] However, the agency was an amalgamation of several bodies with their own traditions of environmental protection and styles of regulation. Such separate traditions are reinforced by the training of those who work in particular parts of the organisation. Engineers may have an expertise in water pollution and meteorologists in atmospheric pollution, but neither has a strong incentive to become familiar with the work of the other and neither is likely to be sympathetic to a reorganisation that involves the learning of new standard operating procedures. Given these organisational pressures, it is not surprising that the shape of the EPA was a compromise, with some offices based upon control in respect of specific media (air, water and categorical programmes) and others based upon functions (management, enforcement and research and development) that cut across approaches by specific receiving medium. To have created a new form of organisation in the early days would have required a great investment of time and energy by top management at a period when there was considerable political pressure to develop substantive policies. The urgent simply drove out the important. Over time new programmes and offices were created, for example solid wastes, and the single medium approach was organisationally entrenched.[18]

The limits on integrated pollution control do not derive simply from bureaucratic inertia, however. Members of the policy community find it advantageous to invest their reputations and expertise not in the health of the environment as such, but in the health of specific aspects of the environment. Thus, politicians develop an interest in a particular component of environmental policy and acquire political capital to the extent to which they succeed in defending the cause to which they are attached, as is instanced by the example of Congressman Bob Roe's campaign to prevent New York City dumping its sewage sludge off the coast of New Jersey.[19] Integrated pollution control depends upon the assumption that the correct way to go about policy is by means of 'nicely calculated less or more' of the balance of pollutants entering the environment. Political campaigns thrive on absolutist demands. 'No nukes here' or 'No sewage dumping in the sea' have a persuasiveness in politics that 'A graduated reduction of toxics in sewage sludge by 90 per cent over five years, provided that no adverse effects show up in the meantime', does not. It is difficult to mount a political campaign on complex statistical parameters.

These features of political campaigning are carried over into the type of legislation that is passed in the US. When EPA was established one of its first tasks was to implement the National Ambient Air Quality Criteria required by the 1970 Clean Air Amendments. These legislative amendments had been passed against a background of political disillusionment with the traditional New Deal style of regulation. In particular this meant that Congress no longer trusted to the expertise of regulators to come up with a policy strategy that accommodated the conflicting interests of affected parties. Instead, it required the implementing agency to set quantitative clean air targets and fulfil them by 1977 at the latest.[20] The new Air Quality Criteria came out on schedule, but only at the cost of absorbing the agency's attention in a single-medium problem. Since there is less political momentum in the US for general consolidating legislation than for highly visible attacks on single-issue problems, it is perhaps not surprising that the organisational capacity of the EPA is hamstrung by its legislative mandate.

If the EPA story illustrates how important certain types of political constraint can be in preventing structural reorganisation, the history of Britain's pollution inspectorate illustrates yet other sources of restriction. British environmental policy has been less prone to the populist political style that is characteristic of the US, and the political controversy over the creation of integrated pollution control took place among a small and select policy elite. Nevertheless, the political constraints on moving to integrated pollution control have been as strong in their own way as those in the US.

The topic of integrated pollution control emerged seriously on the policy agenda when the Royal Commission on Environmental Pollution reported on arrangements for controlling air pollution.[21] It had been invited to examine this topic in 1974 by the then Secretary of State for the Environment, after the work of the agency responsible for controlling the most serious forms of air pollution, the Industrial Air Pollution Inspectorate (IAPI), had come under attack from public interest groups for the secrecy and ineffectiveness of its work. During the time the Royal Commission was conducting its review, IAPI had been located with inspectorates related to occupational health and safety as a result of the

Robens Committee report on occupational health and safety. The Royal Commission was opposed to this location and it argued that for IAPI to be able properly to protect the environment it needed a line of accountability to the Department of the Environment:

Environmental policy is properly the concern of the Department of the Environment, and the expert knowledge of the inspectorate we propose would be crucial to the Department's work. It would clearly be unacceptable for the inspectorate not to be directly responsible to the Department.[22]

In other words, according to the Royal Commission, there was a clear need for an administrative capacity distinct from that of occupational health and safety if the function of protecting the environment was to be performed adequately.

One of the reasons why the Royal Commission was anxious to relocate IAPI was that it hoped that it would become the centrepiece of a new pollution inspectorate responsible for regulating pollution discharges from complex industrial processes into all receiving media. The Royal Commission identified instances where water pollution problems had been worsened by the IAPI's attempt to improve atmospheric pollution control, and it hoped that a body given responsibility for regulating the total environment would be sensitive to the trade-offs involved. It proposed that the name of the new inspectorate should be 'Her Majesty's Pollution Inspectorate'. The traditional principle that IAPI and its predecessors had used in regulating air pollution was that of the 'best practicable means' by which inspectors could require firms to install certain technologies for pollution control provided the state of the environment warranted it and the financial implications for the firm were acceptable. The Royal Commission borrowed from this traditional principle and proposed that in future the principle of regulation should be that of 'best practicable environmental option'. The idea was to produce a comprehensive approach to pollution control that would allow the new pollution inspectorate to set optimal controls for environmental protection through the adoption of an holistic approach to emission limitation.

If the textbook accounts of British public policy style are to be believed, the approach of the Royal Commission was a classic illustration of consensual, elite incrementalism. The existence, let alone the work of IAPI, was hardly a matter of public knowledge and the numbers of parliamentary participants in the debates surrounding the Robens reforms were few.[23] IAPI itself was unhappy with its location with the Health and Safety Executive (it never physically moved its offices from the Department of the Environment) and the support of the prestigious Royal Commission for its return to the Department should have counted for something. Moreover, the reform proposals of the Royal Commission were framed in a cautious incremental way. The logic of the Royal Commission's proposal was that the earliest national environmental regulatory agency in the world, with its well-established traditions and respected expertise, would form the heart of a new regulatory body whose operative principle would be adapted from tried and tested techniques of pollution control. Much of what had been considered definitive of the excellence of the familiar ways of working would remain in place: a collaborative relationship with industry; a professional inspectorate organised nationally and trained to high standards; and a dependence upon the pragmatic application of standards as circumstances warranted rather than the imposition of uniform emission limits.

Despite these features, the response to the suggestions of the Royal Commission could hardly be described as enthusiastic or speedy. It took two governments over six years to pen a reply that was negative, turning down both the ideas of an integrated environmental inspectorate and the principle of best practicable environmental option. In a passage reminiscent of Lewis Carroll's Red Queen, the reply acknowledged that the logic of the Royal Commission's proposals was unassailable, but asserted, in flat contradiction, that there was 'little evidence that the present system is failing in terms of achieving a sensible balance in the control of pollution in different forms'.[24] The reasons for the resistance to the Royal Commission's proposals largely reflected vested institutional interests, partly from industry, which had a good working relationship with the HSE, partly from the local authorities, who were also anxious not to have good working relationships disrupted, and partly from within the civil service itself, where awkward questions of pay scales would be raised by the creation of a new inspectorate.[25]

Eventually these set-backs were to be overcome with the establishment on 1 April 1987 of Her Majesty's Inspectorate of Pollution. Again, the political pressures leading to this outcome were as various as the sources of resistance to the original idea, but they included political embarrassment over the failure adequately to regulate discharges from the nuclear reprocessing plant at Sellafield, the 'product championship' of Mr William Waldegrave as minister and the return of the Royal Commission to the fray in its 1986 report. Seizing the opportunity of a review of the cost-effectiveness of regulation, a joint ministerial initiative between the Department of Employment, which had the responsibility for occupational health and safety, and the Department of the Environment referred the issue to a team examining the efficiency of the government machine and thereby found a mechanism for breaking the log-jam.[26]

The unified inspectorate that emerged from this process could be described as the germ of a comprehensive environmental protection agency, but could hardly be characterised as a fully ripe specimen. Its constituent units comprised the Industrial Air Pollution Inspectorate, the Wastes Inspectorate and Radioactive Substances Inspectorate and a fledgeling water quality inspectorate. Thus, its organisational arrangement was essentially medium-specific, despite its original inspiration in a vision of integrated pollution control. As Susan Owens characterised it, it was originally little more than an amalgam of existing inspectorates.[27] Perhaps this was only to be expected given the political difficulties that had surrounded its creation. There was, however, a variety of reasons why it could not be expected to develop comprehensive integrated pollution control quickly, quite apart from the intrinsic difficulties of the process to be discussed in the next section.

The first was the existence of a separate regulatory body, the National Rivers Authority, which had responsibility for controlling pollution into watercourses. The National Rivers Authority had emerged after a complex political wrangle, following the Conservative government's decision to privatise the water industry. The National Rivers Authority was intended to be a body having responsibility both for the management of water resources, for example flood protection, and the regulation of discharges into water under prevailing pollution control legislation. It was clear that given this remit, there was an inherent ambiguity in the relationship between Her Majesty's Inspectorate of Pollution and the National Rivers Authority, an ambiguity not made any the easier by the National Rivers Authority being some ten times

larger in terms of staffing than HMIP. An early indication of the
problems inherent in the relationship came with the controversy
over 'red list' substances, identified by the EC as being especially
dangerous when released to water and the subject of a Council
Directive. Under the new administrative arrangements it was
unclear whether HMIP or the National Rivers Authority would
have responsibility for regulating such discharges. Eventually
HMIP was assigned the task as part of its responsibility for
integrated pollution control at 'scheduled works', that is complex
processes requiring a high level of technical competence in respect
of pollution control. The National Rivers Authority was given a
consultative role in respect of these processes.[28]

The controversy over the allocation of responsibility for the red
list substances illustrates a general point about integrated pollution
control, namely the problem of defining the boundaries between
an agency responsible for taking an holistic perspective on environmental pollution and other agencies whose work necessarily
has an environmental dimension. Thus, the management of natural
resources cannot easily be separated from issues of pollution control in relation to those same natural resources. Decisions on land
drainage and the management of water courses will have implications for the pollution loads that rivers can bear. There was, therefore, considerable merit in linking together within the National
Rivers Authority the functions of river management and pollution
control. The problem is that such a linking of functions necessarily
precludes the possibility of integrating pollution control functions in
an agency working on a multimedia basis. The political dilemma
inherent in this problem was revealed when the Prime Minister, Mr
John Major, announced on 24 June 1991 that there would be yet
another reorganisation of pollution control, involving both HMIP
and the National Rivers Authority, the outcome of which seemed
likely to take some two or three years.

Apart from these difficult organisational and administrative
questions, a second problem revealed by the British story is the
one familiar from the US comparison, namely the need to give a
unified agency the legislative capacity to regulate in a multimedia
way. The 1976 Royal Commission report had anticipated this, but
the implementation of the legislative changes was slow when it
eventually came. The establishment of HMIP was announced on
7 August 1986 and the new organisation came formally into being

on 1 April 1987. The legislation giving HMIP new powers was not passed until the 1989–90 session of parliament, and did not come into force until April 1991, four years after the new organisation was established. New legislation was needed independently of the creation of the unified inspectorate in order to bring the UK into line with an EC directive on air pollution control. As it was, the legislation implementing the EC directive was later than it should have been, so that there is a chance that, without the quite fortuitous incentive provided by the EC directive, the legal instruments to bring about integrated pollution control would have been even more delayed.

The US and British examples have some features in common. In both cases organisational 'turf' disputes within the system of regulation displace the attention of policy-makers away from the substantive tasks of devising and implementing adequate procedures of integrated pollution control. Although the political barriers to the creation of suitable legal instruments for multimedia pollution control are greater in the US than the UK, both systems reveal how the quality of administrative reorganisation is dependent upon ad hoc conjunctions of political circumstances that cannot be guaranteed to support an agency in the difficult tasks of building up the capacity and the expertise to conduct integrated pollution control.

Similar political and organisational constraints are likely to occur in other systems. Thus, it has been argued that it would be impossible to create a fully integrated agency in The Netherlands because control of watercourses and canals is vested in the Ministry of Transport, with responsibility for the historically important *Waterstaat*. In Germany the strong position of the *Wassergenossenschaften*, established at the beginning of the twentieth century, would make the creation of a national body with full multimedia responsibilities politically difficult. In consequence, the administrative reorganisation that has occurred in these countries has taken place at the subnational, provincial level.

Thus the Swedish ability to create a body that would have free-standing responsibility for regulating environmental pollution in an holistic way rested upon specific political conditions that are not generally replicated elsewhere. The factors presenting complete integration in Sweden have proved even more constraining in other countries. One lesson that might be drawn from these experiences is that the development of integrated pollution control should not depend upon the creation of unified agencies, whose establishment is bound to lead to unproductive 'turf' disputes, but should instead depend upon changes in organisational process and the invention of new procedures that will facilitate the task of multimedia regulation. In other words, structural reorganisation is often infeasible, and therefore attention ought to focus on process innovation. It is to the experience of such process innovations that we now turn.

Integration and organisational process

The simplest type of process innovation to contemplate is integrated permitting. This involves the licensing of potentially polluting activities or processes according to one single procedure, instead of involving several regulatory agencies in issuing licenses under sectoral legislative mandates. There is no assumption in integrated permitting that the approaches and decision criteria contained in the sectoral legislation are consistent or, taken in sum, represent the basis for optimal pollution discharges. All that is involved is that one authority takes care of all the stages of licensing, thus saving the licence applicant the task of dealing with a number of authorities who might impose mutually inconsistent requirements. The need for integrated permitting obviously becomes more important the wider the scope and details of the specific sectoral legislation.

Sensing the problems of multiple permitting, the Dutch political authorities passed the General Environmental Provisions Act (GEPA) in 1979, which came into force in 1980. GEPA contains a uniform procedure for applying for and granting licences to be issued under the sectoral environmental acts. Applicants for a licence may request that procedures under the sectoral legislation be co-ordinated within the procedures specified by GEPA. An example of how integrated permitting in this sense works is provided by Graham Bennett's study of the decision to license the Rotterdam municipal authority to deposit contaminated sludge dredged from the Rhine/Meuse estuary on a site known as the Parrot's Bill.[29] The depositing of this sludge required authorisation under a waste act, administered by the Rijnmond Public Authority and water pollution legislation, administered by the Ministry of

Transport. Under the provisions of GEPA, it was possible for the Rijnmond Public Authority to co-ordinate the licensing process. When it turned out that the sludge to be deposited might contain substances that would be classified as toxic under the Dutch Chemical Wastes Act, the environment ministry also had to be involved in the licensing process. In principle, therefore, the application was potentially administratively complex.

The process of obtaining the final permit took three years, although the delay involved was partly occasioned by the unanticipated problem of the toxicity of the sediment. However, as Bennett and von Moltke note, the rigorous assessment of a complex proposal is almost inevitable in such a case. The reasons why the Rijnmond Authority was able successfully to act as the co-ordinating body were threefold. First, there was early notification from Rotterdam over the scheme, which enabled Rijnmond to initiate consultations with other regulatory agencies. Second, the existence of uniform permitting procedures provided the necessary legal and administrative conditions. Third, intensive consultation between the agencies involved was aided by clear agreements about how decisions were to be taken and good personal relationships between key officers.[30]

The Rijnmond example shows that integrated permitting is possible although the issues involved can be complex and generally a number of agencies operating under diverse legislative authorisations will be involved. However, integrated permitting is only a short step along the road of fully integrated pollution control. Consider for example the following definition of the concept of best practicable environmental option (BPEO) advanced by the UK's Royal Commission:

A BPEO is the outcome of a systematic consultative and decision-making procedure, which emphasises the protection of the environment across land, air and water. The BPEO procedure establishes, for a given set of objectives, the option that provides the most benefit, or least damage, to the environment as a whole, at acceptable cost, in the long as well as the short term.[31]

The Royal Commission is insisting in this passage that a comprehensive approach be taken towards the environment and that cost-effective reduction strategies in pollution control be adopted as the centrepiece of the substance of decision-making. This is clearly a far cry from streamlining administrative procedures in the application of what are basically medium-specific standards. It implies the possibility of developing techniques and procedures of pollution control that take cognisance of the holistic nature of the environment and the cycling of substances through different media.

The US Council on Environmental Quality advocated a similar approach in its *Sixteenth Report*. Arguing that the approach embodied in the policies of the 1970s needs to be modified to cope with new problems, the Council urges the principle that environmental protection policy must recognise the interconnectedness of the environment and emphasise multimedia approaches to pollution control. It also urges that the main business of environmental protection is the reduction of risk:

... when we require that pollution be removed from one environmental medium we are obliged to determine where it goes and what it does when it gets there, in quantitative risk terms, whenever possible ... Risk-based cross-media analysis must become prospective, and the programs must be given a positive responsibility to generate the information that will make this a reality.[32]

Later the Council goes on to urge that EPA adopt a strategic approach in which it concentrates its resources on a few obtainable and measurable objectives.

Both the Royal Commission and the Council on Environmental Quality appear to be pursuing parallel themes, albeit with different emphases. In order to highlight the similarities, it is useful to identify what would be the opposite of a cross-media, cost-effective, risk-reduction strategy. In essence, the opposite would be medium-specific uniform emission limits based upon an estimate of the technological possibilities of control. The differences are identified in Table 4.1. The approach towards integrated pollution control that is advocated by the Royal Commission and the Council on Environmental Quality aims at both an optimising of the effects of pollution upon the environment and at a risk-analysis that aims to ensure that resources are devoted most efficiently to the reduction of the most hazardous pollutants. In the case of the Royal Commission, this approach is couched in terms of the development of the traditional British regulatory approach, whereas in the case of the Council on Environmental Quality the

Table 4.1 *Integrated pollution control versus uniform approaches*

	Integrated pollution control	Uniform approach
Focus of control	All receiving media, considered in their interrelationship; substances	Specific media; substances
Aim of control	Environmentally optimal risk-reduction of pollutants	Reduction of emissions to specified target levels
Environmental quality objectives	Relevant to determining optimal levels of pollution	Only relevant if application of emission controls would be insufficient to secure acceptable environmental quality
Cost considerations	Imposed as constraint, implicitly or explicitly, on pollution reduction effort	Not relevant unless 'excessive'

attempt is to seek to get away from what are perceived to be the inefficiencies of uniform emission standards currently operative in some US policy and legislation, particularly air and water pollution.

Advocating integrated pollution control is clearly intended to be a prescription for rational environmental management, but it will only be superior in its rationality to the uniform emission limits approach if it can be implemented in the political and administrative conditions that obtain in the real world of policy-making. From this point of view there are likely to be three problems: a scepticism among many of those active in parts of the policy community about the good faith of those advocating risk-reduction strategies; the difficulties of information deficit and the dangers of 'paralysis by analysis'; and the divide between the technical rationality of environmental management on the one hand and the political rationality of effective policy development on the other.

Scepticism in the various policy communities that surround the making of environmental policy has been well expressed by Ronald B. Outen at a conference organised on multimedia pollution control:

It may startle some of you to hear that risk assessment is itself a fairly dirty word in some circles. There is a concern that it is a stalking horse for less real control of pollutants, especially toxic pollutants. Critics of risk assessment argue that it is a highly inexact and therefore misleading form of analysis, and that it asks the wrong question. The issue is how much waste reduction we can possibly achieve, not how much exposure we can stand. And critics fear that it leads naturally to comparative risk analysis, which is another form of the question 'Where do you want it put?' That is not the question that many environmental policy leaders want to ask until they are assured that all possible opportunities for waste reduction of the source have been exhausted.[33]

An example of this attitude among environmental leaders is provided by the attitude of Greenpeace towards the dumping of sewage sludge in the North Sea. Greenpeace has campaigned for the ending of sewage sludge dumping in the North Sea, even when recognising that the scientific evidence for environmental damage arising from the practice is slim or ambiguous. The attitude of Greenpeace does not rest on a view that there is an alternative, less risky disposal route, but on the principle that a natural resource like the North Sea should not be regarded as a dumping ground. This attitude is quite consistent with recognising that, in the present state of understanding and given a certain level of investment in sewage treatment, the North Sea disposal route offers the best practicable environment option. It questions the fact that the present state of understanding and the prevailing level of investment should be taken as fixed points to which all other considerations have to be adjusted.

It may be argued that the attitude of Greenpeace and similar campaigning groups is counterproductive, because the closing of one disposal route does nothing to ensure that alternative disposal routes are environmentally superior. Thus, it may be argued that spreading sewage sludge on land is potentially hazardous for crop growth given contamination of the sludge by heavy metals, like mercury, that adversely affect plants, although the same sludge might be satisfactorily disposed of to a marine environment in which the metals were dispersed. But this argument neglects Outen's point about trust, as well as the characteristic incentives that face a campaigning organisation. To advocate cost-effective, risk-reduction strategies presupposes that regulators are trusted by the general public and, in particular, that portion of the attentive public that belongs to campaigning organisations. Often, however, this trust is lacking. Sometimes, in order to maintain public confidence, regulators have to devote much effort to the regulation of some risks about which there is special public concern, even when they are convinced on 'objective' grounds that the relative returns in risk-reduction are not worth the effort they are expending. Thus, the UK's Health and Safety Executive devotes more resources to nuclear regulation than it believes is warranted by the hazards posed, because it recognises that the public attaches special importance to nuclear safety and it would not be doing its job unless regulatory effort was high.[34]

The incentives facing campaigning organisations are also important in this context. Issue attention cycles in environmental politics rise and fall unpredictably. To ask a campaigning organisation not to take advantage of public concern about a specific receiving medium is rather like asking the clothing industry to ignore changes in fashion. Campaigning groups are most effective when they ride on a wave of public concern, and they are unlikely to hold up a campaign that has caught public attention because public regulators believe that the particular pollution problem it addresses is low down the list of rationally determinable priorities. After all, there is no log-rolling mechanism between governments and pressure groups by which the former can trade action on a high priority issue for a reduction of campaigning on a low priority one.

The second problem is that integrated pollution control requires a great deal of information, and in any serious regulatory decision there is an inevitable information deficit. Collecting and analysing data is time-consuming and expensive. The EPA, which has more resources than most other environmental protection organisations in the world, has only completed analysis on a small number of the chemicals that it ought to be concerned with. The experience at Rijnmond showed that integrated permitting was time-consuming, let alone integrated pollution control. Shortly after it was established, HMIP launched two trial BPEO investigations, one involving a small experimental nuclear facility at Winfrith in Dorset and the other a chemical complex at Dow-Corning in South Wales. The analysis was primarily technical, intended to discover how to incorporate the cross-media approach into plant regulation. The results showed that, although an integrated solution to effluent limitation was possible and desirable from the management point of view, it was time-consuming and hence costly in terms of personnel.[35]

The problems of delay are increased when the criterion of cost-effectiveness is taken seriously, since that criterion requires a combination of natural science and economic information which can be expensive to obtain and difficult to analyse. Moreover, by the time that econometric estimates have been superimposed upon environmental models derived from sampling regimes that may have been designed for other purposes, the policy-maker has to take an awful lot on trust. From the viewpoint of the policy-maker what matters is not the intrinsic value of the information, which to the natural scientist or economist may be the most interesting feature of the exercise, but the extent to which waiting and paying for the information produces a commensurate improvement at the margin to a decision that might have to be taken with other considerations in mind. As Arild Underdal points out, when governments fix upon a reduction target for a particular pollutant, they probably have no policy criteria stipulating whether and how much the target should be modified in response to a more exact estimate of damage or abatement costs.[36]

Here we touch upon the third consideration, namely the distinction between technical rationality and political rationality. The demand for integrated pollution control really amounts to the claim that technical effectiveness and economic efficiency should be the two most important values in the making of pollution control decisions. Even as an abstract normative proposition this is contestable, since it ignores the possibility that other values, for example due process, might also be relevant. But if it is contestable in logic, it is impossible in practice. Governments within liberal democracies are inevitably subject to the demands of a wider range of values than technical effectiveness and economic efficiency, not least the demands to be responsive to popular preferences and concerns. No doubt, eventually, the British government would have responded in time to the steadily accumulating evidence of the damage to human health caused by lead in the environment, but the activities of CLEAR almost certainly contributed to a speedier decision than would have otherwise occurred. Similarly, it was the scientifically unsubstantiated link between sulphur dioxide and forest death in Germany in the early 1980s that led to policies with substantial benefits. Had the German government not been responsive to popular preferences, decisive action might not have been taken.

It may be argued that the optimising approach advocated by those who favour integrated pollution control is inherently prone to passivity in the face of complex problems, whereas the relatively crude principles of the uniform emission limits approach will lead to significant policy developments. Ronald B. Outen urges this point of view. Contrasting the US Clean Water Act with the Toxic Substances Control Act, he points out that the latter has contained within it the legislative capacity to conduct cross-media analysis, at least in the case of toxics, whereas the former is an example of technology-based controls. But whereas the Clean Water Act has led to the removal of large quantities of pollutants from waste streams, only a few pollutants have been regulated under toxic substances legislation. The very complexity of the analysis induced by the cross-media approach may lead to regulatory passivity.[37]

Essential to political rationality is the problem of trust, and this can be especially serious where international relations are concerned. An optimising risk-management approach may mean being willing to countenance lower standards of control in respect of one form of pollution, judged to be not as serious as another form of pollution in which tighter standards are applied. Here again, the case of sewage sludge dumping in the North Sea provides a clear example. It may appear from the viewpoint of environmental science that heavy metal contaminants in such sludge are better dumped in the North Sea, where they form only a small proposition of the total heavy metal input, than being spread on the land as part of a fertiliser or incinerated and thereby contribute to an air pollution problem. The North Sea may be better able to receive the pollutant input as a receiving medium than either high grade farming land or the atmosphere. But it is one thing to come to a calculated judgement about the optimal balance of environmental risks, and another thing to persuade the representatives of other nations around a bargaining table that this is a good faith estimate of the situation rather than a device for avoiding carrying one's share of a common burden or a simple unwillingness to shake off bad habits. In the international context uniform emission limits, including the special case of zero emissions into a particular receiving medium, may be the only basis upon which general agreement can be secured. In Schelling's terms, uniform emission limits may represent 'focal points' on which the expectations of diverse parties can converge.[38]

Although there may be a powerful case from the viewpoint of the environmental sciences for integrated pollution control, the political conditions under which policy decisions must be made mean that the approach based upon uniform emission limits, set in the light of the best available technology may often prove more feasible. Does this mean that there is a stark choice between the two approaches? Not necessarily. One way of seeking a reconciliation is to see the optimising approach as one to be applied within the constraints of uniform emission standards. The uniform standards set the boundaries of the permissible, and the decision on risk-management provides an idea of the desirable. One reason for favouring this reconciliation is that within the process of implementation there may well be factors favouring a move towards optimisation. Since those responsible for an implementation will usually have a technical background, they can be expected to derive professional satisfaction from the challenge of optimising within a given set of constraints.

Experience from the German system of pollution control tends to confirm this interpretation. The German system favours uniform emission limits, based on a judgement about what is technically possible. These uniform emission limits are set by the national, federal government, but their implementation is a matter of provincial, *Land* governments. In their case study of Hamburg, Bennett and von Moltke showed that the permitting process is more subtle in implementation than the legal specification of emission limit values would suggest in the abstract. Taking account of the environmental and economic gains below the specified emission limits is part of the permitting process, and cross-media effects are taken into consideration. For example, a major combustion plant, with a relatively short future life, was allowed to fit a technology producing a dry waste that had to be landfilled in order to secure gains in air quality more quickly, it being judged better to create an increase in solid waste than to place a heavier burden on air or water. As Bennett and von Moltke note, part of the explanation for this more discretionary approach at subnational level is to be found in the professional backgrounds of those involved. Whereas legal expertise, which favours uniform single-medium controls, is prevalent at the national level, process engineering predominates at the level of the permitting authority, and process engineering is not medium-oriented.[39]

Synoptic rationality and social learning

The synoptic ambition at the heart of the demand for integrated pollution control faces a number of barriers to its realisation. For a variety of political, constitutional and administrative reasons it may well not be possible for many countries to achieve the centralisation of organisation that characterises the Swedish system. Moreover, in so far as integrated pollution control involves a change of organisational process, there are political problems in moving towards the environmental risk-management model that is currently favoured among influential policy elites. Countervailing trends, most notably the increasing demand for greater public and international accountability in pollution control, favour a uniform emissions standards approach, based upon a judgement of technical possibilities, which is often thought to be the antithesis of environmental rationality in these matters.

The suggestion that a synthesis is possible between the two approaches, and that optimising decisions may be made within a framework of uniform emission standards, is little more than a hint of an organisational possibility. But this reinforces a more general point about environmental protection policy, namely that its form and substance is a matter for invention and research, and this in turn has implications for the terms in which we understand and analyse pollution control policies. The advocacy of integrated pollution control has been an important element in the policy discourse of influential elites, just as the claims about the compatibility of environmental protection and economic growth were an important element in the ideology of ecological modernisation. However, in the case of integrated pollution control, the formulation of the new policy discourse has not been sufficient to secure reform, but has instead encountered the harsh realities of bureaucratic politics and the incentives that confront leading policy actors like politicians and pressure groups. Both the turf disputes that have surrounded the reorganisation of environmental protection agencies, and the difficulties of changing standard operating procedures in the direction of a putatively more rational risk-management approach indicate the institutional barriers to reform led by intellectual speculation.

This does not mean, however, that we need only pay attention to the rationality of the incentives facing key politics actors or to the resistance of institutional practices to change. To make sense of the controversy over integrated pollution control we need to understand it as a demand that arises from a perception of failure of fragmented administrative systems in the face of the interrelationships to be found in the natural world. The difficulties raised by that disjunction will not go away. Hence, there is likely to be a continuing search for regulatory reform, and much experimentation, even though it is not conscious, in administrative structures and processes. Policy controversies cannot be understood simply as the application of pre-existing belief systems. They must also be seen as the discovery and exploration of the implications of belief systems. The same message applies to the next topic, namely the ways in which environmental policy is, or is not, integrated with other sectors of public policy.

Notes

1   R. H. Harris, 'Multimedia Exposures at Hazardous Waste Dump Sites', in Committee on Mulitmedia Approaches to Pollution Control, *Multimedia Approaches to Pollution Control: A Symposium Proceedings* (Washington, DC: National Academy Press, 1987) pp. 42–53.

2   R. C. Loehr and C. H. Ward, 'Waste Treatment Processes and Cross-Media Transfer of Pollutants', in Committee on Multimedia Approaches to Pollution Control, *Multimedia Approaches to Pollution Control*, pp. 8–23.

3   L. A. Teclaff and E. Teclaff, 'International Control of Cross-Media Pollutants – An Ecosystem Approach', *Natural Resources Journal*, 27:1 (1987), pp. 21–53, especially pp. 24–7.

4   A. Weale, T. O'Riordan and L. Kramme, *Controlling Pollution in the Round* (London: Anglo-German Foundation, 1991) pp. 184–96.

5   R. B. Outen, 'Environmental Pollution Laws and the Architecture of Tobacco Road', in Committee on Multimedia Approaches to Pollution Control, *Multimedia Approaches to Pollution Control*, pp. 139–43.

6   J. Salzwendel, 'The Approach of the Federal German Republic –

Anticipating Environmental Effects', in T. J. Lack (ed.), *Environmental Protection: Standards, Compliance and Costs* (Chichester: Ellis Horwood, 1984), p. 173.

7 Cited in Council on Environmental Quality, *Environmental Quality*, Sixteenth Report (Washington DC: Government Printing Office, 1985), p. 10.

8 Royal Commission on Environmental Pollution, *Air Pollution Control: An Integrated Approach*, Fifth Report (London: HMSO, 1976) Cmnd. 6371, especially at p. 76.

9 See the quotations in F. Irwin, 'Introduction to Integrated Pollution Control', in N. Haigh and F. Irwin (eds.), *Integrated Pollution Control in Europe and North America* (Washington DC: The Conservation Foundation, 1990), pp. 6–7.

10 Irwin, 'Introduction to Integrated Pollution Control', pp. 15–18.

11 D. Hinrichsen, 'Integrated Permitting and Inspection in Sweden', in Haig and Irwin (eds.), *Integrated Pollution Control in Europe and North America*, pp. 147–68. This article provides the source for subsequent material on Sweden's pollution control structures and history.

12 See S. Kelman, *Regulating America, Regulating Sweden* (Cambridge, Mass.: The MIT Press, 1981), pp. 118–23.

13 Irwin, 'Introduction to Integrated Pollution Control', pp. 21–4.

14 A. Underdal, 'Integrated Marine Policy. What? Why? How?', *Marine Policy*, 4:3 (1980), p. 162.

15 The classic discussions of which are to be found in: C. E. Lindblom, 'The Science of Muddling Through', *Public Administration Review*, 19 (1959), pp. 79–85 and D. Braybrooke and C. E. Lindblom, *A Strategy of Decision: Policy Evaluation as a Social Process* (Glencoe: The Free Press, 1963).

16 P. Szanton, 'So You Want to Reorganize the Government', in P. Szanton (ed.), *Federal Reorganization: What Have We Learned?* (Chatham, NJ: Chatham House, 1981).

17 A. L. Alm, 'The EPA's Approach to Cross-Media Problems', in The Conservation Foundation, *New Perspectives on Pollution Control* (Washington DC: The Conservation Founation, 1985), pp. 7–13.

18 A. Alm, 'The Multimedia Approach to Pollution Control: An Impossible Dream?', in Committee on Multimedia Approaches to Polution Control, *Multimedia Approaches to Pollution Control*, pp. 114–116.

19 Outen, 'Environmental Pollution Laws and the Architecture of Tobacco Road', p. 140.

20 B. A. Ackerman and W. T. Hassler, *Clean Coal/Dirty Air* (New

Haven and London: Yale University Press, 1981), p. 9.

21   Royal Commission on Environmental Pollution, *Air Pollution Control.*

22   Royal Commission on Environmental Pollution, *Air Pollution Control*, p. 72.

23   Weale, O'Riordan and Kramme, *Controlling Pollution in the Round*, p. 57.

24   Department of the Environment, *Air Pollution: An Integrated Approach. The Government's Response to the Royal Commission on Environmental Pollution's Fifth Report*, Pollution Paper 18 (London: HMSO, 1982), p. 2.

25   Weale, O'Riordan and Kramme, *Controlling Pollution in the Round*, pp. 151–6.

26   Weale, O'Riordan and Kramme, *Controlling Pollution in the Round*, pp. 150–1.

27   S. Owens, 'The Unified Pollution Inspectorate and Best Practicable Environmental Option in the United Kingdom', in Haigh and Irwin (eds.) *Integrated Pollution Control in Europe and North America*, pp. 169–98, especially at p. 191.

28   S. Owens, 'The Unified Pollution Inspectorate and Best Practicable Environmental Option in the United Kingdom', p. 192.

29   See G. Bennett and K. von Moltke, 'Integrated Permitting in the Netherlands and the Federal Republic of Germany', in Haigh and Irwin (eds.) *Integrated Pollution Control in Europe and North America*, pp. 105–45.

30   Bennett and von Moltke, 'Integrated Permitting in the Netherlands and the Federal Republic of Germany', pp. 115–16.

31   Royal Commission on Environmental Pollution, *Best Practicable Environmental Option*, Twelfth Report (London: HMSO, 1988), Cm. 310, p. 5.

32   Council on Enviromental Quality, *Environmental Quality*, Sixteenth Report, p. 20.

33   Outen, 'Environmental Pollution Laws and the Architecture of Tobacco Road', p. 140.

34   J. D. Rimington, 'Innovation and the Public Perception of Risk' in L. Roberts and A. Weale (eds), *Innovation and Environmental Risk* (London: Belhaven, 1991), p. 14.

35   T. O'Riordan and A. Weale, 'Administrative Reorganization and Policy Change: The Case of Her Majesty's Inspectorate of Pollution', *Public Administration*, 67:3 (1989), p. 290.

36   A. Underdal, 'The Politics of Science in International Resource

Management: A Summary', in S. Andresen and W. Østreng (eds.), *International Resource Management: The Role of Science and Politics* (London and New York: Belhaven Press, 1989), p. 256.

37   Outen, 'Environmental Pollution Laws and the Architecture of Tobacco Road', p. 140.

38   T. C. Schelling, *Strategy of Conflict* (London: Oxford University Press, 1960), Chapters 1 and 2.

39   Bennett and von Moltke, 'Integrated Permitting in the Netherlands and the Federal Republic of Germany', pp. 130–1.

5
Turning government green

Pollution has many sources. Most of these find their origins in the otherwise legitimate activities of social actors, industry, farmers, transport and consumers. Around these activities there grow up regulation and political control, in the form of ministries for agriculture, industry, transport and so on. Concern for the environmental consequences of these activities is high on the agenda of the environment ministry or environmental regulators, but it need not be high on the agenda of those ministries, like transport and agriculture, whose function is in part to protect the interest for which they are responsible. Hence, if pollution is to be controlled at source, rather than mitigated in terms of its effects, environmental considerations need to be integrated across the whole range of government policy. An emphasis upon controlling sources, rather than effects, therefore promises, or threatens, a substantial departure from many of the implicit assumptions of the 1970s.

The extent of this departure can be judged by considering current pollution problems. Global climate change and the possibility of greenhouse warming find their origin in extensive fossil fuel burning. Hence, controlling emission of greenhouse gases requires consideration of transport and energy policy. Similarly, the problem of eutrophication, the overenrichment of waters with nutrients, requires agricultural policy to be sensitive to environmental considerations. Soil pollution offers yet another example. The sites of chemical plants cause serious problems of pollution, and industrial policy, when it is concerned with regional development, needs to take these problems into account. These examples provide just a few instances where environmental considerations extend broadly into government and public policy.

Effective environmental policy cannot be simply left, then, to an environment ministry or other specialist agency of government. Although the tasks of regulation and the defining of environmental quality objectives are specialised tasks, so that there undoubtedly has to be one particular branch of government that undertakes these activities, the pursuit of improvements in environmental quality goes wider than any one industry or specialised agency is likely to accomplish. Moreover, environment ministries, where they have existed, have been relatively junior in government, and the corresponding cabinet portfolio has not been as significant as industry or even transport and agriculture. In any conflict of wills, therefore, between the environment and other ministries, it would be unlikely that environment would emerge as the unscathed victor.

One solution to the scale of problems posed by environmental problems is to increase the size and competence of the environment ministry. In effect offices, bureaux or other parts of the machinery of government are shifted around in order to strengthen the environmental function. Some reorganisation of this sort has taken place in many countries in recent years. In the UK Her Majesty's Inspectorate of Pollution was created in 1987, and lodged within the Department of the Environment. The Ministry of Environment, Nature Protection and Reactor Safety was created in the Federal Republic of Germany in 1986. In other countries environment ministries have also been created or strengthened recently. Restructuring the machinery of government becomes a method by which the demands of environmental protection can be integrated into the workings of government.

However, it should be clear that, though some reorganisation of the machinery of government is occasionally necessary, the approach that requires reconfiguring the hardware of government cannot be an adequate solution. If the seriousness of environmental issues is something that affects the whole of government, it is implausible to think that restructuring the machine is the solution. The chief difficulty is that substantive issues of policy are displaced by territorial disputes about turf. Instead of focusing upon the goals of policy and the best way of achieving them, partisans from different ministries concentrate on keeping as much responsibility for their organisation as possible. This tendency towards baronial protectionism can be observed in all governmental processes, and examples include disputes within the US bureaucracy over pesticides regulation, the long-running antagonism in Britain between the Department of the Environment and the Department of Employment over the location of the pollution inspectorate or the disputes in the Federal Republic of Germany over the issue of whether there should be an environment ministry or not.[1]

Instead of changing the responsibilities of government departments, emphasis can be placed upon policy co-ordination, to be achieved by various changes in the organisational structure of government. For example, cabinet committees may be established, interdepartmental working groups set up and departmental ministers assigned the responsibility to take care of the environmental aspects of the ministry's work. In essence this is one of the main planks of the approach adopted by the British government in its 1990 white paper on the environment.[2] The proposals contained within the white paper included: the establishment of a cabinet committee chaired by the Prime Minister to oversee the implementation of policy; the establishment of a committee of ministers, chaired by the Secretary of State for Energy, to draw up a programme for greater energy efficiency; and the nomination of ministers in each department to take responsibility for the environmental dimensions of the department's work. However, the chief difficulty with this approach is political. The creation of new parts of the government machine is directly threatening to the established interests of affected departments. Given this constraint, it takes a great deal of political will to overcome political resistance and inertia. It is therefore likely that initiatives will be stifled, and this appears to have happened with the UK government's proposal. Nearly ten months after the announcement of the establishment of the cabinet committee, it was revealed by a journalist that the committee had never met, and the British secrecy laws were so strict that it could not even be officially confirmed that such a committee existed!

The question arises, therefore, as to whether there is an alternative way of seeking to integrate environmental concerns into the heart of government. How might this goal be achieved? Since restructuring the machinery of government is only a partial answer to this question, it is also necessary to identify processes or procedures that will have the desired effect. Rather than reconfiguring the existing hardware, or even bolting on some new device to our government machine, we need to look at the operating software to see whether it can be improved. In other words the standard operating procedures of public programmes can be changed, and the problem is to identify the best way of doing this.

In this chapter we shall consider one attempt to change standard operating procedures of government that is perhaps the most serious attempt to integrate environmental concerns into the full range of public policy. The example in question is the Dutch National Environmental Policy Plan (NEPP).[3] This has attracted widespread interest for its radical approach to the problems of pollution control. As we shall see, the Plan has emerged from a distinctive political and institutional set of conditions, and it is unlikely that any other country could simply follow the Dutch example without adapting and transforming the approach. On the other hand, it can be argued that all developed economies require something like the functional equivalent of the Dutch NEPP, and from this point of view something of value can be gained by considering in some detail the features of the Dutch approach.

Outline and logic of the Dutch National Environmental Policy Plan

The NEPP was published in 1989 and takes the form of a report to the Dutch Parliament, the *Tweede Kammer* (the Second Chamber). It is signed by four cabinet ministers, one each from Environment, Transport, Agriculture and Economics (the last being the industry ministry). Its chief role is to specify environmental policy objectives in quantitative terms, with targets to be achieved by the year 2010. These targets are identified both in terms of their implications for public spending and in terms of the costs that will be displaced on to industry, consumers and agriculture. Underlying the environmental policy objectives are a set of environmental quality objectives, but the principal form that the planning targets take are in terms of specified percentage reductions from 1980 levels of pollution. For example, one part of the NEPP is concerned with policies to reduce acidification, and the target is set in relation to reductions in the level of emissions of SO_2, NO_x, NH_3 and VOCs. The scale of the emission reductions are often substantial, and in this respect the acidification programme is typical. Table 5.1 provides the details.

It can be seen from Table 5.1 that substantial reductions, typically between 50 and 70 per cent, are required by the year 2000
over 1985, and these are to be regarded as intermediate targets for
the year 2010 when the level of emission reductions aimed at can
be of the order of 80 to 90 per cent. This example illustrates both
the scale of the proposed reductions and the fast pace at which the
NEPP anticipates their being achieved. Goals of a similar strin-
gency are set in relation to other major environmental problems.
Thus, in addition to an action programme on acidification there
are specific programmes on climate change, eutrophication, the
diffusion of hazardous substances, waste disposal, noise and odour
pollution, dehydration, and sustainable resource use. To each of
these programmes there are attached quantitative costed targets
for pollution levels, which in many cases extend to the year 2010.
The NEPP in sum, therefore, is a plan aiming at a substantial
commitment to environmental improvement.

To understand the development and character of the NEPP, we
need to understand both its internal logic and the institutional
conditions under which it was produced. The internal logic is
significant in itself. Theories of cause and effect are often implicit
in the development of public policies. One of the distinctive features of the NEPP is that it goes to some effort to set out explicitly
the theory of environmental pollution on which it is based. According to the thinking of those who drew up the plan, the causes
of environmental degradation are to be found in the breaking of
substance cycles. Substance flows occur over various periods of
time in the absence of human activities.[4] Human intervention
alters these substance flows, either by the introduction of new
substances or by the acceleration of existing substance flows. An
adequate understanding of these substance flows during the course
of human intervention leads to 'run-off' or 'leaks' in which substances end up in the environment at the wrong place, the wrong
time or in the wrong form. In other words, human intervention in
breaking the substance cycles prevents the environment from per-
forming its natural cleansing function. This analysis replicates the
views of environmental writers like Commoner that there are
competing principles at work between the natural ecosphere, to be
regarded as a slowly evolving cyclical system, and the technos-
phere, to be regarded as a rapidly expanding linear process.[5]

One way of thinking about these issues, according to the theory

Table 5.1 *Emission targets under the NEPP acidification programme (k tonnes / year)*

	SO$_2$		NO$_x$		NH$_3$		VOCs	
	1985	2000	1985	2000	1985	2000	1985	2000
Total	276	105	544	268	253	82	459	194[1]
Industry and refineries	164	51	83	37	6	3	198	85[2]
Power plants	65	30	82	40	–	–	10	10
Traffic	47	24	272	112	–	–	195	80[3]
Households	–	–	24	11	9	9	32	15
Agriculture	–	–	–	–	238	70	24	6
Other	–	–	83	68	–	–	–	–

[1] Assumes additional contribution from related project

[2] Of which 80 (1985) and 40 (2000) by small firms

[3] Of which: passenger cars 138 (1985) and 35 (2000); trucks 42 (1985) and 30 (2000); other traffic 15 (1985) and 15 (2000)

Source: Calculated from National Environment Policy Plan ('s-Gravenhage: SDU Uitgeverij, 1989), pp 133–4

behind the plan, is to conceptualise the problem in terms of sources and effects. Since the breaking of substance cycles is to be found in human intervention, the sources of pollution are ultimately to be found in human activities. These activities are linked by chains of cause and effect to observed pollution effects. These effects occur at different levels of social and spatial organisation and there has been a growth in the last few decades in the scale on which effects occur. Environmental degradation is occurring not only at the level of the locality, the region or the river basin, but also at the level of continents and the globe itself. Moreover, the nature of the pollution at these levels is not simply that of a waste stream out of proportion to the capacity of the receiving medium to absorb it, but also takes the form of accumulation resulting in the irreversible loss of part of the environment's carrying capacity.[6]

The theoretical basis of the NEPP is therefore a form of general systems theory. The natural and social worlds are seen as a large, complex, interlinked system in which disturbance at one point can cause malfunctioning at another. To the extent to which we can understand the system we should seek to rectify the malfunctioning not at the point of effects but at the point of sources. This means modifying or eliminating the human activities that are responsible ultimately, as sources, for environmental degradation. In other words, from this general systems perspective, the integration of environmental considerations with the full range of public policy, and indeed by extension their integration into corporate policy and personal morality, is not a luxury or optional extra; it is an essential precondition for the satisfactory resolution of environmental problems. Sources need to be modified if effects are to be avoided.

One problem with a general perspective is that taken on its own it does not indicate priorities for action. If everything is involved in one big system, it is a problem for decision-makers to know how to proceed in terms of policy and action. To be useful as an aid to policy development, a plan should indicate priorities for action.

The NEPP has an elaborate specification of how this general systems perspective is to be brought to bear on environmental problems. In order to summarise this, we suggest that the approach of the NEPP be thought of as specifying certain stages of a decision analysis comprising the following steps:

- problem identification
- problem elaboration
- assessment of scope for feasible intervention
- involvement of target groups for policy change
- definition of policy objectives and targets
- identification of costs
- specification of policy instruments

Thus one way of understanding the NEPP is to see it as attempting to undertake each of the above steps in respect of a specific policy problem. At each of these steps certain questions may be asked. Thus, at the stage of problem identification it is important to specify not only the nature of the problem but the geographical level on which it occurs. The problem is then elaborated in the light of the general theory underlying the plan to do with the breaking of substance cycles, and three principles of pollution control are given priority: a reduction in the use of energy; the need to manage waste streams over the production or product cycle; and the need to rectify a bias in production against quality improvements. Having achieved some understanding of the problem, the next stage is then to assess the scope for feasible interventions in terms of source, volume, emission or effect oriented measures. This assessment will provide a guide to the available policy options. The next stage is to involve target groups, like industry or consumers, in specifying policy objectives and targets as well as policy instruments. The last stage in the process is the writing of a plan for the specific policy problem which can serve as an indicative reference point for policy development. A diagrammatic representation of this process is set out in Figure 5.1.

To present the approach of the NEPP in this way is rather over-stylised in the sense that it provides too tidy a picture of what is a complex process. For example the relationship between identifying policy objectives and negotiating with target groups is not one that can be neatly separated into discrete stages. However, the stylisation is intended to highlight certain features of the plan which may be taken as defining some of its distinctive characteristics.

The first of these is the importance of elaborating a scientifically

Figure 5.1 *Schematic outline of Dutch environmental process*

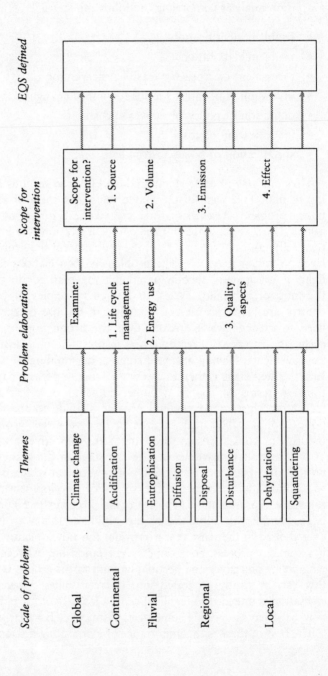

informed understanding of the nature of policy problems before seeking to devise policy solutions. This is illustrated not only from the statement of the background theory of substance cycles but also by the attention paid to elaborating the nature of particular problems in terms of their life cycle, energy use and quality aspects. These aspects are seen to be ways of focusing attention upon the underlying systematic features of pollution problems, and identifying what might be the most important policy interventions. A similar point can be illustrated by the assessment of the feasible scope for intervention. It is an implication of the theory underlying the NEPP that source oriented measures are preferable where these are possible, since they serve to reduce the occurrence of an environmental problem and not simply mitigate its effects. However, the plan recognises that source oriented measures are not always feasible and that it is necessary to identify explicitly what alternative measures might be taken if a source oriented approach is not possible. Clearly one of the most important features of writing any plan is that the process of writing itself forms part of the elaboration of the problem and in the present case this augmentation of understanding arises through an elaboration of an underlying general systems theory and its application in terms of a sources and effects analysis.[7]

The involvement of target groups in defining policy objectives, specifying objectives and selecting policy instruments is also an important feature of the planning process. In this respect the involvement of three ministries other than the environment ministry is a significant feature of the Dutch plan. To prevent substantive questions of policy being displaced by issues of administrative turf protection, the involvement of other ministries in the planning process was regarded as essential. By being involved in the specification of objectives, the ministries responsible for transport, industry and agriculture are given an opportunity to protect the core of their own policy programmes whilst participating in a process that forced them to look at the environmental dimension of their activity. For the environment ministry the advantage of the arrangement was that it was seen as having a say in these broader public policy questions. This can be particularly important in relation to a policy area like energy, since otherwise the tendency of government involvement in extraction and use is to maximise the exploitation of available resources, rather than aiming at their conservation.[8] Since the plan is intended to be indicative, rather than directive, it is unlikely that the precise targets specified will be met. Moreover, planners at the environment ministry found that the involvement of target groups forced it to accede to less stringent measures than it otherwise would have proposed, but reasoned that the political and policy advantages of securing inter-ministerial involvement outweighed the disadvantages of having to compromise on targets, particularly when the latter were likely to change anyway in the light of new scientific understanding and changing economic circumstances. There was therefore an implicit exchange accomplished by the process: the environment ministry secured co-operation, but at the expense of conceding on some targets.

A further advantage of the target groups approach is that it can help with the problem that some ministries may be 'more royalist than the king' in their policy stance. In common with ministries in other liberal democracies, Dutch ministries take on a sponsoring role in respect of their interests for which they are responsible. Thus the agriculture ministry will see its mission as the protection of agriculture and the industry ministry will see its mission as the protection of industry. Since the NEPP involved increasing consid-erably projected costs on industry, the responsible ministry was naturally anxious that the interests of those for whom it was responsible were adequately protected. At one point in drawing up the plan this threatened to create a serious rift between the plan-ners in environment and their counterparts in the industry minis-try. The rift was avoided by the environmental planners meeting representatives of industry directly who accepted the increased costs with a much greater equanimity than their ministerial repre-sentatives.

The choice of instruments also represents an interesting feature of the logic of the NEPP. In its appearance the NEPP looks as though it is simply an extension of the traditional system of administrative regulation. Environmental quality objectives or emission levels are specified and the plan draws out the conse-quences for the economy and society of these specified norms. By and large the legal instruments necessary to impose more stringent norms already exist under Dutch environmental legislation, and so it would seem that the plan merely extends in a more comprehens-ive way the existing system of pollution control. Moreover, the

NEPP only gives a limited role to economic instruments, which during the preliminary stages of the planning process the finance ministry had argued would be too complex to administer. However, appearances are deceptive in at least two respects. The NEPP was developed within a context of ideas, stemming from the liberal environment minister Winsemius, that stressed the concept of *'verinnerlijking'*, that is the internalisation by social actors of responsibility for their actions. It therefore moved away from the assumption that effective protection of the environment can be achieved simply by the imposition upon industry of a politically and administratively determined set of norms.

The NEPP extends this notion of the internalisation of responsibility beyond industry and producers to embrace consumers, again moving beyond the operational assumptions of traditional administrative regulation. The NEPP envisages consumers and citizens taking a much higher degree of personal responsibility for the protection of the environment than hitherto. The movement of thought is well illustrated by the following passage:

It is no longer simply an issue of the responsibility that individuals bear relative to one another. The distance between source and effect has become so great – in terms of both space and time – that the issue is now the responsibility borne by individuals as members of a society relative to societies elsewhere in the world and as members of a generation relative to future generations. Individuals will have to give this responsibility substance by doing everything reasonably within their possibilities to prevent pollution as a direct or indirect consequence of their activities.[9]

The notion in the plan is that there should be a partnership between government, industry and consumers to create the circumstances in which industry and consumers come to realise that the level of pollution is a consequence of their joint decisions.

In implementing this strategy, stress is laid upon the role of consumer organisations in pressing for improved environmental performance in their contact with government and the plan also talks about improved information and publicity targeted at consumers. However, the plan is clear in expecting that there will be significant shifts in consumer behaviour, and it draws some support for this view from shifts in attitudes and behaviour in respect of smoking. In specific terms, it expects that the consumer contribution will take specific forms, for example in a willingness to participate in separation schemes for household waste, including separate disposal of batteries, small chemical waste, tin, glass, textiles and paper, an increase in the composting of waste and a greater predilection for public over private transport. The stress placed upon personal responsibility in the NEPP raises obvious issues of political feasibility.

This issue of feasibility in turn raises what is perhaps the central feature of the NEPP, namely the ambitiousness of its targets for environmental improvements and its discussion of the cost implications of seeking to achieve those targets. The percentage reductions for a range of emissions that are envisaged for the planning period are considerable. What led the planning team to the conclusion that pollution control on this scale and across such a wide range of activities was both desirable and feasible?

The necessity of such stringent targets has emerged in what may be termed the pre-planning stage of the policy process. As part of their preparation, the planning team asked the Dutch State Institute for Public Health and Environment Protection (RIVM, *Rijksinstituut voor Volksgezondheid en Milieuhygiene*) to conduct a review of the environmental consequences of current policy options. RIVM was asked to look in particular at two options: the first involved no change from current practice in pollution control standards and the second involved the application of all known end-of-pipe technologies. When RIVM was given this task, it was anticipated that these two policy options would define the full spectrum of what policy ought to be chosen, and that somewhere between these two extremes a publicly acceptable policy could be defined. In practice the work of the RIVM turned this expectation on its head. They discovered that *even with the full application of existing end-of-pipe technologies* it would not be possible to prevent a decline in environmental quality in the Netherlands. For example, acidification was such a serious problem that by the year 2010 there might only be some 20 per cent of woodlands in the Netherlands that were undamaged. The same type of result was repeated for other environmental problems, including contamination of ground water, eutrophication and soil protection.[10] The option that seemed to define the limits of the feasible options suddenly became a measure of the inadequacy in the way problems were being approached.

The results of the RIVM forecasting were presented to a group in the environment ministry, and their policy implications discussed. The main conclusion to be drawn was that emission reductions by means of the application of end-of-pipe technologies were inadequate, and that volume and structural changes were needed in the economy. Politically this did not seem an attractive conclusion since it threatened to put the cause of environmental protection on a collision course with economic development, and environmental policy would therefore return to the old zero-sum conflict with other public policy objectives. It was at this point that the influence of the Brundtland report was felt.[11] The main message of the Brundtland report is that concern for the economy and concern for the environment should not be seen as opposing one another, but that protection of the environment is an essential condition for sustainable economic development. The planners reasoned that if it was possible to devise a planning process that incorporated the representatives of economic concerns, then it should be possible to build on the Brundtland philosophy. After two months of work within the environment ministry, the planning task force groups were broadened to include representatives from agriculture, transport and economic affairs. The participation of these groups did not rest upon the premiss that they should have responsibilities for the environment, but on the assumption that properly to promote their responsibilities for economic development they needed to take into account the environmental dimension.

Perhaps the most significant manifestation of this union of economy and environment is to be found in the attempt to cost the cumulative loss of marketed output on the assumption that the NEPP was implemented. The Netherlands Central Planning Bureau (CPB) was asked to look at the effects on Dutch GNP from implementing the NEPP. It conducted its analysis using two assumptions. The first was that there would be no similar implementation of measures in other countries, and the second that other countries took similar measures. Clearly such an analysis must be highly conjectural, but the results are important none the less. On the assumption of no other country taking similar measures the cumulative loss to the growth in GNP by the year 2010 was estimated to be 2.6 per cent. If other countries were to take similar measures, the cumulative loss by the same date was estimated to be 0.9 per cent.[12] These figures have to be set in context, since they represent accumulated losses not to current standards of living but to future growth in the standard of living. Alongside these figures must be set the CPB estimate of the cumulative growth in the economy to the year 2010, which appears to be 99.4 per cent. In other words, over a twenty-year period it would be possible both to implement in the full range of measures in NEPP and simultaneously achieve virtual doubling in the average standard of living.

There are two points to be made about the economic logic contained in the NEPP. In the first place the costs are presented as extra net costs. They do not show separately the economic savings that result from the implementation of environmental policies, of which energy conservation and the recovery of materials from waste recycling represent the most important aspects. Secondly, they show the costs of environmental measures, but they do not include an estimate of the benefits that might flow from environmental improvement, and which would in a full cost-benefit analysis be deducted from the costs. If environmental amenity is a superior good, then the benefits it produces ought to be set against the cost of its achievement. The estimates presented in the NEPP, therefore, represent, if they are accurate, a strict upper bound as the economic costs of a stringent environmental policy.

Having looked at the logic of the NEPP, it is now time to step back from its detailed exposition and seek to analyse the political and institutional conditions under which it emerged. The successful pursuit of environmental policy depends not only on the intellectual cogency of the arguments advanced in its favour but also on the circumstances within which it is developed. It is to the analysis of those circumstances that we now turn.

The circumstances of the National Environmental Policy Plan

In order to understand why and how the NEPP took the form that it did we need to place it in its institutional, political and policy context. This is important partly to identify what gave it its distinctive character and partly to separate what in general can be learnt from the experience as well as what the process tells us is specific to the Netherlands.

Perhaps the first place to begin is with the policy tradition of planning in the Netherlands. At various times sine 1945 economic planning has occupied a central place in public policy in the Netherlands, although by the 1980s such planning had gone out of fashion. By contrast land use and development planning continues to be important, as one might imagine in a densely populated and heavily urbanised society. In particular, given the historic importance attached to waterways and flood protection, the zoning of land for development purposes has traditionally occupied a prominent place in Dutch public policy. The idea of environmental planning could thus hope to find a congenial intellectual and institutional reception in the Netherlands, and in this sense its emergence as a tool of public policy is not surprising.

The immediate forerunners to the NEPP were the Indicative Multi-Year Plans (IMPs). These had first been developed in 1984, and their purpose was to achieve some co-ordination of environmental regulation and policy. The problem to which they were a response was the one discussed in the previous chapter, namely that multiple licensing procedures and cross-media pollution flows can lead to problem displacement in environmental policy rather than problem solution. The solution adopted for this dilemma was not to focus upon the particular receiving medium, but to identify *themes* that had implications across policy and organisational boundaries. For example, instead of a focus upon sulphur emissions, the theme would be acidification, of which the control of sulphur emissions would form one component.

The purpose of the IMPs was to use the occasion of having to present a plan to parliament to provide a process within which interdepartmental collaboration could take place. The first and second of the Indicative Plans, in 1984 and 1985, basically therefore provided an opportunity to show how pollution was being dealt with on a cross-media basis. The strategy for different themes was to set priorities and establish environmental quality standards from which emission reduction targets could be derived. Since 1984 several Indicative Plans have been published covering such themes as chemicals, waste management, and eutrophication as well as acidification.

Prior policy developments in the Netherlands not only provided a context within which a new understanding of policy could emerge, they also highlighted the shortcomings of traditional policy instruments and approaches. Although the IMPs took a thematic approach, their ultimate practical implications were in terms of specific targets for a reduction in emissions. They did nothing to integrate environmental concerns into the broad range of public policies. To the extent to which the IMPs provided a mode of policy learning, they suggested what was *not* being done as well as what could be done through new processes and new ways of thinking.

However, the existence of a policy problem does not automatically call forth a solution, even when certain operating procedures have acquired legitimacy within government and bureaucracy. In addition there have to be political conditions favourable to policy development and initiation. One element in these political conditions in the Netherlands is the state of public opinion. For various reasons we might expect public opinion to be sympathetic to environmental protection in the Netherlands. As a relatively affluent European country with a highly educated population, we should expect the Netherlands to include a high proportion of the population with post-materialist values, and this expectation is confirmed by public attitude studies. Moreover, into this generally sympathetic environment two events in the year preceding the publication of the NEPP were important in crystallising public opinion around the need for greater urgency in environmental policy.

The first of these was the Queen's Speech at Christmas, in addition to her formal speech at the annual opening of parliament, which drew attention to the seriousness of environmental problems. Once the environmental message received the royal seal of approval, concern for the environment became respectable and there was a desire on the part of establishment bodies to be seen to be doing something towards the problem. The second event was the publication of the RIVM report which alerted the population to the possible scale of environmental degradation that confronted the Netherlands over the next twenty years. Neither of these events would have been significant had the underlying disposition not been present. Equally, the underlying disposition would not have achieved such a sharp effect had these events not served to crystallise the attitudes of the population. For example, if a study shows that on the most vigorous application of present policies only 20 per cent of woodlands will be undamaged by the year

2000, environmentalists can argue that government policies are allowing 80 per cent of woodlands to be damaged.

Corresponding to this trend in public opinion at the mass level, there were developments among Dutch political elites that were also important in preparing the way for the NEPP, the most important of which was the character of the politicians responsible for the environment portfolio. During the 1980s two politicians, Winsemius and Nijpels, from the liberals (Volkspartij voor Vrijheid en Democratie) held the environment portfolio. The role of Winsemius was to provide the impetus towards the policy of *verinnerlijking*. This had originally started in 1984 when the environment ministry opened discussion with Agriculture on environmental questions. He had also been influential in the development of the IMPs and even after his departure from politics kept a sympathetic interest in the development of the NEPP. Nijpels, as his successor, had been extremely influential in working with other ministers and securing their co-operation on environmental matters. This is an inherently difficult task for any politician since the price that has to be paid for co-operation is a sharing of authority over the development of one's own programmes. He was also placed, as we shall see later, in a difficult position over the breakup of the governing coalition in 1989. From the viewpoint of the NEPP the most important feature of the contribution of Winsemius and Nijpels was their ability to provide intellectual stimulus and diplomatic leadership in relation to other ministries.

At the beginning of this chapter the distinction was noted between structural approaches to the problem of external integration and procedural approaches. In the former the emphasis is placed on reconfiguring the machinery of government to achieve greater co-ordination of policy. In the latter the emphasis is upon devising new process or procedures within the existing machinery without tinkering with the machine itself. Inherent in the strategy adopted by the NEPP planners was a determination to concentrate upon the latter type of reform rather than the former.

The planning team in the environment ministry decided therefore to eschew any ambitions towards changes in the machinery of government. This was partly a sober acknowledgement of the truth that the environment ministry could not go it alone in terms of environmental policy-making, but largely a determination to ensure that policy-makers were not distracted by procedural issues about the limits of ministerial authority instead of substantive issues concerned with the protection of the environment. The hope was that the very process of devising a national plan would create incentives towards co-operation that were not present in the routine modes of policy making within different ministries. This does not mean that the environment ministry simply accepted the prevailing distribution of ministerial authority. Given the centrality of energy conservation to the NEPP strategy, for example, it was important to the planners to ensure that they were seen to have a role in the making of energy policy, but what they wanted to avoid was any suspicion that they were seeking to take over responsibility for that area of policy. Clearly, able political leadership at ministerial level is crucial to this approach.

Two aspects of the planning process were essential to the success of this strategy. The first involved the way in which agreement was secured on the central logic of the NEPP. The logic of the NEPP is driven by and formulated within a specific theory of environmental pollution, from which an understanding of the problems is then elaborated. These general principles are set out in the first four chapters of the NEPP. It was these chapters that were circulated in draft form for discussion and agreement before the subsequent detailed strategy chapters were circulated and discussed. This gave the planners a considerable debating advantage, since they could always say in the face of any opposition to detailed proposals that they were merely the implications of what had already been agreed in principle. One official from VROM said, in interview, that the phrase 'You've already agreed this in principle, these are merely the detailed implications' was used time and time again in debates with other ministries and target groups about detailed targets and policy prescriptions.

The second element in this co-operative strategy was to seek to maintain authority over certain elements of environmental policy being the specific responsibility of the environment ministry. Since co-operative policy-making involves sharing responsibility, the danger is that policy priorities and target will be weakened during the course of co-operative negotiation. The approach adopted by the VROM team was to maintain the principle that it was they who had the responsibility for defining the environmental quality objectives, but that they were prepared to concede and bargain on all other aspects of the plan, for example the timetable for achieving specific targets. It was this aspect of the process that was in part responsible for taking the year 2010 as the limit of the planning horizon, since it provided a sensible context within which the planners could negotiate with industry. It was far enough into the future for managers to adapt their production methods, but not so far that environmental targets and constraints would seem remote and separate from their own responsibilities.

Negotiation and discussion with the target groups, referring both to other ministries and to social interests like industry, is an important aspect of the principle of co-operative environmental policy-making. Since planning takes place in the context of considerable uncertainty, which can cause significant anxiety to industrial managers, the planning team sought to invent a continuing structure of dialogue and negotiation so that industry did not simply feel that it was being handed down targets from on high which it had to meet come what may, but was instead engaged positively in the implementation of the overall strategy. No doubt the relatively co-operative nature of Dutch political culture and the relatively small size of economic and political elites in The Netherlands favoured the development of this co-operative approach, but it is worth stressing that the resolution of uncertainties was not something that the planners felt they could take for granted, but was an issue that had to be confronted explicitly and institutional mechanisms developed as a way of ameliorating the problem.

Even given this co-operative stance, it was not always possible for the planners to ensure that there was a two-way dialogue successfully conducted over the NEPP. The manner of working was to circulate two drafts of the plan to interested parties. These interested parties included the provincial departments of the environment who have the primary responsibility for enforcing environmental regulations. Within the provinces there was some disquiet about the hurried timetable of negotiation and a lack of consultation about the main thrust of the plan. It is noticeable that the NEPP pays relatively little attention to the problems of implementation at the street level. To some extent it assumes that agreement among high level managers and the state in The Hague will automatically translate into effective change in Groningen or Nijmegen. This assumption is far from being validated, and the concern in the provinces illustrates how even well-motivated planners can suffer the effects of limited attention span and scarcity of time.

Political dimensions

To understand the fate and possible future of the NEPP we need to understand the role of politicians and the incentives they face. The political conditions under which the NEPP was developed were fragile, and developments subsequent to its publication need to be understood in the light of the fluid nature of Dutch coalition politics. Among the conditions essential for the NEPP to emerge as a policy initiative was the character and drive of Winsemius and Nijpels as successive environmental ministers. However, it is unlikely that the plan would have evolved in the way that it did had it not been for the involvement of the Prime Minister's office. In the Queen's Speech at the opening of parliament in October 1988 the Prime Minister's office, which is responsible for the contents of the speech, had referred to environmental improvements. The theme was then taken up by the Queen in her own personal message to the nation at Christmas. By this stage the issue was clearly on the political agenda of The Netherlands, just as it was on the political agenda of every developed country. The Prime Minister could not but respond to the rising tide of public opinion. By the spring of 1989 the environment was not just one issue among many for the Prime Minister's office, it had come to dominate among the set of policy concerns. It was clearly necessary in the light of public opinion for the government to be seen to be doing something constructive in the face of environmental problems.

Since the work was already under way, this rising tide of public concern provided a strong impetus to the development of the NEPP. The role of the Prime Minister at this stage was to arbitrate between ministries when disputes could not be resolved in the routine course of the planning process. For example, there was a dispute between the environment ministry and the transport ministry about the baseline date for the stabilisation of carbon dioxide levels. Environment wanted carbon dioxide emissions to be stabilised by 2000 at their 1989 levels, whereas transport wanted them stabilised at their 1990 levels. (Since emissions were rising, it would be easier to stabilise at 1990 levels than at 1989 levels.)

This dispute was unresolved in the course of interministerial bargaining and so it went to the Prime Minister's office for arbitration, where the judgement of Solomon was made and the decision taken to make the target for 2000 the average of the 1989 and 1990 levels. So it appears in the plan.

However, the role of the Prime Minister himself becomes much more important in the wake of the plan's publication. In order to appreciate the significance of this role it is necessary to understand the political composition of the then ruling government coalition. The Prime Minister, Mr Ruud Lubbers, led the largest party represented in the *Tweede Kammer*, the Christian Democratic Appeal (CDA). Its coalition partners were the Liberals (VVD), the party to which Nijpels belonged as environment minister. It was this coalition which was to split apart ostensibly over one of the NEPP's proposals. As Prime Minister, Lubbers could not hold the coalition together over the plan.

The issue was a simple one. For many years Dutch taxpayers had been allowed a tax deduction on their expenses for commuting to work. The deduction had been important in the period of post-war reconstruction when the main objective of city planners had been to move people out from the centre of cities to the newly expanding suburbs. By providing the tax deduction the intention was to reduce the cost of commuting. Consequently, by the time the NEPP was being prepared Dutch taxpayers were allowed a standard tax write-off equivalent to over £200 to cover commuting expenses. As part of its general strategy to discourage private car use, the NEPP proposed the abolition of this tax concession. It can hardly be said that this was a fundamental or leading element in the plan, and yet it was the issue which provided the occasion for the governing coalition to break up.

The VVD fraction in the parliament decided to oppose this provision of the plan, and threatened to withdraw from the coalition unless the proposal was revoked. Among other things this placed Nijpels himself in a difficult situation, and he was forced into the schizophrenic position of having to say that as a member of the VVD fraction he opposed the proposal whilst as a member of the cabinet and as minister of the environment he supported it. In view of the withdrawal from the coalition the Prime Minister had to request a dissolution of parliament and a general election. This is probably the first time in the world's history when a government has fallen as a result of proposing an environmental policy measure. However, this is not to say that the environmental policy proposal was the strict cause of the government's fall. Although this was the way that the press wrote up the story of the Dutch government's fall, there are reasons for thinking that this cannot have been the whole of the story.[13] To see why we have to delve a little more deeply into the character of the governing coalition.

Relations between the Prime Minister and his VVD partners in government had deteriorated during the life of the coalitions. The liberal partners objected to what they perceived as the high-handed style of the Prime Minister in his dealings with them. Moreover, there were clear policy strains within the coalition over other issues, most notably abortion where the CDA inclines to a more conservative position then the VVD. In the opinion of many observers the break-up of the coalition was an event waiting to happen. The proposals in the NEPP were not so much cause as catalyst.

Even if we accept this interpretation, however, there still remains a puzzle about the actions of the VVD faction. The odds against its being electorally rational for any party to cause the breakup of a governing coalition on an environmental issue in northern Europe are surely very long. It is extremely difficult in the conditions of an election to keep clearly in front of the electorate's mind the salience of the one issue that led to the breakup and it can hardly be said that policy towards what is, after all, a relatively technical tax matter is a crusading issue to present to any electorate. Of course it is possible that whatever its objective rationality the VVD perceived it to be rational to be seen protecting the tax allowance, since that stance was likely to be popular with the petty bourgeoisie who comprised its core electoral support. Whatever these subjective calculations may have been, they were shown to be inadequate when the election was held. The VVD lost votes and seats in the legislature, and the CDA gained, leading one influential Dutch weekly to portray the Netherlands as CDA-land and another to portray Lubbers as King of the Dutch (*De Tijd* and *Elsevier*). Whatever else it had done the election had shown that a governing party could face political opposition to environmental measures that threatened to raise the cost of living for ordinary citizens and still come out on top. To that extent the election should be interpreted as a boost for environmental planning, not a set-back.

But it is one thing to win an election in the face of criticism of an environmental programme, and another to implement policies in accordance with that programme. After the usual weeks of coalition bargaining in which Lubbers sought to entice various groups into the governing coalition, including van Mierlo the leader of the Democrats '66, the new cabinet was to be formed from an alliance of Christian Democrats and Labour. This coalition has proved itself less than enthusiastic in its pursuit of a national environmental strategy plan, largely it would appear because of uncertainties about its costs and worries about the scale of transformation in economic and social life that the NEPP envisages. Moreover, with the departure from the governing coalition of the VVD, the cabinet has lost a policy champion for the NEPP in the figure of Nijpels. What at one time seemed the most radical initiative by any government in the world to integrate environmental considerations into a range of public policy threatens to degenerate into something far more routine and far less innovative: an indicative series of policy goals that have relevance to, but do not necessarily guide, policy planning. This need not mean, however, that the epitaph of the NEPP should be written as 'Rest in Peace', not least for the experience that the NEPP provides about how constructive social learning about environmental problems can work in modern politics.

Learning by planning?

Environmental problems are complex and they are now present on a scale and in a form that dwarfs previous experience of legislation and policy-making. There is no reason to believe that the political institutions of modern liberal democracy are capable of responding quickly and effectively to these problems, any more than they have been capable of responding to the mass poverty and unemployment of the inter-war period, themselves novel problems that governments failed properly to understand or to solve in the 1930s. As a device for solving collective problems we should not be too optimistic about the performance of political institutions.

If true, this observation should provide us with a criterion for judging and assessing the Dutch NEPP. Its value as a means of social learning is not limited by the extent to which it is implemented, but by the extent to which it provides the capacity for an improved understanding of the policy issues to which environmental problems give rise. Even if it changes public policy less than might be desirable or necessary from the viewpoint of environmental protection, it may still contribute greatly to the improvement in the quality of policy understanding. Environmental policy is one of those areas in which a little learning goes a long way.

In this context it seems that one of the most important contributions of the NEPP was to provide a general theoretical framework within which environmental considerations could be integrated into the general run of public policy. By making its underlying assumptions explicit and by seeking to articulate a general systems perspective in terms of which to understand the problems caused by pollution the NEPP provided a means to counteract the generally narrowing perspective of department or sectoral responsibilities. Consider by way of illustration one simple example. Sulphur dioxide and nitrogen oxide emissions are usually considered problems of air pollution, which in a sense they are. But they are ultimately problems of soil and fresh water pollution, and locating these polluting emissions in a general systems framework is a powerful way of appreciating that fact. Once the point is appreciated, it can readily be seen how the traditional political and administrative compartmentalisation of the problem is inadequate to cope with the issue of acidification. In other words, the general underlying theory of the NEPP is not just playing a presentational role; it is providing a powerful heuristic device for analysing the character of the institutional and policy response to environmental problems. One important function served by the NEPP, therefore, was to show how a new general theoretical perspective could be incorporated into a process aimed at a practical solution to pressing problems.

During the production of the plan those drawing it up tried out their theoretical perspective on a number of groups and individuals in draft form. They would often meet the response that what they were doing amounted to 'silly ideas' or were 'only theory'. However, during the course of their work they found that a planning team in the Association of Dutch Chemical Industries was working on a parallel approach. It is also worth noting the parallels to the mass balances approached to cross-media transfer provided in the work of the Committee on Multimedia Approaches to Pollution Control, which was a joint body of the Board on Environmental Studies and Toxicology and the Commission on Physical Sciences, Mathematics, and Resources of the US National Research Council.[14] The fact that different bodies with different purposes in mind used a general systems approach when seeking to gain a better understanding of pollution control policy means that there is likely to be a 'deep structure' of underlying logic involved. To criticise the approach as being too theoretical reminds one of Keynes's remark to the effect that so-called practical persons, devoid of theory, are usually the slaves of some defunct economist or political philosopher.

Partly because a coherent theoretical perspective takes time and experience to develop in relation to problems of public policy, it would be unrealistic to expect any political system to move immediately to the stage of developing a national environmental plan of the sophistication and quality that the Dutch have achieved. Moreover, prior to the production of the plan the Dutch bureaucracy had experience of planning in connection with both physical development and the economy, as well as the experience of the IMPs. The IMPs in particular provided a means of policy learning and an opportunity to develop the synoptic perspective that is so central to the NEPP. Indeed the value of the IMPs in retrospect may come to seem not the improvements they made directly to environmental quality, it being difficult in any case to establish the effects from policy outputs on real world outcomes, but the framework they provided for developing the ideas and theoretical approach to be found in the NEPP.

From the perspective of a social learning approach to policy formation one valuable feature of the planning approach is the opportunity and incentive that it provides for policy-makers to cast problems of public choice into an explicit framework for decision. Policy choice often involves choosing among competing objectives. The problem is that policy-makers can often use their general facts about policy to provide cover for making implicit and unarticulated trade-offs. A national environmental plan provides an incentive for policy-makers to ensure that costs and disadvantages are fully weighed in the writing of the plan, but it also forces them to insert the problems and difficulties into the process of deliberation in an explicit and preferably quantified form. Thus, for all its insistence that environmental protection was a necessary condition for economic development, the planners had to accept the arguments of those who insisted that there had to be some economic costs to a policy of stringent environmental protection. The advantage of a formal plan is that it forces the planners to bring those costs out in the open. This has obvious advantages in terms of democratic and public accountability but, just as importantly, it provides an organising framework within which continuing debate and research can be conducted by members of the relevant policy community. Thus, even if it turned out that the planners had been Panglossian in their assumptions about the size of the slowdown to economic growth that the implementation of the NEPP would involve, the explicit treatment of the issue in the plan would provide the framework in which the price of environmental improvement could be weighed against the benefits, and it would present a sacrifice of environmental amenity on the spurious grounds that the benefits were not worth the (unarticulated) costs.

The above considerations identify elements of the NEPP that aid social learning in so far as it is a *plan*. But it is unlikely that every country would be able to borrow or adopt the Dutch approach especially where we are talking about political cultures, like those of the US or the UK, in which there is deep, if not universal, hostility to the very idea of national planning. Does this mean that there are no elements of the Dutch experience from which these societies can learn? Not necessarily, if there are elements of the Dutch approach which, though exemplified in the process of national planning, are none the less distinct from it. Perhaps the most important of these elements relates to the manner of achieving the integration of environmental objectives with the full range of public policies. By explicitly rejecting an approach based on upon the reorganisation of the machinery of government, the Dutch planners have stressed the importance of inventing *processes* of policy planning that secure co-ordination and integration. One way they put this, in a mock form of self-deprecation, is to say that in twenty years they should be out of a job, because by then environmental considerations will be so integrated into the general work of government that their presence will be unnecessary. Of course the premiss need not entail the conclusion: no one supposes that finance ministries are unnecessary because accountability for public expenditure is built into the standard operating procedures of every spending department. Similarly, no one need suppose that an environment ministry can be dispensed with once all the relevant departments of government have proper environmental auditing procedures in place. But the planners' self-mockery has a point: the greater their success the less they will be necessary to adequate environment performance.

If the integration of environmental considerations into the full range of public policies is to be achieved, the Dutch experience of national policy planning suggests that if governments are not going to adopt the same methods, they should at least strive to find their functional equivalents. Attempts to achieve the integration of environmental considerations with the full range of public policies by reorganisations in the structure of government are doomed to failure since the logical implication of that approach is the creation of one mega-environment ministry of which specialist functions were merely subdepartments. Putting particular departments under the authority of an environmental ministry, for example agriculture or transport, is logically conceivable, but almost certainly undesirable from the viewpoint of environmental protection. Indeed, if the UK's experience in the 1970s is anything to go by, brigading environment with transport is at least as likely to make transport interests dominate environment as ensure that environmental considerations are attached to transport. In addition, the danger of displacing substantive policy attention by wrangling over department turf strongly argues for focusing upon procedural devices and processes to attain interministerial co-ordination. The Dutch planning process has been successful in this regard, and it has revealed the implications for transport, agriculture and industry of the pursuit of environmental goals. No one has yet found an alternative device for assembling the information necessary to stipulate the implications of environmental policy in this coherent way. If national planning is shunned, its alternative will have to be invented.

Yet, from another point of view, one lesson to be drawn from the NEPP is that even if national planning is necessary it is far from sufficient to achieve adequate environmental performance. This is the implication to be drawn from the NEPP's stress on the importance of the responsibility for all individual citizens for the quality of the environment. It can be argued, as the plan itself does

F

at some points, that this stress upon the role of the individual is merely an extension of the strategy of *verinnerlijking* from the corporate sphere to the sphere of citizenship. In some respects it clearly is this. However, the move from corporation to citizen can be seen as involving a qualitative shift in the relation of the state to civil society. When applied to the corporate sector the strategy of *verinnerlijking* can be viewed as a means by which the state discharges its regulatory function in a more efficient and effective way. Given the imbalance of information between the corporate sector and the government, some means is needed to ensure the implementation of politically determined environmental standards and instituting systems of internal environmental audit within companies is one way of achieving this objective. When the state affirms the importance of individual responsibility for the protection of the environment, it can be argued that it is doing more than simply seeking efficient and effective means to previously chosen ends; it is instead choosing ends, by selecting a particular interpretation of the network of rights and obligations that bind the state and citizens in an identifiable political unit. It has, to use Matthew Arnold's contrast, gone beyond mechanical reform to moral reform.[15] The object of policy must not simply be a good environment, but good citizens in relation to that environment.

This attempt to provide a moral content to the idea of citizenship is of course a return to an ancient tradition. According to the predominant classical theorists of democracy, the health of the citizen republic was dependent upon the virtue of its citizens, a view that finds echoes in the political theory of Rousseau, Jefferson, J. S. Mill, T. H. Green and A. D. Lindsay. The alternative view, which finds its most dazzling exposition in Hobbes, is that the state is merely a device for harmonising the otherwise discordant desires that individuals pursue and to perform this function it requires the understanding, but not the virtue, of its citizens. It is this second tradition that has dominated recent expositions of liberal thought, for example in the work of Ackerman, Dworkin, Nozick and, even, Rawls. In these writers an essential feature of the liberal state is that it remains strictly neutral between competing conceptions of the good, merely providing a legal and constitutional framework within which individuals can pursue their separate ends. From this perspective the state must not seek to make individuals pursue any particular conception of the good, for that would be to suppose that there is some commonly shared conception of human perfection. This neutralist conception of the relationship between state and citizen has been criticised on the grounds that it provides no method by which irreducibly collective goods, like the tolerance of society, can be secured.[16] Unless, so it is argued, certain types of disposition are fostered in citizens by means of education and social training, the characteristic virtues of a liberal society, many of which are essentially collective in character, cannot be maintained. Not the least interesting feature of the NEPP is its attempt to show how contemporary environmental policy calls for the virtue-based conception of citizenship rather than a conception which secures only a moral neutrality of the state in the face of competing ends of its citizens.

Over all this of course hangs the shadow of politics. Sceptics might argue that what the NEPP shows is that intellectual sophistication, rational persuasiveness and policy commitment are ineffective in a world in which policy requires the sanction of governing politicians who are subject to incentives and motivations at odds with those of effective policy development. Bureaucratic politics or system needs are at odds with policy learning. No doubt there is a measure of truth in this view, but it cannot be the whole truth, if only for the reason that the NEPP would never have got as far as it did without its championing by individual politicians. It is all too easy to underestimate how much effort is required to change the standard bureaucratic procedures of modern government. Even to have secured the co-operation of other ministries in signing an agreed national plan is a considerable achievement. Perhaps the first rule for any government that takes seriously its duties towards the environment is to choose wisely the person who will hold the cabinet environment portfolio.

In addition to the task of fitting the right person to the job to be done there is also the need to provide the legitimating principles, that provide momentum and justification to the task at hand. The role of these political principles is to express a description of a governmental process that makes it intelligible to those who participate in politics or who are subject to its authority. The idea of a national plan, representing a society's chosen response to a common problem, might have provided an appropriate formula in the Dutch case, although weakening the implementation of the plan suggests that the idea was insufficient to the task. Perhaps it is impossible to find such a formula in the circumstances prevailing in contemporary political democracies and no doubt different countries will need different formulae. What is certain is that the ambitions of the Dutch plan are a measure of the scale of problems to be faced.

Notes

1   C. Bosso, *Pesticides and Politics: The Life Cycle of an Issue* (Pittsburgh: Pittsburgh University Press, 1987); A. Weale, T. O'Riordan and L. Kramme, *Controlling Pollution in the Round* (London: Anglo-German Foundation, 1991), chapter 5; E. Müller, *Innenwelt der Umweltpolitik* (Oplahlen: Westdeutscher Verlag, 1986).

2   Her Majesty's Government, *This Common Inheritance* (London: HMSO, 1990) Cm 200.

3   Second Chamber of the States General, *National Environmental Policy Plan. To Choose or Lose* ('s-Gravenhage: SDU uitgeverij, 1989).

4   *National Environmental Policy Plan*, p. 61.

5   B. Commoner, *Making Peace with the Planet* (London: Victor Gollancz, 1990), chapter 1.

6   *National Environmental Policy Plan*, chapters 2 and 3. The identification of scale levels is to be found in the scientific report providing the main analysis behind the NEPP. See Rijksinstituut voor Volksgezondheid en Milieuhygiene, *Zorgen voor Morgen* (Alphen aan den Rijn: Samson H.D., 1988).

7   Compare Haas on the United National Environment Programme: 'In short, UNEP and its ecological colleagues was seeking to promote very sophisticated learning. Maurice Strong repeatedly asserted: "The process is the policy."' P. M. Haas, *Saving the Mediterranean* (New York: Columbia University Press, 1990), pp. 77–8.

8   Compare J. E. Chubb, *Interest Groups and the Bureaucracy: The Politics of Energy* (Stanford: Stanford University Press, 1983).

9   *National Environmental Policy Plan*, p. 87.

10   Rijksinstituut voor Volksgezondheid en Milieuhygiene, *Zorgen voor Morgen*.

11   World Commission on Environment and Development, *Our Common Future* (Oxford: Oxford University Press, 1987).

12   *National Environmental Policy Plan*, pp. 108–15.

13   This is also the way that the story has entered the public policy literature. Compare A. J. Heidenheimer, H. Heclo and C. T. Adams,

Comparative Public Policy (Basingstoke and London: Macmillan, 1990), p. 337.

14 Committee on Multimedia Approaches to Pollution Control, *Multimedia Approaches to Pollution Control* (Washington, DC: National Academy Press, 1987).

15 For some relevant quotations from Matthew Arnold, see P. Day and R. Klein, *Accountabilities* (London and New York: Tavistock Publications, 1987), p. 168.

16 J. Raz, *The Morality of Freedom* (Oxford: Clarendon Press, 1986), pp. 198–200.

6

Implementation, economic instruments and public participation

When T. S. Eliot wrote that between the idea and the reality falls the shadow he had some rather exalted metaphysical problems in mind rather than the mundane problems of public policy.[1] Yet the thought that things do not always turn out as expected applies just as much to public policy as it does to the topics about which T. S. Eliot wrote, and environmental policy has proved no exception to this rule. Thus, the US Clean Air Act of 1970 set a 1977 deadline for achieving a 90 per cent reduction in urban carbon monoxide, hydrocarbon and ozone levels. By 1977 compliance had not been achieved, and the deadline was moved to 1982, and then in turn to the end of 1987 and, in the case of three cities, a further twenty-year grace period was allowed.[2] In the 1970s in Germany Renate Mayntz and her colleagues were able to show that bargaining and compromise characterised the implementation of what in theory were formally strict emission limit values.[3] In the United Kingdom important provisions of the 1974 Control of Pollution Act, relating to public access to environmental information, remained unimplemented for more than ten years.[4] These examples are replicated widely through many different political systems. They are also replicated in many different sectors of public policy.

These examples relate only to policy *outputs*, the product of government activity in the form of regulations, laws, inspections and procedures. When we consider policy *outcomes*, that is changes in the environment itself, the assessment is more telling. Even those aspects of the environment that have been a substantial focus of public concern, for example Lake Erie, have failed to show signs of significant improvements in environmental quality.

Despite the stringent application of new emission standards in Germany in the 1980s, air quality showed little sign of improvement. And many problems, for example the preservation of bio-diversity, have become worse because there has been little explicit policy development.

These examples have led analysts to identify implementation failure or implementation deficit as significant features of the policy process. The origins of such implementation failure are various. Sometimes they stem from a failure of political will, reflecting other policy priorities or political pressures. Sometimes they stem from the inevitable limits of ignorance and uncertainty to which organisations are subject. And sometimes they stem from the psychology and professional background possessed by those with the responsibility to implement policy. These factors interact in the case of environmental policy, as they do with public policy more generally, to produce the patterns of failures that we observe.

However, apart from these general features, critics of the environmental policy strategies of the 1970s have alleged some specific defects in the approach adopted. The 1970s pollution control strategies tended to follow traditional models of regulation by administratively determined standards and as they were implemented, many people became critical of the assumption that this approach was the best way to pursue the goals of environmental policy. There were two distinct types of criticism in particular. On the one hand, economists began to develop the case for using economic instruments in the reduction of pollution rather than administratively defined standards. The argument was that economic approaches would remedy some of the economic inefficiencies associated with traditional modes of regulation, and so bring greater economic protection at lower cost. On the other hand, critics of the typically bureaucratic mode of regulation argued that implementation deficit reflected a deeper democratic deficit, and new ways would have to be found to increase public participation in the making and implementation of environmental protection policy.

Although both these approaches imply criticism of traditional regulatory strategies, they stand in a complex relation to one another. On the one hand, they may be seen as criticisms that pull in quite opposite directions. Those favouring the development of economic instruments have to presuppose the technical work of the economics profession and therefore the logic of their position involves the imposition of a particular type of technical rationality upon policy processes, whereas those who criticise administrative regulation for its democratic deficit often wish to demystify and deprofessionalise the processes of policy-making. A concern with economic instruments and a concern with public participation may be seen as quite contrary concerns therefore. On the other hand, there are potentially serious economic costs consequent upon a misestimate of public expectations and concerns. For example, frequent revision of environmental standards to meet rising public expectations can be both administratively costly and costly to firms who have to adapt their production processes more frequently. In so far as innovative methods of public participation promise to correct these misestimations, they can lead to a reduction of economic costs, and therefore the two lines of critique can be seen as complementary.

Moreover, both the use of economic instruments and innovative public participation presuppose that certain political conditions and circumstances apply, and it may be that these presuppositions are not always sustainable. The purpose of this chapter is to investigate the relationships between these critiques of the conduct of pollution control policy and the political conditions under which alternative strategies may be developed.

Economic approaches and instruments

The need to consider the role of economic approaches to pollution control becomes inevitable once we consider the implications of seeking to integrate environmental considerations into the broad range of public policies. Since many public policies involve the use of economic instruments, for example taxes or subsidies, it is natural to ask whether the incentive effects induced by these instruments are environmentally benign. This was the question raised about the commuter's subsidy in the Dutch National Environmental Policy Plan, and it is also the question that a number of commentators have raised about agricultural subsidies under the European Community's Common Agricultural Policy, which, because it has offered guaranteed purchase of commodities produced, has encouraged intensive production, for example by using fertilisers for increased wheat production, and thus increased some pollution problems. To raise the question of economic instruments in relation to pollution control policy is therefore often just another way of raising the question of whether such economic instruments as are used in public policy are consistent with a concern for environmental quality.

However, in discussions on the use of economic instruments in environmental policy, the focus of concern has usually been expressed the other way round: not how can we assure the environmental benignity of economic instruments, but can economic instruments supplement or supplant existing administrative devices to make pollution control policy more effective and efficient? At this point, it is important to distinguish two approaches, since each is likely to relate in quite different ways to the question of political feasibility. The first approach is the more ambitious and comprehensive of the two, and aims to integrate environmental considerations into our concept of social welfare. Its very ambitiousness, I shall argue, raises serious questions about its political feasibility. The second approach is more strictly related to the idea that taxes and other economic devices are really *instruments*, and it is concerned with the extent to which such instruments may provide a more cost-effective way of achieving politically or administratively determined objectives. By that token there are fewer problems of political feasibility, although there are none the less some crucial issues in that respect.

In order to see the logic of the social welfare approach, it is useful to consider the case of market failure, as discussed in chapter 2 when considering the rational choice idiom. Market failure occurs when there is a competitive equilibrium in the processes of production and exchange (that is, no economic agent has an incentive to change his or her behaviour given what other agents are doing) and yet social welfare is not at a maximum.

In the context of pollution control policy the most important condition that might not be satisfied is the absence of externalities or neighbourhood effects. A textbook example of an externality is the smoking factory chimney which deposits pollution in the neighbourhood. These external or neighbourhood effects impose economic costs among those who live in the town. Windows, buildings and cars have to be cleaned more frequently, stonework is damaged and has to be repaired and the incidence of chest-related diseases increases necessitating greater spending on medicines and visits to the doctor. In the conventional analysis of economic welfare, the incidence of these costs is unimportant, since neo-classical economics eschews any judgement about the distribution of welfare.[5] What is important is that the citizens of the town would be willing to pay for a reduction in these economic costs, that is there is an economic value assigned to clear air as a resource. If the sum of the willingness to pay exceeds the costs of the appropriate clean-up measures, then the economy has a sub-optimal level of welfare. There is a potential gain from trade between the factory owner and the citizens that is not being secured. Welfare gains are unrealised.

Cleaning up pollution depends upon solving a collective action problem. Since conventional economic theory suggests that voluntary collective action in the production of public goods is unlikely to occur at an optimal level, the suggestion has been that there is a role for government in a market economy in solving the collective action problem. Where markets fail, governments might succeed. Hence, on this account, the task of government is to ensure that externalities are internalised, either by a system of corrective taxes and subsidies or by means of administrative regulation, thus achieving the optimal level of welfare of which the economy is capable.

The existence of public goods, including environmental protection, is one of the reasons why uncorrected market prices might fail to produce overall allocative efficiency. However, there are other reasons. Among these is that not all factors of production are priced, so that they are treated as free goods. Uncontrolled use of the environment as a disposal route illustrates one way in which factors of production remain unpriced. On orthodox analysis, an unpriced good will be consumed at a greater rate than a priced good, and so we should expect environmental degradation. Moreover, some of the losers from environmental degradation will be members of future generations, who currently do not exercise any purchasing power, and whose welfare is thereby ignored in current economic decisions.

The tradition of economic analysis in which these arguments have usually been developed stems from Pigou's *The Economics of Welfare*.[6] According to Pigovian analysis, one way for the government to rectify the inefficiencies of a market economy subject to externalities in the form of pollution is for them to impose a system of taxes and subsidies that would discourage the use of polluting goods and encourage the use of non-polluting goods. Yet, as Majone has pointed out, it has not been possible for governments to follow the logic of this analysis.[7] Nowhere do we find a system of Pigovian taxes in place. Instead, we find specific taxes placed on certain polluting commodities, for example leaded petrol, but without any attempt to relate the value of those taxes to broader estimates of the optimal allocation of resources within the economy. This universal absence of Pigovian instruments is significant. It suggests that there are structural characteristics implicit in the workings of modern political systems that inhibit or prevent the development of the Pigovian approach.

To understand in more detail the nature and extent of these structural impediments, it may be useful to consider the fate of some of the proposals in the UK government's white paper on the environment, *This Common Inheritance*, which explicitly addressed the issue of allocative efficiency and pollution.

This Common Inheritance proudly announced itself as 'Britain's first comprehensive White Paper on the Environment'[8] and was presented by the Departments of Trade and Industry, Health, Education and Science, Transport, Energy, Employment and the Ministry of Agriculture, in addition to the Department of the Environment and the territorial ministries for Wales, Scotland and Northern Ireland.

The white paper had been long awaited, and, ever since Christopher Patten was given the position of Secretary of State for the Environment, its strategic importance had been stressed around Whitehall and in the relevant policy communities. On the relationship between the economy and the environment, *This Common Inheritance* adopts a positive tone, premissed on the need to attain an integration of environmental and economic considerations: 'There is ... no contradiction in arguing both for economic growth and for environmental good sense. The challenge is to integrate the two.'[9]

Although, unlike the Dutch National Policy Plan, a framework of environmental theory is absent from white paper, it is not innocent of all theoretical connotations. Implicitly in many places and explicitly in some, the issue of compatibility between a market orientation and a concern for environmental protection is addressed. The usual style is one of straightforward assertion, as is revealed in the following typical passage:

In the Government's view, market mechanisms offer the prospect of a more efficient and flexible response to environmental issues, both old and new. There is nothing new about markets being influenced by environmental factors: houses in the quieter parts of town have generally commanded the best prices; and, recently in particular, people across the world have been voting with their purses and wallets by preferring merchandise which seems environmentally-friendly, and manufacturers and suppliers have responded. Many Governments are now considering going a stage further by deliberate government intervention to establish a new set of price signals.[10]

However, behind this passage, there is both a complex set of issues and an essential part of the story.

As part of the background preparation for the white paper, The Secretary of State for the Environment had published a report by the economist David Pearce called *Blueprint for a Green Economy*, which essentially consisted of a review of economic issues and approaches to environmental protection, much of it within the Pigovian tradition of analysis.[11] It had been clearly part of the Department of the Environment's strategy to promote the cause of economic evaluation of the welfare losses due to environmental damage. One of the consequences of the publication of the Pearce report was the establishment of an interdepartmental committee of officials, chaired by the Treasury, to examine the feasibility and scope for a greater use of economic instruments. As things turned out, Treasury opposition to the raising of taxes to correct for externalities, on account of its inflationary potential, prevented the Department of the Environment from pressing home its original strategy and the white paper is left stressing its potential significance, but only developing a limited number of concrete proposals where the integration of environmental concerns in the management of the economy looks possible.

It is this disjunction between the promise of economic analysis and the level of detail contained in the white paper that makes it plausible to deny that neo-classical economic theory played the same central role in the intellectual construction of the white paper that general systems theory did in the Dutch National Policy Plan. Although the ideological predilections of the Thatcher administration made a concern with market-based incentives compulsory is British policy thinking, the extent to which the neo-classical framework provides the intellectual driving force, rather than the rhetorical veneer, of policy is limited. This can be seen in the fact that administrative regulatory strategies are also endorsed in the white paper, so that there is a pragmatic acceptance of a pluralism of policy instruments without any guiding idea or elaboration of the basis upon which competing policy instruments might be chosen.

There might have been more theoretical elaboration in the British case had the original impulse towards the development of economic instruments been sustained, but the powerful opposition of the Treasury with its fears about inflation was effective in preventing an extensive development in this direction. Moreover, it can be argued that it had been a political mistake in the summer of 1989 to lay so much weight on the potential of economic instruments. Whatever their theoretical attractiveness as efficient instruments of environmental protection, their practical difficulties are considerable. They presuppose more information about cause-and-effect relations in environmental systems than is usually available to policy-makers, except in the most straightforward case, and the process of determining levels of taxation or fines rests inevitably upon uncertain techniques for evaluating costs and benefits. For example, Turner has surveyed a number of approaches to the economic valuation of wetlands, in which a variety of estimated values occurs.[12]

Although only one example, the explicitness of the strategy adopted by the Department of the Environment suggests that the UK case contains more general lessons. One of these is that the technical complexity associated with a regime of Pigovian taxes means that the timetables of professional economists will be out of synchronisation with those of professional politicians. Properly to develop estimates of the damage functions and cost estimates will take longer than policy-makers feel they have available. It may be urged that this merely provides an argument for a more long-term approach to the development of research, but this raises yet other problems.

Pigovian taxes are essentially tied to a conception of an economy that is static in terms of its production technologies. The problem in Pigovian terms is, *given* a body of technology, how can one extract optimal value from its functioning? Yet, as Joseph Schumpeter notoriously pointed out, capitalism is a process of 'creative destruction', in other words it is a process, or rather series of processes, in which technology is constantly undergoing change and modification.[13] As John Felton has put it, innovation is the life-blood of the industrial enterprise and the 'ability to do a little more, a little better, perhaps a little differently, a little more effectively, a little more economically, is what differentiates success from failure'.[14] From this perspective the search for an optimal allocation of resources within an existing technology seems otiose, for the competitive struggle for innovation will quickly render the technology obsolete. The setting of administrative standards is much easier from this point of view, because emission levels can be set in the light of new developments in technology, without the need for a series of intermediate calculations about the implications of these changes for the allocative efficiency of resources at large. To be sure, the setting of standards in the light of developing technological standards has its own problems, not least the potential for 'cartels of refusal' among producers who collectively restrict innovation to prevent the imposition of ever more stringent emission limits.[15] But this is a pragmatic problem, and raises few of the methodological difficulties involved in the constant adjustment of schemes of putatively optimal taxation.

The Pigovian analysis also abstracts from distributive considerations, and looks only to the possibility of a net gain in social welfare from reducing pollution. Thus, Coase was able to demonstrate that, in the absence of transaction costs, it made no difference to the optimal level of production in a polluting industry whether polluters were required to compensate those affected by the pollution for the damage they caused, or whether those affected had to pay the polluters to desist from their activities.[16] There would of course be a difference in terms of the distribution of advantage, but in the Pigovian framework, in which what matters is the total sum of welfare, the distribution of well-being between different individuals and groups is immaterial. However, from the viewpoint of political incentives and action, the distributive questions may well be the ones that are to the fore. Political parties gain their support differentially from distinct economic groups within the community. Proposals to increase costs on the consumption of polluting commodities will hit some economic groups harder than others, and hence will affect the well-being of some groups more seriously than others. Those political parties who draw their support disproportionately from groups seriously affected by pollution taxes therefore have an incentive to resist the imposition of such taxes, just as the Dutch VVD, with its suburban support, resisted the phasing out of a tax allowance on commuting.

The problem of political support can go beyond the calculation of electoral advantage, however. For social democratic and other left-wing parties committed to principles of economic equality, the use of taxes to discourage or deter consumption leads to serious ideological dilemmas, as the various proposals for a carbon tax show. Carbon taxes are not strictly Pigovian taxes, but they do involve the principle that the tax system should be designed explicitly to discourage the consumption of fossil fuels. The difficulty with such proposals, from the viewpoint of social democrats, is that deterring certain forms of consumption hits the poor harder than upper or middle income groups. There is no point in saying that compensating variations can be made in the distribution of income via the social security system for a variety of reasons. Social security is not well targeted on the poor. There may not be the political support to make the compensating payment. And if the compensation is adequate it may be used merely to sustain consumption of the polluting product at previous levels, and therefore involve sacrificing some of the environmental gain. For these reasons social democrats would find more appealing a publicly funded programme of energy-conservation in domestic houses than the imposition of tax, in discouraging the consumption of fossil fuels, providing merely an incentive towards individual householders adopting their own energy-conservation measures. As this example shows, ideological commitments can affect the choice of policy instruments and in particular the disposition to use economic instruments as much as they can affect the choice of ends.

For these reasons, as well as the example of the UK's white paper proposals, there are good reasons for supposing that a Pigovian approach will encounter political resistance, and that this resistance will be difficult to overcome. The same objection ought not to apply to the second approach to economic instruments, however. In this second approach the idea is not to use economic techniques to obtain a valuation of environmental resources, but instead to use economic instruments to achieve objectives that have been determined by an independent political or administrative process. Baumol and Oates call this the standard-tax approach.[17] The aim here is to use economic instruments to achieve

specific pollution reductions in a cost-effective way. In this case
there is no question of placing an additional tax burden on the
economy. Instead the idea is to use economic instruments to
achieve more cheaply the goals of environmental policies that
traditionally employ administrative regulation.

The traditional administrative approach to the control of pollution in the US or Germany has been to impose uniform performance standards on sources. This administrative approach has
been criticised for not taking advantage of the fact that some
pollution sources find the marginal cost of reducing pollution
much lower than others. Uniform reductions imposed on all
sources are inefficient because the same total volume of reductions
could be achieved at lower overall cost by greater reductions in
the low cost firms and lower reductions in the high cost firms. To
take advantage of these variations in marginal cost of pollution
abatement, one solution has been the proposal to introduce tradable emission permits. This technique has been adopted in the US
under the 1977 Amendments to the Clean Air Act, for those
regions that had not met specified gains in air quality.[18]

Although there are many detailed ways of applying the policy
of tradable emission rights (some of which receive quixotic names
like 'bubble', 'off-set' and 'banking'), the basic idea is quite simple.
Permitted emission levels can be traded among polluters in a given
locality, provided that the results of the trading improves, or at
least does not worsen the quality of the air. Since plants faced
varying marginal costs in controlling emissions, those plants that
can control quite cheaply find it in their interest to reduce their
pollution below the level that would be implied by the imposition
of a uniform emission limit, because they can trade their surplus
emission permits for a profit. Empirical studies on the workings
of the US emissions trading policy suggest that air quality objectives have been achieved at less cost than a uniform emission
standard, usually of the order of $3 million of capital costs at
1981 prices.[19]

Given these cost advantages, the issue arises as to why economic
instruments are not more extensively used. One obvious answer is
that not all administrative systems use the technique of uniform
emission limits, and so there is little incentive to develop the
flexibility that emissions trading implies. Neither Sweden nor the
UK operates with strict limits, and even in Germany the uniform

standards have not always been rigidly applied. To that extent the US policy is a way of overcoming the inflexibility built into the timetables of the 1970 Act, which, as Lundqvist pointed out, erred towards the desirable rather than the practical.[20] However, there may be other, more general factors. For example, one barrier to the use of emission permits is that many activists in the pro-environment lobby, and perhaps members of the general public as well who tend to have a healthy scepticism about the dismal science, object to the idea that firms can acquire by trading a 'right' to pollute. In strict logic, of course, this cannot be a well-founded objection. Pollution control by traditional administrative regulation gives a 'right' to pollute in the same sense, in so far as it permits any discharges at all.[21] But the trading of rights for economic advantage may give the sense that polluting firms 'own' some portion of the environment which is theirs to use as they please. Perhaps these apparently unfounded suspicions could be allayed by suitable policy innovations, but the mistrust that currently exists between many pro-environmental groups and large capitalist firms means that someone would have to be very inventive to find ways of making workable pricing solutions to all parties.

There are, however, other political obstacles to the use of tradable emission permits, particularly as they bear on the question of transactions costs. Following Arrow and Williamson, we may define transactions costs as the costs of operating an economic system, including the costs of the price system itself. In relation to pollution control, transactions costs are likely to include a number of elements (for example, the clean-up costs associated with mistakes in previous environmental policies, compensations costs to those damaged by externalities, and the costs of running a legal system to enforce claims), but one set of costs will be particularly significant in the present context, namely the administrative costs to the state of operating a system of tradable permits.[22]

Transactions costs, in the form of the costs of administration, may be higher under tradable permits than with uniform emission standards or enforced technology. The essential reason for this is that pollution control has to be as much concerned with *where* pollution occurs as with the *total volume* of a pollutant emitted.[23] With tradable permits increases in pollution may cluster around certain pollution 'hotspots'. To monitor for this effect and to take action if it occurs may well be considerable more expensive than present pollution control regimes. It is possible to overcome this problem with the framework of tradable permits, by restricting the geographical scope of trading, but this reduces considerably the gains from trade that can be realised, with the consequence in one study that tradable permits appeared only marginally cheaper in sulphur dioxide emission reduction than conventional administrative regulation.[24] Just as significant may be the fact that increased transactions costs are likely to be borne disproportionately by the political authorities, who are therefore going to be resistant to the reform.

From the viewpoint of legal values like due process and democratic values like public accountability the use of economic instruments instead of administrative rules can also cause problems. Michael Kloepfer has raised the question of whether economic instruments are compatible with the norm of equal treatment before the law in the German legal system.[25] Where there is a rule involving the imposition of uniform emission limits there is an obvious sense in which all those subject to the rule are being treated in the same way. Tradable pollution rights, by contrast, are premissed on the assumption that some firms find it more difficult, that is costly, to comply than others. Of course, if tradable pollution licences work efficiently, they will equalise the marginal burden of pollution control. (That is to say, every firm within the scheme would find that it had to pay the same amount to make its next incremental reduction.) But the estimate of marginal equivalences is inherently more complex and contestable than the imposition of a uniform rule.

Interestingly enough the German courts have been prepared to countenance the use of effluent taxes. These are rather different from tradable permits since they are not related to environmental quality objectives and are merely charges imposed on polluters for the effluents they discharge to water. Opschoor and Vos note that they are structured in order to provide an incentive to reduce the volume of pollution by providing a discount on the charge if minimum standards of discharge are exceeded. Despite these incentive effects, the charge basically functions in order to raise revenue, and this is even more true for the 90 per cent of German firms who discharge into the sewerage system of the municipalities.[26] This tends to be a pattern with effluent charges: they do not supplant the administrative determination of standards, merely provide one way of achieving them that is acceptable for broad historical reasons.

As well as conventional cost recovery charging in the case of water discharges, other uses of economic instruments in a number of countries include: deposit refund schemes, recently introduced in Sweden and Norway for car hulks, and used extensively for bottles; tax differentials between leaded and unleaded fuels; and the Italian tax on plastic bags.[27] From the economic point of view these tend to be crude devices, with no attempt to ensure that the charge or tax levied achieves any kind of optimality. But the neglect of efficiency properties, which is what gives such instruments low status in economic terms, is an advantage in political terms. Freed of the constraints to demonstrate superior efficiency, such instruments can become one of a number of flexible devices for discouraging polluting behaviour, and they have the advantage that they provide a tool to control non-point sources of pollution, where there are few other effective instruments available.

If the logic of this conclusion is accepted, it is unlikely that economic instruments can replace, rather than supplement, the traditional forms of administrative regulation. Viewing administrative regulation and economic instruments as complementing one another has a number of advantages, not least in highlighting the need to ensure that economic taxes and subsidies do not provide a perverse incentive to environmental policies being pursued by other methods. For example, unleaded petrol has at times been more expensive than leaded petrol in France, a differential that has now been removed by tax changes. Avoiding these perverse incentives is important, but it hardly amounts to the comprehensive substitution of administrative regulation by economic instruments that has sometimes been proposed. Moreover, the technical complexity of issues implied by a stress upon economic instruments can be viewed as posing problems for democratic accountability and participation, which is the next topic to be examined.

Public participation

The emergence of the environment as an issue in the 1970s was accompanied by an enormous growth of political activism, burgeoning pressure groups and essentially the emergence of Green political parties. The origin of these movements is often to be found in the public's reaction to instances of environmental damage or to land use planning and developments, for example the construction of nuclear power stations or waste disposal sites. Their origins are also to be found in currents of ideas that capture the public imagination, as was evidenced by the publishing success of Rachel Carson's *Silent Spring*.

In Germany in the late 1960s, for example, public interest in environmental issues was aroused not only by the political interest in developments in the United States but by fish poisonings in the Rhine resulting from industrial discharges of toxic wastes and other scandals involving private waste removal firms. In response to local issues of town planning, redevelopment and traffic management, citizens' action groups were formed and in 1972 the network organisation of the Association of Citizens' Initiatives in Environmental Protection was formed. In the mid-1970s, co-operation among civic groups dealing with a variety of policy areas – including health, environmental and security policy – developed, and the expansion of the nuclear power programme in the wake of the OPEC oil price rise of 1973–74 prompted mass demonstrations and protests on a national scale. From 1977 the first environmental political party groups participated in federal elections, and the Greens first entered the *Bundestag* in 1983, creating a new force in the electoral dynamics of German politics.[28]

In 1969 in Denmark the new wave of environmental activism was inaugurated when a group of students took over the final plenary session of the annual conference of a natural history society, locking the doors, filling the room with polluted air from burnt waste and spraying the audience with water from a polluted lake. From this a new environmental organisation, NOAH, was born. The growth and development of the environmental movement in Denmark reflected the growth of social criticism more generally and affected established patterns of political co-operation, not least that of the Danish Conservation Society which began to respond to the new concerns by reporting on the effects of pollution on wildlife. From a small group of twenty students in Copenhagen University, NOAH developed as a grass roots organisation along with other new social movements in the 1970s. In common with many other countries there was also a growth of opposition to the development of nuclear power, which would have been entirely new in Denmark, and which focused in one organisation, OOA. An important element in the various strands of the environmental movement was an open, participatory political culture in which the emphasis was upon using scientific knowledge in the interest of society as a whole.[29]

These specific examples represent facets of a general trend throughout the developed world in an increase in the demand for public participation and accountability in the making of environmental policy. One sign of this is the greater public use of political opportunity structures to challenge the decisions of policy elites. The earliest manifestation of this was in challenges to nuclear power programmes in many Western countries, as well as project developments like the trans-Alaska pipeline or projects that involved the draining of wetlands and other natural habitats.[30]

These same trends are also revealed in the growth in consumer awareness, with changing public values and rising levels of education demanding improved environmental performance in the economy. In the UK these trends became quickly apparent when in 1989 the retail sector underwent a series of shocks. The rise of green consumerism left many retailers unprepared, although it should have been clear that the underlying development had been taking place for some time. The cross-national significance of this development can be seen in the volume of sales of Elkington and Hailes's *The Green Consumer Guide*.[31] Moreover, many members of modern populations now have the educational and technical competence to understand the environmental significance of product and process developments. The skills necessary to understand such developments, including skills of numerical and statistical analysis, computer modelling and information retrieval, are widespread throughout the economy because they are increasingly demanded by the jobs that people do. The combination of a growing public concern with the environment and the technical skills to understand the environmental significance of economic processes and products means that firms are increasingly liable to see their environmental performance come under public scrutiny.

The effect of these trends is to question the operating principles of the traditional environmental policy process. Many questions of pollution control and environmental protection had traditionally been settled with relatively closed policy communities comprised

of specialist public officials, industrial representatives and, depending upon the independence of legislature and executive, the few
interested participants in the legislature. The technical competence
of the new environmental movements had the effect of challenging
the assumptions on which traditional policy elites operated. This
was most obviously true in the case of nuclear power in the late
1970s and early 1980s, but it came to apply to air, water, soil and
marine pollution.

The example of nuclear power suggests that institutional factors
were important in explaining the differential ability of environmental groups to mobilise support and affect outcomes. Thus,
Kitschelt has shown that 'political opportunity structures' are
important in understanding anti-nuclear protest. Political opportunity structures are defined as being 'comprised of specific configurations of resources, institutional arrangements and historical
precedents for social mobilisation, which facilitate the development of protest movements in some instances and constrain them
in others'.[32] An example of variability of opportunity structures in
this sense would be provided by the institutional processes that set
pollution control standards or determined project developments.
In some societies, for a variety of historical and institutional
reasons, these processes are open to judicial review and constitutional scrutiny, whereas in others the processes are relatively closed
and controlled by the executive.

There tends to be a large gap between the openness of North
American processes on the one hand and the closedness of European processes on the other, but even within Europe there are
significant variations. For example, the Austrian corporatist style
of policy-making has come under criticism within Austria for
excluding environmental interests in the deals that are struck
between capital and labour. In Sweden by contrast the concerns
of the new environmental movement were rapidly assimilated into
the traditional structures of policy formation, symbolised by the
early establishment in Sweden of administrative structures to deal
with environmental protection.[33] Yet, open or closed decision-
making structures have all had to cope with the changing character
of environmental policy-making and the felt need to respond to
the demand for great public participation in decision processes. In
looking at the nature of the response to these demands, I shall
consider three different types of environmental decision: project

developments; the setting of pollution control standards; and the determination of policy principles.

Project developments are large-scale changes of land or resource use including such facilities as dams, factories and power stations, airports, or pipelines. An important aspect of project development is that there is typically a process of public consultation necessary before the project is allowed to proceed. This consultation takes the form of planning and appeal processes for land use development in which the developer is required to show that various substantive and procedural requirements have been met. Moreover, such traditional processes have been supplemented in many countries in the last twenty years by the development of environmental impact assessments, in which developers are required to demonstrate that the project will not have an adverse effect upon the local ecology, for example in terms of pollution caused.

Bruce Doern has pointed to three characteristics that often make projects developments subjects of political and economic controversy: they usually involve a multiyear physical planning cycle; they are especially sensitive to problems of financing and capital markets; and they involve high political risk.[34] Given these characteristics, it is possible that significant transaction costs will be imposed in the implementation of projects, to the point that if the projects are not designed with sufficient environmental concern, their development will be aborted, with initial expenditures incurred and no returns secured. The existence of these costs may well be important in the search for new political and policy structures.

Since many project developments currently require formal planning agreement by the public authorities, there is an opportunity for public participation within the formal planning procedures. However, for a variety of reasons, such procedures may not solve the problems of ensuring that controversy and competing perspectives are brought out into the open. Often the existence of formal processes may leave parties to the dispute dissatisfied. Experience in the US and Canada suggests that the selection of the chief individual responsible for conducting the planning enquiry will be important in addressing such issues. Mr Justice Berger in Canada was able to use the opportunity of the Mackenzie Valley Pipeline Inquiry to open the planning process to participation by native peoples and others who might otherwise have been disenfranchised

by the conventional planning procedures.[35] The selection of those
responsible for conducting planning enquiries then becomes an
important aspect of policy. It is not simply a question of appoint-
ing outstanding individuals, but also of ensuring that the qualities
they exemplify are identified and their importance conveyed in the
training of other individuals.

Environmental impact assessment takes the process of planning
one stage further by requiring developers to demonstrate that their
development will not have an adverse impact upon the environment. In such processes, project developers are usually required to
show what the estimated effects of their development will be upon
local flora and fauna and to demonstrate that the best available
steps have been taken in planning the project to avoid or minimise
adverse environmental effects. Over time environmental impact
assessment can be expected significantly to influence the nature
and type of project development. Thus, Taylor has shown that the
introduction of environmental impact assessment into the US ad-
minstration changed the nature and type of project development
by providing a professional core of assessors with a background
in environmental science who changed both the culture and the
policy orientation of the departments of state within which they
were placed.[36]

An important aspect of the environmental impact assessment
process is that it also shifts the balance of power between developers on the one hand and environmental protection groups on
the other by providing the latter with an opportunity to challenge
developments and to investigate the technical basis of the proposal. Since the technical skills necessary to assess environmental
effects are now fairly widespread throughout the economy, environmental protection groups have found themselves able to interpret the evidence in such a way as to demonstrate unforeseen
problems with the project. Moreover, the introduction of environmental protection groups with the formal opportunity to challenge
developments, occurs not only through the administrative processes of the review itself but also by means of a judicial review
of the administrative process where that is possible.

The country that has demonstrated the highest consistent level
of challenge to environmentally threatening project developments
has been the United States. This has a number of sources. It stems
partly from a traditional neglect among US business interests of

the demands of environmental protection and partly from the fact that US environmental protection groups have been well funded by large philanthropic foundations so that they can afford the specialist staff and expertise to make use of administrative and legal procedures. Finally it stems from the institutional opportunities provided by a constitutional and legal system in which the courts have been far more willing to overturn administrative decisions than has often been true in Europe.

Given the openness of the US system to challenge and conflict between project developers and environmental protection, both traditional planning controls and environmental impact assessment, as formal processes, have been seen to lead to delay and increased cost. It is therefore not surprising that the United States has been at the forefront in seeking to develop new institutional processes of an informal kind to try to overcome the delay and costs inherent in the formal processes. The most important of these has been the technique known as environmental dispute resolution.

The term 'dispute resolution' is used to refer to a variety of processes 'that allow the parties to meet face to face in an effort to reach a mutually acceptable resolution of the issues in a dispute or potentially controversial situation'.[37] The processes are voluntary and they take place outside of conventional administrative or planning processes. Such processes may involve a mediator or facilitator as third party, or they may simply involve the parties to the dispute meeting on a bilateral basis.

Environmental dispute resolution in the US has been developed by the Conservation Foundation in particular, and it has covered a wide range of project-specific developments. A typical example was the development of the extension to the subway system operated by the Massachusetts Bay Transit Authority (MBTA). MBTA planned an extension of its subway system to a major suburban highway loop, with an important stop planned for the Alewife area in north western-Cambridge. Residents, businesses and environmental groups were concerned about a variety of effects that construction and operation of the extension would have, including flooding, loss of open space, disruption of railroad freight and traffic flow and safety. Over a period of eighteen months a 54-person taskforce which brought together government, residents, business and environmental groups, chaired by Professor Susskind of the Massachusetts Institute of Technology, debated policy alternatives in the design of the project. The agreed plan included a linear park that would connect open space areas and soften the impact of parking facilities. In practice, the agreement was not implemented in full, but the process did provide an example of how some of the conflicting interests could be mediated.[38]

Project-specific environmental dispute resolution has not always been successful in the sense that it has not always reconciled competing interests or remedied delays in the process of making decisions. However, it has shown that parties to a site-specific group may agree on some things, even if they are in disagreement over the substantive proposal. Gail Bingham has shown from reviewing the experience of environmental dispute resolution that all parties care about the representation of interests, as well as the fairness, legitimacy, efficiency and effectiveness of the process. Even where the conflict is necessarily zero-sum, so that the gains of one party are purchased at the expense of another party, a satisfactory process of decision, in which parties to the dispute feel that their interests have been fairly represented, will help soften the effects of the decision.[39]

There have been cases in the US where the technique appears to have had great success, and some states now require a process of dispute resolution by law in cases where there are conflicts of interests over project developments. Successful dispute resolution, however, depends upon a willingness of those who participate to agree at some level, and it works less well when there are fundamental issues of principle or value at stake, where there is relatively little room for manoeuvre. This has led some commentators to conclude that dispute resolution is appropriate for only a small number of cases. There are other criticisms that have been identified. Douglas Amy, for example, has stressed the threat to values like those of due process. There are procedural safeguards built into the operation of legal systems that protect the interest of parties to a dispute. The informality of dispute resolution processes means that weaker parties to a dispute may lose out, for example if the stronger party feels able to bear the costs of delay in getting to an agreement.[40]

Does environmental dispute resolution reduce the administrative and transaction costs associated with project development? There is little evidence on this point, and what there is does not point in one direction. Dispute resolution is not costless. The parties to the dispute have to devote time and resources to the process, and often professional mediators are involved. More importantly, there is no simple comparison with the cost of administrative and legal approaches, since the threat of legal action may be one of the factors bringing the participants to the process of mediation, so that it would be misleading to take simply the marginal cost of dispute resolution procedures in the absence of legal costs. Where the dispute process works well, it may generate a sense of trust between the parties that will spill over into other issues, thereby reducing the potential for further conflict, but it is of course difficult to assess the value of the improvement in the quality of decisions that are made through dispute resolution by comparison with more traditional and formal procedures. Advocates of the approach certainly ascribe a marked improvement to the quality of decision-making as a result of mediation techniques. The more detached observer would perhaps want to say that this is an interesting approach to project disputes which deserves to be tried in a wide variety of circumstances to see under what conditions it can secure better quality decisions with lower transaction costs.

Site-specific or project issues are important in environmental policy, but the changing character of the relevant policy communities means that disputes are no longer restricted to the specifics of development but extend to the question of the *setting of pollution control standards* under which firms operate. This provide an opportunity for 'regulatory negotiation', a technique that has been developed in North America.

Regulatory negotiation is an adaptation of the traditional ways in which performance standards are set. The traditional method is for public officials to propose standards after bilateral consultation and discussion with interested parties. Regulatory negotiation seeks to bring together these interested parties in a series of meetings convened by an independent mediator. As Douglas Amy has written, the aim of the meeting is to produce a consensus about a proposed rule or regulation.[41]

The origins of a regulatory negotiation are to be found with the dissatisfaction that a number of parties felt with traditional rule-making in the United States. The traditional method of rule-making allows the opportunity for interested parties to challenge the proposed rule by means of judicial review. Indeed, the litigation that is such a prominent feature of US environmental policy typically occurs at the rule-making, rather than enforcement, stage, as interested parties seek to use the courts to pursue their own point of view. Business asserts that the delays associated with this process are costly and increase the uncertainty surrounding business decisions. Environmental protection groups assert that the implementation of protection standards is delayed. Agency officials feel they are in a no-win situation as parties to the dispute will accuse them of favouring the other side. And many people feel that administrative courts are inappropriate places to review complex scientific and factual questions.[42]

Early examples of regulatory negotiation occurred in the early 1980s over regulations concerning the control of atmospheric emissions and regulations concerning the register of pesticides. Observers claim the process as a success. Many participants felt the negotiated outcome was better than they could have expected had they gone to court and, although participants were surprised by the time and effort that it took to negotiate a consensus rule, they felt that the overall amount of time absorbed was less than with the traditional process.[43] A more extensive application of regulatory negotiation occurred in the development of a management plan to reduce NO_x and VOCs emissions in Canada. Essential to the development of the plan was the participation of government, industry and environmental groups in a workshop in April 1990 to discuss the details of the management plan, with an extensive process of consultation around the plan.[44]

At present it is too early to say whether a more extensive use of regulatory negotiation will improve public participation. It may be that the successes of the present examples spring from a variety of specific causes that cannot easily be generalised. To some extent, for example, the issues that have been dealt with through regulatory negotiation have been chosen precisely because key actors in the process believed they would make suitable candidates. However, regulatory negotiation is an important technique, because it addresses directly the question of legitimacy. The legitimacy of rules from this perspective depends upon the participation of interested parties in a process and not upon the presumed superior expertise of a superior authority. There are difficult questions still to be addressed here about the relationship between technical expertise and popular confidence.

A problem with all environmental regulation is that the knowledge of the public authorities lags behind technological innovation. Those responsible for potentially polluting substances are characteristically in a better position to appreciate what new controls can be applied than are the public authorities. This is an example of the bounded rationality that affects all forms of public regulation.

One way around this dilemma is to establish a system by which effective responsibility for improvements in environmental management is developed within those firms that are potential polluters. The chemical industry has played an important role in developing systems of environmental management as is evidenced by the example of Bayer AG and Royal Dutch Shell.[45] However, from the point of view of the public regulators, this does not address the problem of opportunistic behaviour: how can the public authorities be sure that appropriate measures are being taken, given the asymmetry of information between regulated and regulator?

The logic of this question is to lead towards a requirement on all firms to install systems of responsible environmental management. Already there are plans within the European Commission to introduce annual environmental audits for industry, many of which would be voluntary, but some of which would be compulsory for larger companies in 'eco-risk' sectors, for example chemicals.[46] However, the development of such systems of internal management and audit is likely to lead to a new relationship between public regulation and industry. Some interesting thinking went on in the Netherlands in the late 1980s on this topic under the principle of *verinnerlijking*, or the internalisation of environmental responsibility, a notion that, as we saw in the last chapter, had more widespread application in Dutch policy.[47] As the principle of *verinnerlijking* is developing in Dutch regulatory practice, it is leading to a change in the quality of regulation. Regulators focus less attention upon emissions and more attention upon the adequacy of the system of environmental management. In the successful cases this approach leads to a reduction in costs for firms. As they think through the basic nature of their production in an attempt to improve their environmental performance, they identify opportunities for production changes that increase profitability. It is usually possible to identify a number of recycling opportunities, as Sterling Organics is currently finding with its current environmental programme.[48]

Both regulatory negotiation and the internalisation of environmental management can be regarded as anticipatory management strategies. By internalising responsibility for environmental management, the firm is forced to consider the problems that it will face in the future and the actions that it needs to take to overcome those problems. Similarly by participating in regulatory negotiation, firms are exposing their practices to potential criticism. However, this anticipatory practice may well reduce costs in the medium to long term if it brings a greater level of stability to the regulatory standards that are set. From the point of view of the public authorities, successful innovations in the setting of standards promise to reduce the costs of overcoming the asymmetries of information that are such a pervasive feature of the regulatory process.

The determination of policy principles provides the third aspect of public participation. The purpose here is not to resolve specific disputes but to identify points of agreement and disagreement about a broadly identified policy area, looking at the evidence and the arguments that proponents of different courses of action draw upon. Approaches that may be used here including informal discussion and policy dialogues.

Informal discussion is perhaps the most obvious and least practised technique. It consists of representatives from different organisations meeting face to face to exchange views and to identify common or contrasting perspectives. This approach was adopted by the UK's National Radiological Protection Board in the 1980s during the debate over the future of nuclear power. In 1987 the NRPB started a series of informal discussions with environmental groups who had expressed concerns about the effects of radiation. Representatives of the environmental groups were drawn from Friends of the Earth, Greenpeace as well as the Consumers' Association. NRPB also invited representatives from professional associations, like the Royal Society of Chemistry, who had environmental interest branches. The purposes of the meetings was to explore the concept of acceptable or tolerable risks in the context of the development of new nuclear power stations. The Director of the NRPB, Dr Roger Clarke, has commented upon those dialogues as follows:

We would like to think that three years on we have achieved rather more of a rapport and trust with these groups. I think we've learned from talking to them and probably to some extent modified our ideas, and I honestly think they've modified some of their ideas too .... We were both exploring tolerable risks and not violently disagreeing with each other, but searching from our different perspectives forward where an agreement might be found ...[49]

Such informal discussions do not have a specific practical purpose, but they do provide a context within which general issues can be explored and trust built up. It is also worth noting that the discussions have to be undertaken in good faith, from all parties in a situation in which there is an identifiable consensus to be worked towards. The Department of the Environment sought to reproduce the experience of the NRPB, but the experiment was a failure because nobody believed that the Department was serious about the issues.[50]

It is possible to take these informal discussions a stage further by establishing a formal 'policy dialogue'. Often convened under the auspices of an independent mediator, the purpose of these policy dialogues is to bring together representatives from government, industry and environmental groups to see whether it is possible to agree on policy questions. Such policy dialogues have been used in the United States to develop policies towards the use of water resources in Colorado, the health and environmental implications of pesticide use and the siting of hazardous waste sites.[51] In the successful instances of policy dialogue, participants have been able to agree a plan of action or issue codes of practice or guidelines. Industry has found, therefore, that it can address and meet the concerns of environmental groups.

Perhaps the major example of a policy dialogue took place in the United States in the form of the National Coal Policy Project. The project arose out of a joint concern by industry and environmental groups over the expanded use of coal to meet energy demands. Out of initial informal meetings there grew the five-year National Coal Policy Project which was able to produce a report bringing together the deliberations of nine taskforce groups addressing over 200 specific issues.[52] Despite this high measure of agreement, it is difficult to know if the National Coal Policy Project was a success or not. Few of the project results have been implemented successfully and the project has been criticised by some environmental groups who did not participate in the process. On the other hand, as Bingham notes, it did provide a model for co-operation in an area in which it was assumed there could only be controversy. Moreover, it might be argued that the National Coal Policy Project was simply too ambitious given the time and circumstances in which it took place. To expect a high degree of consensus and implementation may simply have been asking for the impossible given the relatively short period of time, less than ten years, in which concern with the environmental impact of expanded coal use had emerged.

Policy dialogue is a costly device, and although informal dialogue is less costly, it is also less precise in terms of its intended effects. Unlike the implementation of projects and the setting of standards, techniques related to the general formulation of policy may not seem directly related to the resolution of practical questions and therefore there may be a tendency to dismiss them as simply raising administrative and transactions costs without any tangible benefit. However, this is likely to be a mistake. New methods for debating the formulation of policy are essential if one is to bring out into the open the differences of belief and perspective that lie behind much of the distrust that characterises environmental policy-making.

All of the approaches surveyed attach great significance to the *process* by which decisions are made and policies determined. The difference between successful and unsuccessful applications of these approaches often seems to depend upon process factors, most importantly the willingness of parties to meet each other in good faith. Moreover, even when outcomes are disappointing, participants do attach importance to the processes by which issues were confronted and problems identified. How different policy systems adapt and use these approaches will depend upon the institutional and historical context within which problems are confronted. However, if difficult issues of legitimacy are to be addressed, then new techniques for public participation will be needed.

Analytical implications

Problems arising from the implementation of traditional regulatory strategies have led to the search for new policy instruments, of which economic instruments are a key example, as well as means by which public participation and confidence may be increased in the regulatory process. The political and policy system has been seen to fail in terms of its ability to implement improved pollution control standards, but critics have also pointed to economic inefficiency as well as deeper process failures in securing public legitimacy. Thus, high and unnecessary political and economic costs are associated, it is alleged, with traditional regulatory strategies.

Reform is not so easy to achieve for a variety of reasons. Often the rational choice of key actors within particular institutional settings can consist of frustrating attempts at innovation. Finance ministries, conscious of the tax burden that the increased use of economic instruments entails, may be one of the key actors opposing their introduction. Similarly, members of a policy community who benefit from the closed nature of policy formation will often be resistant to reforms that create an increase in opportunity structures for greater public participation.

Looked at in this way, it might seem that we would need little more than a combination of the rational choice and institutions idioms in order to account for the barriers to instrument and institutional innovation. This is to neglect one important point in the systems perspective, however, namely the requirement for legitimacy if a political and policy system is going to be able to function across a wide range of decisions with any degree of competence. A consideration of rational strategies of action, given their institutional resources, may explain how some key actors are able to keep reform initiatives off the political agenda, but it cannot explain how the issue of reform insistently returns to centre stage as the failures of traditional policy processes become manifest. It is at this point that we may need to consider broader issues of system functioning and the prerequisites of legitimacy. It should also be clear that innovatory policy strategies will not emerge from the pursuit of rational strategies within given institutional contexts, since innovation by definition implies an attempt to think creatively, beyond existing constraints, about the solution to certain problems. Here it looks as though we shall also have to draw upon idioms of policy discourse and social learning. Hence, we are likely to find a complex mixture of analytic categories involved in the understanding of implementation dilemmas. How to sort out these potentially contradictory strands of analysis is a topic to which we shall have to turn in the final chapter – but not before looking at one further, and potentially fundamental, change to the politics of pollution, namely its internationalisation.

Notes

1   T. S. Eliot, 'The Hollow Men', in *The Complete Poems and Plays of T. S. Eliot* (London: Faber and Faber, 1969), p. 85.

2   B. Commoner, *Making Peace with the Planet* (London: Victor Gollancz, 1990), p. 27.

3   R. Mayntz u.a., *Vollzugsprobleme der Umweltpolitik* (Wiesbaden: Rat von Sachverständigen für Umweltfragen, 1978).

4   R. Levitt, *Implementing Public Policy* (London: Croom Helm, 1980).

5   R. H. Coase, 'The Problem of Social Cost', *Journal of Law and Economics* 3 (1960), pp. 1–44.

6   A. C. Pigou, *The Economics of Welfare* (London: Macmillan, 1920).

7   G. Majone, *Argument, Evidence and Persuasion in the Policy Process* (New Haven and London: Yale University Press, 1989).

8   Her Majesty's Government, *This Common Inheritance* (London: HMSO, 1990), Cm. 1200, p. 8.

9   Her Majesty's Government, *This Common Inheritance*, p. 8.

10   Her Majesty's Government, *This Common Inheritance*, p. 14.

11   D. Pearce, A. Markandya and E. Barbier, *Blueprint for a Green Economy* (London: Earthscan Publications Ltd, 1989).

12   R. K. Turner, 'Valuation of Wetland Ecosystems', in J. B. Opschoor and D. W. Pearce (eds), *Persistent Pollutants* (Dordrecht: Kluwer Academic Publishers, 1991).

13   J. Schumpeter, *Capitalism, Socialism and Democracy* (London: George Allen and Unwin, 1954 edition), chapter 7.

14   J. C. Felton, 'Acceptance of Innovation: An Industry View of Environmental Aspects', in L. Roberts and A. Weale (eds), *Innovation and Environmental Risk* (London and New York: Belhaven Press, 1991), p. 31.

15   G. R. Wagner, 'Entrepreneurship and Innovation from an Environmental Risk Perspective', in Roberts and Weale (eds), *Innovation and Environmental Risk*, p. 142.

16   Coase, 'The Problem of Social Cost'.

17   W. J. Baumol and W. E. Oates, *Economics, Environmental*

Policy and the Quality of Life (Englewood Cliffs, NJ: Prentice-Hall Inc., 1979), pp. 354–56.

18   T. H. Tietenberg, *Emissions Trading. An Exercise in Reforming Pollution Policy* (Washington, DC: Resources for the Future, 1985). See also J. B. Opschoor and H. B. Vos, *Economic Instruments for Environmental Protection* (Paris: OECD, 1989), pp. 88–94.

19   Tietenberg, *Emissions Trading*, pp. 54–5.

20   L. Lundqvist, *The Hare and the Tortoise. Clean Air Policies in the United States and Sweden* (Ann Arbor: University of Michigan Press, 1980).

21   M. Jacobs, *The Green Economy* (London: Pluto Press, 1991), pp. 150, 160.

22   A. Marin, 'The Choice of Efficient Pollution Policies', *Journal of Environmental Economics and Management*, 5 (1978), p. 53.

23   Marin, 'Efficient Pollution Policies', pp. 51–2.

24   See for example, E. G. Dolan, 'Controlling Acid Rain', in W. Block (ed.), *Economics and the Environment* (Vancouver, BC: The Fraser Institute, 1990), p. 226.

25   M. Kloepfer, 'Rechtsstaatliche Probleme ökonomischer Instrumente in Umweltschutz', in G. R. Wagner (ed.), *Unternehmung und ökologische Umwelt* (Munich: Franz Vahlen, 1990), pp. 241–61.

26   G. M. Brown Jnr and R. W. Johnson, 'Pollution Control by Effluent Charges: It Works in the Federal Republic of Germany, Why Not in the United States?', *Natural Resources Journal*, 24:4 (1984), p. 950.

27   Opschoor and Vos, *Economic Instruments for Environmental Protection* pp. 82–8.

28   See E. Müller, *Innenwelt der Umweltpolik* (Opladen: Westdeutscher Verlag, 1986).

29   See A. Jamison, R. Eyerman, J. Cramer, with J. Laesso, *The Making of the New Environmental Consciousness* (Edinburgh: Edinburgh University Press, 1991), chapter 3.

30   Compare P. D. Lowe and W. Rüdig, 'Political Ecology and the Social Sciences – The State of the Art', *British Journal of Political Science*, 16:4 (1986), pp. 513–50.

31   J. Elkington and J. Hailes, *The Green Consumer Guide* (London: Victor Gollancz, 1988).

32   H. Kitschelt, 'Political Opportunity Structures and Political Protest: Anti-Nuclear Movements in Four Democracies', *British Journal of Political Science* 16:1 (1986), pp. 57–85.

33   P. Gerlich, E. Grande, and W. C. Müller, 'Corporatism in

Crisis: Stability and Change of Social Partnership in Austria', *Political Studies*, 36:2 (1988), pp. 209–23 (on Austria); Jamison, Eyerman, Cramer, with Laesso, *The Making of the New Environmental Consciousness*, chapter 2 (on Sweden).

34   G. B. Doern, 'Canadian Environmental Policy: Why Process is Almost Everything', *Commentary*, 19 (1990), p. 5.

35   R. Paehlke, 'Democracy and Environmentalism: Opening a Door to the Administrative State', in R. Paehlke and D. Togerson (eds), *Managing Leviathan* (Peterborough, Ontario:Broadview Press, 1990), p. 43.

36 , S. Taylor, *Making Bureaucracies Think* (Stanford: Stanford University Press, 1984).

37   G. Bingham, *Resolving Environmental Disputes* (Washington, DC: Conservation Foundation, 1986), p. 5.

38   Bingham, *Resolving Environmental Disputes*, pp. 175–6.

39   Bingham, *Resolving Environmental Disputes*, p. 68.

40   D. Amy, *The Politics of Environmental Mediation* (New York: Columbia University Press, 1987).

41   D. Amy, 'Decision Techniques for Environmental Policy: A Critique', in R. Paehlke and D. Togerson (eds), *Managing Leviathan* (Peterborough, Ontario, 1990), p. 70.

42   L. Susskind and G. McMahon, 'The Theory and Practice of Negotiated Rulemaking', *Yale Journal of Regulation*, 3 (1985), pp. 133–65.

43   Susskind and McMahon, 'The Theory and Practice of Negotiated Rulemaking', pp. 142–51.

44   G. B. Doern, 'Regulations and Incentives: The NO_x – VOCs Case', in G.B. Doern (ed.), *Getting It Green: Case Studies in Canadian Environmental Regulation* (Ottawa, Ontario: C. D. Howe Institute, 1990), pp. 89–110.

45   E. H. Rohe, 'Entwicklungstendenzen des praktischen Umweltschutzes in der Chemischen Industrie', in G. R. Wagner (ed.), *Unternehmung und ökologische Umwelt* (Munich: Franz Vahlen, 1990), pp. 97–112; J. C. Felton, 'Acceptance of Innovation: An Industry View of Environmental Aspects', in L. Roberts and A. Weale (eds), *Innovation and Environmental Risks* (London and New York: Belhaven Press, 1991), pp. 31–7.

46   'Commission Tries to End Row over Where to Site Environmental Agency' *Financial Times*, 8 April 1991, p. 4.

47   Commissie Bedrijfsinterne Milieuzorgsystemen, *Milieuzorg in Samenspel* ('s Gravenhage, 1988).

48   'Sterling Organics: Taking Control of its Environmental Im-

pacts', ENDS *Report* 193 (February 1991), pp. 16–18.

49   Dr Roger Clarke in Roberts and Weale, *Innovation and Environmental Risk*, p. 174.

50   Dr Roger Clarke in Roberts and Weale, *Innovation and Environmental Risk*, p. 174.

51   Bingham, *Resolving Environmental Disputes*.

52   Bingham, *Resolving Environmental Disputes*, p. 17.

7

The international dimension

The new politics of pollution now have an inescapable international dimension. This is not to say that the policy activities of the early 1970s entirely ignored the international dimensions of pollution. There were, for example, significant international agreements on marine pollution and the pollution of the seas from land-based sources, represented by the establishment of the Oslo and Paris Commissions for the North Sea as well as the International Agreement on Dumping of Waste at Sea, the Convention to Prevent Marine Pollution from Ships. Moreover, the United Nations Conference on the Human Environment in Stockholm in 1972 was an important impetus to international and national action.[1] However, many of these developments presupposed the framework of the nation state and rested on the assumption that the focus of activity would be the national community. International treaties, like the London Dumping Convention or the Convention to Prevent Marine Pollution from ships imposed few restraints on national action, but left genuine regulation to instruments yet to be negotiated under continuing international diplomacy.[2]

Moreover, the major and distinctive legislative activities of the period were conceived of in national terms. The control of air pollution, the cleaning of surface waters or the regulation of toxic chemicals were a product of conventional systems of domestic policy-making. The most common feature of the legislation of the period was the *nationalisation* of pollution control arrangements, which modernised the previously local systems of nuisance control, and introduced national uniformity into previously variable arrangements. This was just as true of US legislation on water pollution as it was of German legislation on air pollution or British legislation on waste disposal. Although international dimensions were far from absent in the first wave of environmental policy-making, the primary focus was the domestic control of pollution. Indeed, tall smokestacks, as devices to disperse pollutants from localities, provide one example of how domestic pollution problems might be solved by displacing the problems internationally.

Since the 1970s the *internationalisation* of pollution policy has proceeded at great speed. In part, this reflects more general trends in the making of public policy.[3] For reasons to do with techno-logical developments in communications, the border controls of nation states are less capable of restricting transactions in goods, services, ideas and cultural exchange, and the expansion of trans-national capital and transnational actors limits the ability of na-tion states to pursue their own objectives, for example Keynesian full employment policy. These trends have led to the emergence of regimes of international political co-operation, particularly at the regional level. The most obvious example here is the development of the European Community, but the move towards the economic integration of North America also provides another example.

Pollution control is no exception to these trends. Since the imposition of controls may be perceived to have significant cost implications for the industries to which they are applied, it is hardly surprising that national industrial organisations have been anxious to ensure the application of equally stringent pollution control measures to their competitors in other countries. In other words, as general economic integration takes place across national boundaries and systems of international government are estab-lished to manage the processes of integration, it becomes more difficult to avoid the environmental implications of international economic activity. This process has been most obvious in the case of the European Community, and later in this chapter I shall examine the ways in which environmental policy has been nested in the development of the EC.

However, the internationalisation of pollution issues during the 1980s also reflects the growing appreciation of the fact that pol-lution itself is often an international problem. The most striking example here is the prospect of global climate change consequent upon the increasing emission of 'greenhouse gases', most notably carbon dioxide, methane, chlorofluorocarbons (CFCs) and nitrous oxides stemming from human activities as diverse as electricity generation and wet rice cultivation. Greenhouse gases are those that absorb the infra-red rays of the sun reflected from the surface of the earth, and there is no doubt that they play an important role in determining the temperature of the earth. There is also no doubt that concentrations of infra-red absorbing gases have been increasing since the industrial revolution, and, if current trends continue, concentrations of carbon dioxide will double from pre-industrial levels by around 2075.[4] There appear to be a number of sound reasons for believing that changes in the concentrations of infra-red absorbing gases in the atmosphere will lead to an increase in mean global temperatures of 1.5 to 4.5 degrees celsius.[5]

Global climate change can be regarded as an international problem in a number of diverse respects. Firstly, the world's climate is an obvious public good, and there is no exclusion from the consequences that climate change might impose. Moreover, given the present uncertainties about the specific regional effects that might arise from climate change and global warming, there is a clear sense that no one nation or group of people can rationally expect to benefit from the change. Of course, small island micro-states in the Pacific can be expected to be definite losers, but Western Europeans expecting warmer summers ought soberly to contemplate the prospects of ocean tidal changes that might induce sharp falls in European temperatures. Not only are the effects public, therefore, but everyone has a reason for wishing to prevent such effects, if possible, or at least prevent a further worsening of the problem. In this sense all nations are united behind a 'veil of ignorance', or at least a 'veil of uncertainty'.

Global climate change is also an international issue because the causes of global atmospheric change are to be found in all continents and in all nations. Although some countries are responsible for a greater output of greenhouse gases than others, either absolutely or per capita, no country fails to contribute to the problem, and existing patterns of development mean that those who currently contribute least can in the future expect to contribute more.

However, although global climate change is the most striking example of the internationalisation of pollution control issues, it is by no means the only one. The transboundary character of acid rain has been recognised for many years, although it is only with the establishment of such activities as the European Monitoring and Evaluation Programme (EMEP) that it has been possible to identify with precision the sources, flows and depositions of sulphur dioxide emissions. Regional seas have also provided a focus for recognising the international public goods nature of environmental resources. Thus, when the 'Stella Marris' left the port of Rotterdam in 1971 laden with 650 tonnes of chlorinated hydrocarbons to be dumped in the northern part of the North Sea, it caused a public outcry and led a number of governments to call for the international regulation of the dumping of wastes in the North Sea. Other examples of international public goods include the stratospheric ozone layer and the genetic material locked up in bio-diversity. A significant international public good is also contained in the accumulated knowledge of scientific communities about the earth's environment.

How well might we expect political institutions to respond to the international character of environmental problems? In the dominant realist and neo-realist traditions of analysis springing from the work of Morgenthau in international relations theory, we might expect a poor response.[6] On this account, the international system is regarded as one of pure power and nation states are usually represented as being within a Hobbesian state of nature with respect to one another since by definition they have no 'common power to keep them all in awe'.[7] In a Hobbesian world, common action to provide public goods can be represented as an N-person Prisoners' Dilemma and on the standard analysis of such dilemmas no set of individuals has any incentive to make provision for public goods. Thus, just as in Hobbes's own state of nature, individuals lack an incentive to abide by common rules in the absence of a sovereign, so in the Hobbesian state of nature represented by the international system the conventional analysis suggests that we should not be optimistic about co-operative activity on the part of nation states to protect a regional or global commons.

In practice, the development of international co-operation is longer lasting and more extensive than the bleak Hobbesian analysis would suggest. Although international agreements for the prevention of international pollution are comparatively recent, so that the first international agreement on air pollution was the Convention on Long-Range Transboundary Air Pollution (LRTAP) agreed in November 1979, other forms of co-operative arrangements and agreements on international resource use have been in existence for a number of years. Early examples of inter-

national organisations include the International Council for the
Exploration of the Seas formed in 1902, the International Association of Meteorology and Atmospheric Physics formed in 1919
and the International Commission on Radiological Protection
formed in 1928. These bodies are not only of long-standing, but
often their activities play a significant role in the activities of
national governments, as is demonstrated by the way in which
national governments have adopted recommendations of the International Commission on Radiological Protection.

Although international arrangements for the control of pollution
are relatively few in number, other forms of what Oran Young has
termed 'resource regimes' extend the list of relevant institutions to
some extent. 'Resource regimes', according to Young, 'are institutional arrangements governing the human use of natural resources
and environmental services; international resource regimes are
those resource regimes that deal with natural resource and environmental issues cutting across the jurisdictional boundaries of the members of international society or involving the global commons.'[8]
Internationally important resource regimes in this sense include the
International Whaling Commission (formed in 1946), the International Maritime Organization (1948), the International Commission
for the Conservation of Atlantic Tunas (1969), the International
Commission for the Southeast Atlantic Fisheries (1969) and the
International Arctic Committee (1979). Taken together resource
regimes form an important part of the pattern of governance for
the international environment.

The existence of a complex variety of international resource
regimes is a challenge to the Hobbesian picture of international
relations. This is not simply because international regimes of
co-operation have emerged in the absence of a sovereign to provide to necessary means of enforcement, but also because, in
Young's words, regimes are 'interlocking sets of rights and rules
that govern interactions among their members with regard to
particular issue areas'.[9] In other words, international resource
regimes establish rules and norms that have consequences for the
behaviour of states, even though such norms and rules are not
commands supported by the threat of force as they would have to
be in a Hobbesian world.

There may, of course, be a number of reasons why observed and
emerging patterns of political co-operation are out of line with a

simple Hobbesian picture. The Hobbesian view is one of rational individuals competing with one another for security, and it may be simply a mistake to regard anything as complex as the governments of modern nation states as unitary actors endowed with a coherent rationality. It may also be that the conventional view about international relations as comprised solely of the interplay of power politics is mistaken. Other factors, including cognitive and intellectual factors, may come into play. If, as Young asserts, regimes 'are social institutions governing the actions of those involved in specifiable activities or sets of activities', then we shall need to give weight to the place of institutional norms in determining behaviour as well as self-interested rational calculation.[10] Moreover, since relations between nation states are conducted at many levels including not simply the high diplomacy of international agreements but also the low politics of expert and advisory working parties, we may well find that looking at the organisational processes at work turns out to be crucial.

Alternatively, it may be that a modified Hobbesian idiom is the appropriate one in which to explain the development of international co-operation. Repetitive playing of the prisoners' dilemma can make it rational for actors to co-operate even under 'anarchic' conditions, provided that they are sufficiently long-sighted to see the benefits of long-term gains over short-term victories.[11] Moreover, it may be that problems of international co-operation correspond not to the pure prisoners' dilemma, but to what Sen has termed an 'assurance game'.[12] In an assurance game co-operation is an individually rational strategy provided that the actor contemplating co-operation can be assured that others will co-operate. Thus, contrary to the prisoners' dilemma where it is rational *not* to co-operate if others are going to co-operate (since the benefits are secured anyway), an assurance game makes co-operation contingent upon how others behave. Thus, even within the rational choice idiom, if we wish to understand the emergence and functioning of international resource regimes we cannot rely upon a simple picture of the anarchic order of international relations. Instead, we shall have to analyse empirically key features of their operation.

Conditions of international environmental co-operation

There are a number of possible reasons why international action to protect the environment might emerge in the form that has been observed. These include: the nature of the issues being dealt with; the role of key types of actors, particularly scientific policy elites, in the formation of national government policy preferences; the changing pattern of domestic political actors; or the willingness of a subset of international actors to bear disproportionate collective costs. We can look at each of these factors in turn.

Turning first to *the nature of the issues*, it is apparent from the listing of international organisations for environmental protection that the emergence of such organisations has historically shown certain patterns of development. Thus, the earliest international organisations tended to be scientific bodies concerned with the exploration of the seas or 'remote' regions like Antarctica. The next type of international organisation to emerge was concerned with the management of collective resources, most importantly fisheries stocks. Finally, by the end of the 1960s international regimes began to emerge to control pollution into the seas or the oceans, either from shipping or from the dumping of waste.

It is useful here to distinguish what Ostrom has called 'common-pool resources' from other types of resource concern:

The term 'common-pool resource' refers to a natural or man-made resource system that is sufficiently large as to make it costly (but not impossible) to exclude potential beneficiaries from obtaining benefits from its use ... Examples of resource systems include fishing grounds, groundwater basins, grazing areas, irrigation canals, bridges, parking garages, mainframe computers, and streams, lakes, oceans, and other bodies of water.[13]

The point about common-pool resources is that they provide a source of benefit to those who have access to them, and in order to prevent collective inefficiency in their use some way has to be found of effectively regulating the behaviour of the beneficiaries.

The sort of international environmental goods that are properly counted as common-pool resources include such things as fish stocks, fauna, forests and other flora. The benefits that societies derive from the existence of these stocks are commonly obtained by withdrawing them from the common pool, and the problem of regulation is to ensure that no set of individual actors draws resources at a rate faster than a collectively prudent use of re-sources would dictate. In other words, when we are talking about common-pool resources we are talking about benefits that can be individually appropriated. By contrast, we can compare international environmental goods that are pure public goods, either for the world at large like the composition of the atmosphere or for some portion of it like the quality of a regional sea. As Wettestad and Andresen say, compared to fishery resources, clean air and clean water share the characteristics of joint supply and non-appropriability.[14] The quality of these resources is affected not by the individually appropriable resources that individual actors withdraw, but by the extent to which individual actors make use of them to dispose of their own waste material. For this reason, they may be called 'common-sink resources', since the problem is not to regulate the withdrawal rate of a stock but to control the use of the resource for the purposes of disposal.

Common-pool resources may be distinguished from common-sink resources in a number of respects. Firstly, the protection of common-pool resources can more easily be turned from a prisoners' dilemma game into an assurance game than is usually possible with common-sink resources. Since the benefits of common-pool resources are individually appropriable, it is possible to establish monitoring arrangements to assess whether individuals are taking their commonly agreed share or not, and, given that everyone else is taking their share, it becomes rational for all individual actors to take their share, so that the resource regime itself becomes a source of security. By contrast, there is typically no way in which the benefits of common-sink resources can be individually allocated and there is often no easy way in which the use of common-sink resources can be collectively monitored, and in this situation individual actors can reason that their restraint is merely providing an opportunity for others to use more than their fair share. In the absence of monitoring possibilities, it is therefore difficult to escape the prisoners' dilemma problems in the case of common sinks.

The difficulties of non-appropriability contribute to a second problem of common-sink resources. It is a frequent practice in international negotiations to seek to invent some measure that will stand proxy for an individual resource allocation of the common-pool type. One such proxy is to take current pollution levels as a given, and to negotiate proportionate reductions from that base. This, in effect, is giving individual countries a 'right' in their present volume of pollution and asking them to cede a portion of this right on condition that other countries cede a similar portion of their rights. Thus, the original draft proposal for the EC's Large Combustion Plant Ordinance was that all member states should reduce their sulphur dioxide emissions by 60 per cent from a baseline date. The problem with this approach, as was so clearly revealed in subsequent negotiations over the draft directive, is that proportionate reductions from a given baseline are only a poor proxy of the value to an individual country of its current use of a common-sink resource. Since different economies face different marginal costs in achieving any particular reduction target, there is a considerable incentive for those bearing the higher marginal cost to refuse to agree to proposed reductions.

A third distinction concerns the question of where and how the effects fall in the two cases.[15] Over-exploitation of common-pool resources will primarily hit those who benefit from extraction. If fishing-stocks are over-exploited or land is over-grazed, then fishing or farming communities will feel the effect, and economies in which fishing or farming are important have an incentive to rectify the situation. If common-sink resources are over-exploited by contrast then the problems will often fall on actors other than those who create the problem. Thus heavy metal residues in industrial waste dumped in the seas is a problem for fishing communities, not the dumping industries. To be sure, some waste disposal practices will rebound to the disadvantage of those causing the waste, as when sewage disposal is inadequate in seaside holiday resorts, but even here there is likely to be a transfer of some costs from one section of the community to another.

These three differences between common-pool resources on the one hand and common-sink resources on the other suggest that international agreement ought to be easier in the common-pool case than in the common-sink case, and this is one of the reasons, I conjecture, why organisations to manage common-pool resources, like fisheries stocks, emerged earlier in the system of international relations than did organisations for the control of access to common-sink resources. This is not to say that one can expect common-pool resource regimes always to function more effectively than common-sink resource regimes, since there may be other factors bearing upon the functioning of the regime, for example scientific uncertainties or the intensity of competition for available stocks. Thus, Wettestad and Andresen assess the effectiveness of the International Whaling Commission as low through two of the three phases of its activity, partly because in the first phase whale stocks continued their serious decline and partly because in the latter phase political considerations prevented the emergence of a management strategy based upon a sound scientific assessment.[16] However, in this context it is worth noting that common-sink regimes, like the Convention on Long-Range Transboundary Pollution, also have a long way to go in demonstrating effectiveness in solving the large problems with which they are confronted.

The place of key actors in international co-operation can be best examined by looking at *the role of scientific policy elites*. It is striking that international co-operation in the field of international resources developed early in the case of scientific research. Many of the early international bodies dealing with international resources were scientific organisations, like the International Council for the Exploration of the Seas, and in this respect the organisation of resource regimes at the international level parallels developments at the level of the nation state, where early national action also tended to be based upon scientific work.

The reason for the early development of the scientific dimensions of international co-operation is probably to be found in the fact that institutional science has developed a number of powerful incentive systems for individuals and organisations to contribute towards the public good of scientific knowledge. The practice of citation and acknowledgement, the naming of new discoveries after prominent individuals and the establishment of a paradigm or agreed corpus of knowledge that none the less still leaves scope for individual problem-solving constitute some of the main devices of these incentive systems. Moreover, there are considerable economies of scale to be derived from international co-operation in scientific research, but, since these are only available when the system of scientific communication is good, the gains from international trade in scientific research often depend upon international institutions. Thus, international scientific organisations both provide the public good of facilitating research, for example by providing a forum for publications falling within a particular area of expertise and so eliminating a significant amount of search costs, and also provide some of the incentives for individuals to contribute to the maintenance of the self-same public good.

Although it is possible to see why scientific research might provide the earliest and most long-lasting forms of international resource co-operation, it is another question to understand why scientific communities might play a crucial role in the formulation of international treaties protecting the environment, which always require action by non-scientifically motivated politicians. Here there are two important points. The first is that a government's policy preferences in respect of an environmental policy question are influenced by the professional scientific advice it receives. Typically, one of the first actions of governments confronted by environmental dilemmas at the end of the 1960s was to create institutions of technical and scientific advice to advise on the problems, and subsequent experience has shown that the influence of scientific policy advisers can be considerable. Economic costs were an important element in the UK's resistance to international action to reduce sulphur dioxide emissions, but a powerful buttressing element was the advice the British government were receiving from its own scientists. It is possible to regard the use of this advice purely as a legitimating device, designed to secure the public facade of respectability (the hypocritical homage that vice always pays to virtue), but not something that was taken seriously by the actors involved. However, after a while this becomes too strained an interpretation. The British government was obstinate on the issue partly because the scientific advice it was receiving about the uncertainties involved made it feel that it was right to obstinate.

The second important element in the role that scientific communities are likely to play in negotiations on international treaties is a substantive one. Where there is an international scientific consensus, this is likely to be an important element in creating the preconditions for a successful international agreement. Underdal identifies the existence of consensual knowledge among the relevant scientific elites as one of the important conditions leading to a strong impact of science upon the decision-making process.[17] Similarly, the EMEP process has maintained the impetus towards improvements in controlling transboundary air pollution by providing firm evidence about the extent and character of international depositions. Finally, it is clear the scientific consensus on the seriousness of ozone stratospheric depletion and the link with CFCs was a major element in creating the conditions for the conclusion of the Montreal Protocol, although scientists did not play an important part in the final, and conclusive stages of the negotiations.[18]

This dual role of scientific bodies in both creating an understanding of the policy problem on which government policy preferences rest and securing a transnational expert consensus on solutions to the problem has led Peter Haas to develop the notion of 'epistemic communities' defined as 'transnational networks of knowledge based communities that are both politically empowered through their claims to exercise authoritative knowledge and motivated by shared causal and principled beliefs'.[19] If such epistemic communities are important in shaping the conditions of international environmental negotiation, then we cannot expect to understand the shape of international environmental protection without taking their activities into account.

Haas's study of the Mediterranean Action Plan suggests that epistemic communities may be crucial in creating the conditions that lead to international co-operation. The Mediterranean Action Plan was established under the United Nations Environment Programme, following a request from some Mediterranean states who were concerned about the extent of pollution but knew little about it in detail. UNEP's response was to develop a series of monitoring and research projects, the main importance of which was to shift policy concern from oil pollution resulting from tanker traffic to a more comprehensive range of sources and channels of pollution, including land-based sources, agricultural run-off, river flows and atmospheric deposition. The development of a policy strategy based upon an ecosystem perspective was in essence the work of the scientists employed on the programmes, and since its inception in 1975 the Mediterranean Action Plan has become steadily more comprehensive, developing protocols to cover not only the main routes for pollution, but also specific substances as well.

An important element in the Haas account is that a priori the divergent economic interests of the littoral states seemed as though they would doom international co-operation, and Algeria in particular was wary about participation.[20] However, the process of scientific investigation shifted perceptions of the problem, most notably in identifying land-based sources of pollution as being the most important, but also by providing tangible benefits to some of the poorer countries in terms of the resources that were devoted

to improving their scientific capacity. Thus, complex organisational linkages and incentives established by the process were
themselves crucial in securing international agreement.

One way of reading the Haas study is that it identifies the
importance of cognitive and discursive factors in the making of
international environmental policy, but there is implicit a deeper
message, namely that international institutions and organisations
themselves create the conditions within which epistemic consensus
can emerge. Thus, we should not contrast institutional with discursive approaches, since certain institutional preconditions are
themselves required for epistemic communities to function. Good
international environmental science cannot function in a state of
international anarchy. (Hobbes, who was so much more acute
than the usual run of his contemporary followers, appreciated this
point when he noted that in the state of nature there is 'no
knowledge of the face of the earth; no account of time; no arts;
no letters ...'[21])

Epistemic communities in certain circumstances, therefore, may
be important generators of policy development within an existing
international framework of co-operation, but it may be possible to
secure policy developments without the strict conditions of consensus that Haas specifies. For Haas, epistemic communities are
constituted not simply by agreement on technical questions but
also by a broader vision of appropriate policy orientations and
responses. A less demanding condition of policy development in
the international arena might be simply the existence of an intellectual tool, for example a mathematical and statistical model, that
was acceptable to all the parties. An example here would be the
RAINS model developed by IIASA to map the prevalence of acidification in Europe. This model is used in negotiations on the
Convention on Long Range Transboundary Air Pollution. Although
it suffers from some weaknesses, most notably that it operates on
grids of 150 km by 150 km so that any one grid can contain a
variety of ecosystems, it has a number of other characteristics that
made it a suitable tool in the context of international negotiations:
it covers all types of emissions that influence acidification; it covers
the whole of Europe, and includes data from eastern Europe; it
fitted the EMEP for sulphur dioxide; it was designed to be user-
friendly; and it underwent extensive peer review to establish its
technical credibility.[22]

This last point is particularly important in the international context. Since knowledge is power, participants in international negotiations have an incentive to seek to ensure that their knowledge is used rather than those with whom they may be at odds in discussion. Since models are complex artifacts, inevitably resting on contestable assumptions, it will be to the advantage of a country to have models adopted the assumptions of which are closest to its own. (For example, the determination of the normal acidity of rain in the absence of human induced pollutants is a source of controversy, which has some implications for how much responsibility is laid at the door of particular producers.[23]) This was an issue over the RAINS model, which at one point was in competition with alternative models, one favoured by the British government and the other favoured by the Swedish government.[24]

One way in which the use of RAINS departs from the full requirements of an epistemic community is that it is not embedded in a broader belief system that has normative commitments and more general intellectual commitments. It eschews information relating to cost-benefit analysis, but largely for negative reasons, because some participants in the international negotiations thought that including such information would understate environmental benefits. But this is clearly a far cry from a commitment to, say, an ecological or ecosystems perspective. What it seems to suggest is that international co-operation is facilitated when those professionals who define the detailed terms of debate are comfortable with the scientific and technical processes generating the data on which international agreements have to be based.

The role of technical and professional expertise is likely to be important in one further aspect, namely their place in influencing non-governmental actors. Scientists are active participants in the process by which firms and businesses shape their own policy strategies. Since transnational corporations have a major role to play in the control of pollution through their own self-regulatory and self-auditing activities, it follows that experts and professionals may well be influential in their position as employees of private corporations. In the run-up to the Montreal Protocol the leading international chemical companies used well-financed campaigns to reduce international concern about ozone depletion. However, once the scientific consensus began moving in a particular direction, it became increasingly implausible for firms to continue resisting the policy momentum, and several companies had announced by 1988 that they would phase out production of CFCs by 2000 or earlier.

Participation in international regimes of environmental protection cannot be understood without examining *the changing patterns of domestic politics*. The internationalisation of political life does not simply mean that domestic public policy is constrained by international factors; it also means that foreign policy-making is constrained by domestic factors. Those social groups that have shown the greatest propensity to environmental activism – namely the young, relatively affluent, well-educated middle classes – are also the groups that are most conscious of international issues and are the best placed to take advantage of international travel and international means of communication. Active pressure groups, like Friends of the Earth and Greenpeace, are organised internationally, and have shown remarkable skill in adopting forms of political action that are capable of securing international media attention. The global village may not have arrived, but it is well on the way to development.

Even traditional environmental protection groups can find themselves drawn into international action by policy developments and emerging international regulation and control. The UK's Royal Society for the Protection of Birds is in part an amenity organisation, but it is also a campaigning organisation. Because birds migrate across national boundaries, its interests naturally extend to environmental protection in countries other than the UK, of which the proposals of the Spanish government to allow the draining of wetlands for the purposes of economic development provide one of the best examples. Moreover, as international regulatory regimes develop, national pressure groups can find their bargaining power considerably increased by their ability to appeal over the heads of their national governments to the international regulatory authorities, a technique that was used by British environmental protection groups when they invited the European Commission to inspect Duich Moss on Islay when they were concerned about plans to allow economic development in the area. Organisations like the European Environmental Bureau perform the function of acting as an intermediary between individual European environmental organisations and those involved in formulating EC policies.

Clearly in this sort of pressure group environment there cannot be a sharp separation between the processes of domestic politics on the one hand and the processes of international diplomacy and negotiation on the other. International affairs cease to be the preserve of small and tightly-knit policy elites and become much more a matter of widespread public attention. This is, of course, part of a more general trend, in which, as Smith has argued, publics are increasingly likely to make demands on their politicians concerning action in the foreign policy area.[25] The expansion of the policy communities surrounding the making of environmental policy that has so affected questions of implementation and standard-setting has also left its mark on the freedom of manoeuvre for governments in their international negotiations.

The last factor that may be important in the creation and functioning of regimes of international co-operation is *the willingness of international actors to bear disproportionate costs*. Among theorists of international regimes in general there has been interest in the view that the presence of a 'hegemonic' actor is an important element in the formation of regimes. Thus, the United States has been seen to be important in establishing and maintaining post-war economic regimes, particularly in respect of the international monetary system. Yet, in the environmental case, this proposition does not seem to hold up well.[26] However, this does not mean that individual international actors cannot take the initiative in inaugurating international developments, even if it involves them in disproportionate costs or in the risks of sponsoring an undertaking running the risks of failure.

An example of a single actor taking the initiative in this sense is provided by Germany's convening of the Bremen interministerial conference on the North Sea in 1984, and other examples include the role the Scandinavian countries have taken in convening conferences and meetings on the subject of transboundary air pollution. Initiatives of this sort are often costly, if only in terms of the administrative and organisational resources that have to be devoted to arranging the meetings and preparing the background documents. If the inauguration of a new regime is successful, then the costs may be presumably shared among participating nations, but there has to be some risk attending the early stages of development. The obvious motive explaining the willingness to bear these costs is the fact that the alternative of a null regime is itself costly for the country concerned, either in terms of the continual

pollution damage that may be inflicted, or in terms of the domestic
political costs of being seen to do nothing.

The Scandinavian case for transboundary air pollution is particularly interesting since it emphasises the fact that the willingness
to bear the costs of international co-operation may spring not
from an attempt to secure an advantage, but from an attempt to
lessen a disadvantage. Evidence suggests that Sweden and Norway
import some 80 to 95 per cent of their sulphur depositions from
neighbouring European countries. In this context, recipient countries in asymmetrical relations of cause and effect have little freedom of manoeuvre. One obvious possibility would be to engage
in bilateral negotiations to subsidise the installation of pollution
control technologies in those countries responsible for the
emissions. But such a strategy has obvious drawbacks, since it
would entail not only the direct costs of the subsidy, but also the
indirect costs of further potential subsidies created by the perverse
incentive of paying for someone else's negligence. Given that sort
of option, willingness to bear many of the costs of regime creation
and maintenance may seem like a good bargain.

The nesting of regimes

One way in which international resource regimes may develop is
via evolution within a regime that serves other, more general
purposes. This can be usefully referred to as the 'nesting' of
resource regimes. The most obvious example of nesting in this
sense is provided by the development of environmental policy
within the European Community. From its original inception in
1957 until 1973 the EC had no environmental policy, and the
issues were only placed within the competence of the Community
by a declaration made by the heads of state and government in
October 1972 which called for the formulation of an action
plan.[27] *The First Action Programme on the Environment* (1973–
76) was followed by three further action programmes for the years
1977–81, 1982–86 and 1987–92. Since environmental policy was
not covered explicitly by the Treaty of Rome, it was given a legal
rationale in terms of the requirements of competition policy, in
particular by reference to Article 2 of the Treaty, which required
the promotion throughout the Community of a harmonious development of economic activities with continuous, balanced expan-

sion. In other words, the Community's competence in matters of environmental policy was judged necessary to avoid a situation in which the imposition of environmental protection regulations by one country would serve as a barrier to trade to others. Alongside this economic rationale, the Community was also able to attach itself to the ringingly announced goal of bringing 'expansion into the service of man by procuring for him an environment providing the best conditions of life, and reconcile this expansion with the increasingly imperative need to preserve the natural environment'.[28]

Despite these initial legal and organisational complications, it is clear that the EC developed its own momentum for acting on environmental questions, and its policy decisions are now responsible for regulating matters as wide as drinking water quality, air pollution, solid waste and chemicals. One of the accomplishments of EC policy has been to develop a series of policy principles in its successive action programmes that have developed the themes of anticipation and precaution, as well as stressing the importance of maintaining high environmental standards in the context of industrial competitiveness. Moreover, the development of these policy principles has in turn influenced the progress of national policies in member states. One of the reasons why the UK had to adopt its own pollution control procedures in 1990, for example, was to bring them into line with the requirements of the European Community.[29]

As the international debate over acid rain and forest damage sharpened, the Third Environmental Action Programme put proposals for Community action into more concrete terms.[30] The Directive on the Combatting of Air Pollution from Industrial Plants was the first response of the Community to the problem of acid deposition.[31] This framework directive set down general duties on member states to introduce prior authorisation for certain industrial processes, and it anticipated subsequent daughter directives, the most significant of which was the Large Combustion Plant Directive. When eventually adopted in 1988 after five years of political wrangling and diplomatic bargaining, the Large Combustion Plant Directive required specified proportionate reductions in sulphur dioxide and nitrogen oxide emissions by each individual country within an agreed period of time.[32]

This example shows that one of the main features of international regimes is that they can change the incentives to participation for members. As a member of an international resource regime, a country may find that it has a strong motive to set the agenda at international level. Thus, having adopted the 1983 Large Combustion Plant Ordinance, German policy-makers had an incentive to seek to ensure that large combustion plant operations in other European countries installed pollution control equipment to ensure that German industry was not at a cost disadvantage by comparison with its competitors. Strong regimes induce behaviour rather like federal nation states in this regard, since the environmentally conscious individual states in the USA have an incentive to ensure that regulation operates at the federal level, in order to prevent their own state's industry being put at a cost disadvantage. Perhaps the major point of disanalogy between nation states and provincial governments in a federal system is that the unanimity or super-majority voting rules that operate in international regimes are more inhibiting that the voting rules that operate in federations. Since the style of policy-making within the Commission allowed member states considerable freedom in the formulation of draft legislation, there were clearly many incentives for environmental leaders to use the forum of the EC for their own purposes.

We have in the EC, therefore, an example of a resource regime that is not organised around the need to protect any one natural resource, but which has taken on the broadly based competence of the regime in which it is nested. In this respect, the development of environmental policy can be compared to the development of environmental issues within the nation state, just as the creation of environment ministries or environmental protection agencies established the preconditions for the broadening impact of environmental concerns within the government machine at large. Moreover, much of the expansion of environmental regulation at EC level came during a decade when some member governments, and other governments throughout the world, were expounding the virtues of deregulation.

Another example of the nesting of environmental issues in an existing international regime is provided by the OECD, which in 1972 began research into the long-range transboundary transportation of air pollution. During the 1980s the OECD became one of the principal organisations expounding the principles of ecological modernisation, and which has played an important role in the debate over economic instruments and environmental policy. Although the OECD cannot be regarded as a regime in the fully-fledged sense, since it is not a rule-making body, it does help shape the intellectual context within which individual nations formulate their own environmental policies. Its latest initiative involves the development of environmental policy performance review, analogous to the economic policy reviews it currently conducts, and it began publishing sets of indicators of environmental policy and performance as part of the early stages of this development.

This growth of environmental responsibility within existing international organisations represents a potentially significant qualitative development of the international resource regime system. Although international resource regimes go beyond the nation state, there is a sense in which they are predicated upon the nation state. In international resource regimes nations yield part of their freedom of policy action in order to gain the advantages of international co-operation. The theory implicit in this is still that of sovereign nations who take decisions on international matters by consulting their own interests. With wide-ranging regimes like that of the EC, however, it is clear that nations are yielding their sovereignty, and this marks a new stage in the development of their relations with one another. It is a mark of the centrality of environmental issues that they have played a significant part in driving forward the new forms of national political co-operation represented by the European Community.

Regimes: rational, institutional or discursive?

Oran Young has made the simple, yet powerful, point that international institutions are a fact of life for nation states. In this sense, there is little to analyse in the functioning of regimes. To ask why nation states participate in regimes is rather like asking why soccer clubs participate in league football: the advantages secured clearly outweigh the disadvantages. Yet, the feeling persists that somehow we need to understand why there are such things as football leagues. Given that the institution is there we can see why individual teams participate. But why is the institution there?

This question is perhaps most problematic within the Hobbesian idiom of rational choice theory. The constant temptation to self-interest in that approach creates a puzzle as to why regimes are so extensive. Moreover, to model problems of international environmental goods as a Hobbesian prisoners' dilemma is to assume that nation states behave as unitary actors upon the world stage. Yet, as Allison once pointed out, nations can be reified, but only at considerable cost in terms of understanding.[33] By seeing nation states as unitary actors, we necessarily obscure the role of organisational process and the understanding of policy elites in the making of policy. If epistemic communities or even professional expertise are really important in the identification and understanding of issues, a simple rational actor view of nation states and resource regimes cannot be adequate.

One obvious way to account for regimes is to posit a distinct and separate motive towards government by norms and institutional arrangements, rather than government under a system of unmediated power, rather as Brian Barry has posited a motive to justice in political life generally.[34] The logic here is to say that whatever motives persons have towards government by general norms and principles within the political community are likely to be operative between political communities over the use of international resources.

The specific ways in which this motivation may operate has been well explored in Underdal's work on the politics of international fisheries management.[35] One important element in the motive to be governed by norms under institutional arrangements is a desire to avoid the sense of defeat involved in giving in to naked self-interest. Institutions are important in this context because the sheer assertion of naked self-interest is rare in such negotiations, and arguments, even when they are intended to protect and advance self-interest, are usually couched in terms of fairness or equity. Moreover, there appears to be more consistency in the employment of criteria according to these notions than would be implied if behaviour were only determined on the basis of short-term, issue-specific interest.

To be sure no very strong conclusions can be drawn from these findings, partly because notions like 'equity' or 'fairness' are open-textured in their application to specific issues and therefore their specification can be tailored to the perceived self-interests of nation, and partly because Underdal is referring to common-pool resources, not common-sink resources, and the same orientation towards normative regulation may not carry over from one to the other. However, the analysis is suggestive, particularly when taken in conjunction with the evidence on the importance of cognitive factors stemming from Haas's analysis of epistemic communities.

The suggestion here then is that institutions may be important because they provide the conditions within which the discursive justification of policy is possible. This has general implications for our idioms of analysis, and it is to those general questions that I now turn.

Notes

1 L. K. Caldwell, *International Environmental Policy* (Durham and London: Duke University Press, 1990), chapter 3.

2 S. Boehmer-Christiansen, 'Emerging International Principles of Environmental Protection and their Impact on Britain', *The Environmentalist* 10:2 (1990), p. 99.

3 For a clear summary of issues of interconnectedness, see D. Held, 'Democracy and the Global System', in D. Held (ed.) *Political Theory Today* (Cambridge: Polity Press, 1991), pp. 197–235, especially pp. 201–12. For the effects of economic interdependence on the freedom of manoeuvre of national governments in economic policy, see P. A. Hall, *Governing the Economy: The Politics of State Intervention in Britain and France* (Cambridge: Polity Press, 1986).

4 World Resources Institute, *World Resources 1990–91* (New York and Oxford: Oxford University Press, 1990), p. 12.

5 World Resources Institute, *World Resources 1990–91*, p. 13.

6 H. J. Morgenthau, *Politics in the Twentieth Century* (Chicago and London: University of Chicago Press, 1962), p. 204: '... a theory of international politics must be focused on the concept of the national interest.'

7 T. Hobbes, *Leviathan*, ed. M. Oakeshott (Oxford: Basil Blackwell, 1651 original, n.d.), p. 82.

8 O. R. Young, 'Science and Social Institutions: Lessons for International Resource Regimes', in S. Andresen and W. Østreng (eds), *International resource Management: The Role of Science and Politics* (London and New York: Belhaven Press, 1989), p. 8.

9 O. R. Young, 'Global Environmental Change and International Governance', *Millenium*, 19:3 (1990), p. 339.

10 See O. R. Young, *International Cooperation: Building Regimes for Natural Resources and the Environment* (Ithaca, NY: Cornell

University Press, 1989), p. 12.

11   R. Axelrod, *The Evolution of Cooperation* (New York: Basic Books, 1984); M. Taylor, *Anarchy and Cooperation* (New York: John Wiley and Sons, 1976).

12   A. Sen, *Choice, Welfare and Measurement* (Oxford: Basil Blackwell, 1982), pp. 78–80.

13   E. Ostrom, *Governing the Commons* (Cambridge: Cambridge University Press, 1990), p. 30.

14   J. Wettestad and S. Andresen, 'The Effectiveness of International Resource Cooperation: Some Preliminary Findings' (Oslo: Fridtjof Nansens Instituut, 1991), p.81.

15   This has been pointed out to me by Arild Underdal.

16   Wettestad and Andresen, 'The Effectiveness of International Resource Cooperation', pp. 8–27.

17   A. Underdal, 'The Politics of Science in International Resource Management: A Summary', in S. Andresen and W. Østreng (eds), *International Resource Management: The Role of Science and Politics* (London and New York: Belhaven Press, 1989), p. 259.

18   P. M. Bakken, 'Science and Politics in the Protection of the Ozone Layer', in Andresen and Østreng (eds), *International Resource Management*, p. 201; P. M. Haas, 'Obtaining International Environmental Protection through Epistemic Consensus', *Millenium*, 19:3 (1990), pp. 347–63, especially at pp. 354–8.

19   Haas, 'Obtaining International Environmental Protection through Epistemic Consensus', p. 349. A crisper definition than found in P. M. Haas, *Saving the Mediterranean: The Politics of International Environmental Cooperation* (New York: Columbia University Press, 1990), p. 55.

20   Haas, *Saving the Mediterranean*, p. 72.

21   Hobbes, *Leviathan*, p. 82.

22   L. Horndijk, 'Integrated Environmental Economic Systems', in J. B. Opschoor and D. W. Pearce (eds), *Persistent Pollutants* (Dordrecht: Kluwer Academic Press, 1991), pp. 105–14.

23   C. C. Park, *Acid Rain* (London and New York: Routledge, 1987), p. 26.

24   Horndijk, 'Integrated Environmental Economic Systems'.

25   S. M. Smith, 'Foreign and Defence Policy' in P. Dunleavy *et al.* (eds), *Developments in British Politics 3* (Basingstoke and London: Macmillan, 1990), p. 258.

26   Young, 'Global Environmental Change and International Governance', p. 341.

27   N. Haigh, *EEC Environmental Policy and Britain* (Harlow:

Longman, 1989, revised second edition), p. 9.

28 'Declaration on the Programme of Action of the European Communities on the Environment', *Official Journal of the European Communities*, C112 (20 December 1973), p. 5.

29 Compare the discussion of ecological modernisation in chapter 3.

30 'Resolution on the Continuation and Implementation of a European Community Policy and Action Programme on the Environment', *Official Journal of the European Communities*, C46 (17 February 1983).

31 Commission of the European Communities, Directive on Combatting of Air Pollution from Industrial Plants, *Official Journal of the European Communities*, L88 (16 July 1984), 84/360/EEC.

32 Commission of the European Communities, Directive on the Limitation of Certain Pollutants into the Air from Large Combustion Plants, *Official Journal of the European Communities*, L336/1 (7 December, 1988), 88/609/EEC. For the background story, see S. Boehmer-Christiansen and J. Skea, *Acid Politics* (London and New York: 1991), chapter 12.

33 G. Allison, *Essence of Decision* (Boston: Little, Brown and Co., 1972), p. 253.

34 B. M. Barry, *A Treatise on Social Justice, Volume 1: Theories of Justice* (London: Harvester-Wheatsheaf, 1989), p. 284.

35 A. Underdal, *The Politics of International Fisheries Management. The Case of the Northeast Atlantic* (Oslo: Universitetsforlaget, 1980), especially pp. 115–16 and 141–52.

8
Beyond the tragedy of the commons?

When policy-makers established pollution control regimes in the 1970s, they supposed that they were dealing effectively with the problems they faced. And yet subsequent awareness of the scale and intensity of pollution problems reveals that in many cases solutions lead to more problems. There is now less smoke and grit in the atmosphere, but emissions of sulphur dioxide and nitrogen oxides even at declining rate are still a cause of environmental damage, and the prospect of global climate change has added the formerly 'harmless' carbon dioxide to the list. Sewage treatment facilities have been installed widely to cope with pollution discharges to water, but many of Europe's beaches still fail health tests on coliform bacteria, and sewage treatment works are a primary source of pollution to the atmosphere as concentrated substances are air-stripped. Moreover, eutrophication and pesticide residues have become a serious problem from non-point sources, like farming and domestic garden run off. For soil the legacy of the 1970s was in many respects to create the problems of the 1980s as solid and chemical waste disposal strategies emphasised disposal to land, without thought for contamination.

Hence both the problems and the perceptions of the problems have changed, and this change is one of the key components of the new politics of pollution. Moreover, the continental and global *scale* of problems appears to have outgrown the institutional capacity to deal with them. It is almost as if there is a logic at work by which the displaced externalities of social and economic activity appear at one level higher in the political system than the level with the greatest authority and capacity to deal with the problems. The policy strategies of the 1970s also seem inadequate in terms of their ability to root out the sources of the problems. Here again there appears to be a logic at work by which the concentration of attention necessary to accomplish any action is at odds with the breadth of attention essential to trace back the chain of cause and effect to its origins. Holistic solutions to large-scale problems are not in sight.

These new problems have been accompanied by other wide-reaching changes in the politics of pollution. When laws and regulations, or organisations and advisory bodies were established as part of the policy response to the wave of concern in the 1960s and 1970s, what was established was not simply a configuration of policy institutions, but also a *process* of policy exploration and development. This process has itself contributed to the new politics of pollution, since much that is characteristic of the new politics is related to that problem. Thus, concerns over the integration of environmental policy with other sectors of public policy, insistence on the need to avoid cross-media effects if effective pollution control is to be achieved, or the search for new and more flexible instruments of policy can all be interpreted as reflections on their experience by those who have participated in the making and implementation of policy.

The expansion of policy communities and the rising public profile of pollution politics are also related to the policy processes inaugurated in the 1970s, although in this case there are undoubtedly broader factors at work. Many observers have noticed an increased sensitivity to risk among modern populations, revealed in public concerns about product safety or occupational safety, and rising trends in the pursuit of professional negligence litigation, as well as in worries about environmental pollution.[1] The regulatory institutions and processes of the modern state provide the focus for the political mobilisation of these concerns. Moreover, since these concerns are associated strongly with the well educated and relatively affluent, there is every reason to believe that they will grow in the next two decades.

It is in this context that policy-makers in different countries forged their strategies in the 1980s. The policy strategies of the 1970s may have been inadequate in their own way, but they displayed some commonality of features, within divergent national styles, that evidenced an underlying, if tacit, set of assumptions about how to deal with the problems. No such commonality of response is evidenced in the 1980s. Two of the leading actors in Europe, Britain and Germany, picked out divergent paths of policy development during the decade and, despite some change of policy discourse on the part of the British government, the agreement in action often seems to highlight the difference in thought–world and operative assumptions, amounting almost to radically competing visions of the role of the state and the relation between state and civil society.

Superficially we might say that the US and British governments shared a point of view, and the ideological affinity between Mrs Thatcher and President Reagan, which was such an important feature of the special relationship of the 1980s, might provide some substance to this interpretation. Yet, on closer inspection, the differences seem deeper and more significant. Part of the reluctance of the British government to change the style and substance of environmental regulation reflected the high levels of mutual confidence that small elites in Britain have developed towards one another. Britain's position on acid rain or sewage sludge dumping in the North Sea are simply unintelligible unless we see them against the background of the trust habitually placed by key decision-makers in scientific expertise. Britain's equally dogged attachment to secrecy in the enforcement of pollution control can also only be understood in terms of long-standing features of its political system, not least the social closure practised by policy elites.

In the US the policy system is marked, by contrast, with a pervasive mistrust, which has led to policy strategies quite distinct from those found in the UK. Adversarial and technology-forcing regulation is a symptom of mistrust between social actors, and the willingness to use litigation to contest the standards that are set reinforces the point. With its law-bound political culture and elaborate safeguards for due process in the implementation of regulation, the US resembles Germany more closely than the UK. Yet, it is doubtful whether one would find in Britain or Germany the willingness to experiment with new methods of environmental policy-making that emerged or expanded in the US despite, or maybe because of, a Reaganite hostility to environmental protection. Permit trading, policy dialogues, regulatory negotiation, environmental dispute resolution, consensus conferences, science courts are all ideas that have come from the US, and they are all ideas that have found some support within the policy system. Perhaps the US is so full of solutions because it has so many problems. Were its governmental systems less fragmented and more effective in dealing with social problems, its need for policy innovation might be less.

Whatever the origins of these differences, a common element is to be found in the constraints deriving from politics. Public policy on the environment is not simply an application of the technical rationality of the natural sciences; nor does it instantiate the colourless logic of the utilitarian calculus contained in the axioms of cost-benefit analysis. Public policy is made within the political process, and political action has its own rationality and constraints. In part, this has to do with what is feasible within a given situation, but this is a meaningless notion until we realise that what is feasible is itself something that must be interpreted and decided by political agents, and innovative political agents can redefine the limits of the possible.

The change in the political conditions under which environmental policy is made has almost certainly made the task of policy-making harder for the nation state. Embedded within a growing system of international agreements and conventions on the environment, and now increasingly a part of international regimes with supra-national ambitions, policy-makers face more constraints on their freedom of action, although they also have more opportunities if they can use the fact of international commitments to outwit their opponents. From below policy-makers within the nation state face the growth and diversification of policy communities whose members sometimes represent broad social movements and whose arguments are increasingly sophisticated. No country in this situation has discovered how to combine technical effectiveness with political responsiveness and economic efficiency. The solution to that problem still awaits discovery.

In what idiom, then, shall we describe and account for the trends and patterns we have observed?

Selecting among idioms

In the discussion of the case studies of the new politics of pollution in chapters 3 to 7, it should have been clear that no one idiom can be used exclusively to understand the processes at work, for in each case it was necessary to draw on more than one approach to understand and analyse what was going on. Thus, the transformation of German environmental policy in the 1980s reflected the electoral situation facing politicians, for whom a rational response had to be to place environmental protection and pollution control higher up the agenda. Yet this approach, taken on its own, misses the systemic dimension in the requirement for legitimation, and, more importantly, cannot account for the form and influence of the legitimating ideology of ecological modernisation, let alone the extent to which the principles of ecological modernisation became adopted by a high proportion of policy elites in government and industry. Here the contrast with the UK is striking, and this in turn suggests that institutional dimensions are also important, for the long-standing differences in the way that the state relates to the economy in Britain and Germany plays an essential role in understanding the diffusion of ideas associated with ecological modernisation.

Ideas and institutions do not always work in tandem, however. The idea of integrated pollution control has had a powerful effect upon high level government advisers and environmental policy experts, but its translation into practical and organisational forms has been slow and hesitant, and it looks as though it will be impossible to account for this except by reference to the barriers associated with bureaucratic politics, most clearly expressed in the idiom of institutions. These barriers also have a relevance to the idiom of rational choice, since, in political terms, what could be more rational than trying to defend one's freedom of manoeuvre and span of control?

In these cases, therefore, we need to combine idioms, or at least recognise that not all parts of the story can be told in the same voice. Does this mean that it is entirely a matter of personal whim and predilection which idiom we choose to work with? Not so, I conjecture, for whereas some idioms may be essential when accounting for the context of policy, others may be essential in accounting for its logic. Or, to change the metaphor, one or two voices may give us the melody line, leaving only the accompaniment for the other voices.

Consider, for example, the case of rational choice theory. In 1968 Garrett Hardin published an influential essay, 'The Tragedy of the Commons', in which, using rational choice analysis, he suggested that the metaphor of over-grazing on a piece of common land, in accordance with the logic of an N-person's prisoners' dilemma, provided a paradigm of environmental degradation.[2] The problem that he had in mind was that of over-population, but, as Elinor Ostrom has pointed out, the tragedy of the commons has been taken as a paradigm for a wide range of problems.[3] Precisely because pollution control has a public goods aspect, we might expect it to be an area of public policy where collective inaction is prominent.

And yet those working within the rational choice idiom have been surprised by the high levels of collective action that pollution control has prompted. For example, environmental protection organisations in the US have received high levels of public support. Sometimes this has been ascribed to a tendency on the part of concerned citizens to overestimate their political efficacy.[4] Another explanation offered has been that environmental protection groups have been able to maintain a high public profile by bringing legal suits against regulators or polluters, and this has been funded by a few foundations who do not themselves face the dilemma of collective action.[5] Yet it is difficult to find the same factors at work in the European environmental movement. The German citizens' initiatives were able to secure high levels of participation, without the bonus from foundation funding on the scale that US groups enjoyed. Alan Scott has suggested that one of the reasons why rational actor accounts perform badly in explaining the rise of the environmental groups, and of new social movements more generally, is that they work with an impoverished account of motivation which sees political action as purely instrumental, and therefore ignores the culture and life-style aspects of social movements that secure the affective loyalties of their members.[6]

Perhaps a more striking feature of the new politics of pollution is the growth of international regimes of pollution control, which, as I argued in chapter 7, were inexplicable on a strictly Hobbesian rational choice account of the international order. In part the structure and functioning of international resource regimes suggests that it is not possible for nations to adopt a purely instrumental view of international negotiations, and that the 'rules of the game' that constitute international regimes impose their own influence upon action and events. No one, after all, has shown that Aristotle was wrong to suppose that human beings were essentially political animals.

One problem with rational choice analysis, including public choice theories of the state, is that they do not escape the trap of a mechanistic metaphor. The essential logic of rational choice approaches is to generalise the logic of rational maximising behaviour from the economic market-place to the political market-place. Politicians, pressure groups, voters and bureaucrats are all seen as agents fundamentally concerned to maximise their own preference satisfaction. In consequence, in public choice theory the analysis of government failure replaces the analysis of market failure. From this perspective government intervention will usually fail to solve a pollution problem because concentrated economic interests have a strong incentive to lobby policy-makers to their own advantage and regulators have little incentive to design and enforce optimal roles of control. As we have seen in previous chapters, these public choice pressures are present in a number of aspects of pollution policy, but it would be a mistake to interpret the politics of pollution entirely from a public choice perspective. Although it draws attention to the effects of conflicting and often incompatible interests within the policy-making process, it neglects the cognitive and discursive aspects of policy. Environmental policy is as often about deciding the nature of a problem as deciding between competing interests involved in a problem. The process by which this common understanding is constructed involves both the shaping and determination of policy preferences, as well as their expression.

To some extent the dominance of the economic mode of analysis reflects the particular historical experiences of the Anglo-American democracies. Implicitly it presupposes the norm of laissez-faire and then seeks an explanation of why we observe government intervention. For societies in which industrialisation took place in relative independence of state intervention, this may not be too misleading a starting-point. In both Britain and the US, for various reasons, industrial development did not involve substantial state patronage. In continental Europe by contrast, most notably in Germany, the state was active in fostering industrial development and regulation by legal instruments was extensive. For this reason it may not seem surprising that the analysis of public policy, including environmental policy, in Germany often takes place within a legal, rather than an economic, tradition of analysis. To this extent, neo-classical welfare analysis is the child of the laissez-faire state. One particular consequence of the neo-classical approach is to place a heavy emphasis on the extent to which public policy should be concerned with the static problem of the optimal allocation of resources, rather than the dynamic problem of securing growth and development within the economy. Since the major intellectual change in environmental policy analysis in the 1980s is to stress the extent to which environmental degradation damages economic performance, the tradition of neo-classical analysis threatens to ignore the extent to which a concern with environmental quality can be motivated by a concern for an improvement in economic performance. As we have seen, a significant part of the concern behind the development of environmental policy within the European Community has been motivated by a desire to improve Europe's competitiveness in world markets.

There is of course an ineradicable strategic element in political decision-making, and it is in the treating of this element that rational choice has much to offer. Moreover, the volatility of environmental issues and their proneness to the issue attention cycle can only be accounted for by the recurrent search by politicians for issue dimensions that will upset established majority coalitions – a process on which public choice theory has been so illuminating.[7] Yet the preferences of rational choice theory are fixed, and what we have seen in the new politics of pollution is a change in policy preferences as leading actors have rethought whether their interests are really served by continuing environmental degradation. Policy preferences are not simply tastes like my liking for red wine over white or milk chocolate over plain. Policy preferences are the implications of complex belief systems shared and sustained by actors standing in varying relationships to one another. For these reasons a discourse is needed to perform at least three functions: to define the nature of the policy problem; to conceptualise the relevant interests that agents may have in relation to that problem; and to formulate innovative, and potentially credible, solutions to those problems. The language of that discourse will draw upon a range of vocabularies, including those of natural science, economics and political argument. Without understanding the meaning and function of the competing discourses we are unlikely to be able to understand the changing politics of pollution.

Does this leave any room for systemic explanations cast in terms of the functional prerequisites of a social and political order? The idea that there may be structural and systemic features of the political economy of capitalist societies that distorts the rationality of policy discourse in a predictable way has an obvious intuitive logic. After all, if the rationality of the discourse is not distorted, what can account for the way in which problems have been wrongly identified or mismanaged? In seeking to understand the distorted rationality of policy development, it would seem natural to look for the limits on political discourse implied by the requirements of capital accumulation.

A good example of how these limits might operate is provided by implementation failures following the 1970s reforms. In some cases, as with US air and water pollution controls, the original standards were so high and the timetables so tight that, to the informed observer, it should have been clear that implementation was impossible. However, if the function of the reforms was not to solve a pollution problem but to solve a legitimation problem, then the built-in non-implementability of the policies becomes explicable, for they simultaneously exhibit high political visibility, and hence have symbolic importance in terms of legitimation, whilst taking a form that poses no serious threat to the process of capital accumulation.

Such an interpretation is often possible for particular cases, but it becomes more strained when one considers the cross-national evidence. The Swedish reforms of 1969 assumed the form they did precisely because key policy-makers were concerned about implementability.[8] Similarly the resistance to sulphur dioxide control from German electricity companies was not simple token, but was based upon a recognition that even if there were long-term net benefits to the policy, they would bear tangible short-term costs. What seems to be important here are not broadly conceived structural constraints on all capitalist economics, which there no doubt are, but specific institutional configurations that favour one form and style of policy-making over others. Moreover, when we do observe general trends in different political systems, of which a tendency towards compliance rather than enforcement in the process of implementation is the most conspicuous, the obvious source of explanation is to be found in the institutional role of regulators, combined with a general psychological disposition to be cautious about morally ambiguous situations.[9] In other words, the structure, if there, seems to play only a subordinate role once we locate individuals in their institutional settings.

One virtue of the social systems approach is that it does emphasise the need for the legitimation of public policy. Legitimation has two aspects, however, an external aspect defined by reference to the function it performs and an internal aspect, defined by reference to the reasoning by which it is characterised. If the systems approach has validity, it can only do so by revealing the necessity of an intelligible discourse in terms of which policies are developed.

The institution of discourse

We seem to have arrived at a point at which the melody line is taken by the idiom of discourse, with rational choice and systems approaches playing only background parts. But what of institutions? If ideas and arguments matter in policy processes, their effects are constrained and shaped by the institutional context within which they are deployed. Not matter how coherent and well formed or persuasive to disinterested reason, a policy discourse needs to have force, if it is to be effective in the practice of policy, and force is an institutional matter.

Consider, as an example of this point, the question of implementability. Implementability is a complex notion, but has at least two elements: a proposal cannot be implemented if its administration is too costly or too complex and it cannot be implemented if it is bound to encounter political opposition from important political actors. Lack of implementability seems to be a feature of Pigovian approaches to the valuation of environmental benefits, with its implication that only a comprehensive cost-benefit analysis will provide the appropriate decision framework for environmental quality. Once the assumption is granted that pollution damage should be assessed by reference to its economic costs, where these are defined in terms of willingness to pay, the logic of the Pigovian argument is difficult to fault. None the less, however persuasive in abstract logic, the notion of basing a system of environmental policy on taxes and subsidies has an essential unimplementability. Quite apart from the powerful political opposition it can arouse, as was illustrated in the UK case in 1989–90, the administrative burdens it creates are enormous. Time and resources are necessarily consumed in estimating parameters that, in a world of rapidly changing tastes, are unlikely to remain stable in any case.

Integrated pollution control is a less clear-cut case, although even here it is tempting to say that the implementability problems are considerable. With integrated pollution control, however, a number of intermediate solutions are possible, of which seeking to optimise discharges at the margins of uniform emission limits provides the most obvious example. None the less, the relatively underdeveloped state of integrated pollution control, despite its impeccable intellectual pedigree, indicates that the force of ideas in practice is likely to be severely conditioned by the institutional factors of political acceptability, administrative feasibility and straightforward bureaucratic politics.

In constraining the development of ideas, institutions act analogously to Darwinian processes of natural selection in which some ideas are rejected and others are allowed a life of their own. Probably one of the most important factors here is the professional composition and background of key actors within the policy-making elite. Certain approaches to pollution control will be more appealing to some professions than to others. Lawyers may be sceptical of economic instruments that have different effects on different firms within the same line of production, because they will appear to be discriminatory and hence breach principles of due process. Economists will be suspicious of instruments that do not discriminate among producers, because this would carry the implication that potential efficiency gains were being sacrificed. Similarly, environmental scientists can be expected to be suspicious of engineering approaches to pollution control that are insensitive to the cross-media problems arising from waste residuals.

The professional composition and orientation of pollution control systems varies from country to country for contingent historical reasons. If we are puzzled, therefore, as to why certain ideas take off in some countries but not in others, then a natural set of questions to ask concerns the professional composition of policy elites, and the expertise that is thereby encoded within the system.

Institutions enable as well as constrain, however.[10] More precisely, certain institutional forms are processes that may enable the rational development of policy discourse. Thus, in Germany the administrative courts have played a role in the development of the *Vorsorgeprinzip*, just as administrative review in the US has been important in developing the notion of 'standing'. The latter has been particularly important in identifying an environmental interest that is distinct from an economic interest. Thus, when environmental groups have sought a judicial review of administrative actions, for example the granting of a permit for the construction of a hydroelectric power station, the courts have had to consider their standing in the matter, that is their procedural rights to bring an action for judicial relief in the first place. The tendency of the US courts in the 1970s was to liberalise the rules on standing, even to the point of considering whether trees themselves could have standing, that is whether the interests of nature, and not just human interest in nature, could be given independent representation.[11] The present point of the example is less in the substantive merits of the issues discussed than in the fact that certain institutional arrangements allow the question to be raised and discussed and thereby provide a forum within which the development of ideas can take place.

The metaphor of social learning is not redundant here, provided that we can relate it to the specific institutional conditions within which it can take place. A problem is likely to be better understood when there are appropriate institutional arrangements for key participants in the policy process to come together for discussion and debate. This is the significance of the institutional innovations discussed in chapter 6. They provide a variety of devices by which participants can come together. Conversely, where those institutional devices are lacking, then we can expect the quality of learning to be inhibited. The unstable administrative arrangements for pollution control in the UK in the late 1980s and early 1990 may well reflect the simple institutional fact that there is no neutral, apolitical forum within which key participants can come together to discuss the basic principles involved in the design of an effective and accountable pollution control agency.[12]

Perhaps the most important implication of recognising the institutional preconditions of policy discourse is to be found in its application to international institutions. Underdal's finding that disinterested normative considerations did play some role in international negotiations over fisheries can be interpreted to show that such approaches could become more important with institutional development.[13] At present most international resource regimes are rather poor in institutional structure compared to the nation state:

courts and arbitration play a limited role; there is limited parliamentary accountability; no political competition for representatives; few methods by which even the attentive public can
follow what is going on; and so on. It may be that a richer set of
institutions will increase the capacity for discursive rationality, as
has arguably happened in the European Community where there
are now extensive elaborations of policy principles as well as
specific policies.

To raise the possibility of institutional design is of course to
presuppose that institutions do not go all the way down. Bureaucratic politics, the limitations of organisational process, the struc-
turing of problem perceptions, the bias towards the familiar, the
problems of policy co-ordination and all the other commonplaces
of institutional analysis do not disappear once we acknowledge
that policy has intellectual and cognitive components as well as
motivational interests. But the new politics of pollution shows that
policy actors can step back from their immediate engagement in
playing the game according to established rules and question
whether or not the rules should be changed. The policy innovations that we have examined suggest that policy is not a mechanical matter, but a process guided by the search for intelligible
solutions. Shaping and constraining this process are the institutional factors that restrict its rationality, and hence those factors
must themselves be understood. It is no use in pollution politics
being innocent as doves in your policy intentions unless you are
also cunning as serpents in your understanding and ability to
overcome institutional obstacles: that is, if you want to make the
world safe for either species – let alone yourself.

Notes

1   M. Douglas and A. Wildavsky, *Risk and Culture* (Berkeley:
University of California Press, 1982).

2   G. Hardin, 'The Tragedy of the Commons' *Science* 162(1968),
pp. 1243–8.

3   E. Ostrom, *Governing the Commons* (Cambridge: Cambridge
University Press, 1990).

4   R. Hardin, *Collective Action* (Baltimore and London: The Johns
Hopkins Press, 1982).

5   R. Liroff, *A National Policy for the Environment* (Bloomington,

Ind. Indiana University Press, 1976), p. 144.

6   A. Scott, *Ideology and the New Social Movements* (London: Unwin Hyman, 1990), pp. 117–28.

7   W. H. Riker, *Liberalism versus Populism* (San Francisco: W. H. Freeman and Co., 1982).

8   L. Lundqvist, *The Hare and the Tortoise. Clean Air Policies in the United States and Sweden* (Ann Arbor: University of Michigan Press, 1980).

9   See, especially, K. Hawkins, *Environment and Enforcement* (Oxford: Clarendon Press, 1984).

10   I owe this point to Martin Hollis.

11   C. D. Stone, *Should Trees Have Standing?* (Los Altos, California: William Kaufman Inc., 1974).

12   Compare, P. A. Sabatier, 'Knowledge, Policy-Oriented Learning and Policy Change', *Knowledge: Creation, Diffusion, Utilization*, 8:4 (1987), pp. 679–80.

13   A. Underdal, *The Politics of International Fisheries Management. The Case of the Northeast Atlantic* (Oslo: Universitetsforlaget, 1980).

Index